TEXTILES OF THE MIDDLE EAST AND CENTRAL ASIA
THE FABRIC OF LIFE

TEXTILES OF THE MIDDLE EAST AND CENTRAL ASIA
THE FABRIC OF LIFE

FAHMIDA SULEMAN

With 269 illustrations

This book is dedicated to two remarkable women whose contributions to the project should be acknowledged. My post at the British Museum is funded through the generous bequest of Dr Phyllis Bishop (1927–2007), who was deeply interested in the material culture of the Islamic world and a great supporter of the Museum. This volume will remain a lasting testament to her memory. I also wish to dedicate this work to my dear colleague, Helen Wolfe, Collections Manager for world textiles at the British Museum, who has supported me in all my textile-related projects, helped me narrow down my choices for this book, and provided the artistic direction for its photography. With a career spanning over forty years at the Museum, Helen's passion for the textile collections and her knowledge about their storage, care and display are unparalleled.

First published in the United Kingdom in 2017 by Thames & Hudson Ltd, 181A High Holborn, London WC1V 7QX, in collaboration with the British Museum

Textiles of the Middle East and Central Asia: The Fabric of Life © 2017 The Trustees of the British Museum/Thames & Hudson, London

Text © 2017 The Trustees of the British Museum

Fahmida Suleman has asserted the right to be identified as the author of this work.

Designed by Raymonde Watkins, London

All Rights Reserved. No part of this publication may be reproduced or transmitted in any form or by any means, electronic or mechanical, including photocopy, recording or any other information storage and retrieval system, without prior permission in writing from the publisher.

First published in 2017 in the United States of America as *Textiles of the Middle East and Central Asia: The Fabric of Life* by Thames & Hudson Inc., 500 Fifth Avenue, New York, New York 10110

www.thamesandhudsonusa.com

Library of Congress Control Number 2017934764

ISBN 978-0-500-519912

Printed and bound in China by Toppan Leefung

For more information about the British Museum and its collection, please visit **britishmuseum.org**

ON THE COVER Child's tunic (*kurta*) made of vertical bands of striped silk and lined in cotton, with silk-embroidered patterns and edging along the neck opening, Turkmenistan, 1920s–1930s, Tekke Turkmen people. L 37.5 cm × W 43 cm, 2008,6025.21. The unfinished hem ensures the child's long life.

ON P. 1 Sufi dervish's felt hat inscribed in Persian with pious invocations to Imam 'Ali (d. 661) and poetic verses, wool and silk, Mashhad area, Iran, 1890s–1940s. H 23 cm × D 19 cm, 2017,6002.1.

ON PP. 2–3 Detail of the silk-embroidered bodice of a printed cotton velvet dress, embellished with amuletic elements, including Afghan coin pendants, cowrie shells, glass beads, beaded tassels with bells, beaded discs (*gul-i perons*, "dress flowers") and buttons, Afghanistan, 1980s, Kuchi people. L 115 cm × W 142 cm, 2008,6039.1. The Kuchi are nomadic herders and the women are famed for their flamboyant clothing.

ON P. 5 Detail of a marriage apron of a Zoroastrian bride, made of red and green panels of silk embroidered with sun, moon, fish and bird motifs, Yazd or Kirman, Iran, 1850s–1900. L 60 cm × W 93 cm, As1966,01.524.

Contents

8   Introduction: The Fabric of Life

24   Childhood
42   Marriage and Ceremony
78   Status and Identity
120 Religion and Belief
142 House and Homestead
176 Politics and Conflict

212 A Note on the Collection
213 Notes
224 Bibliography
228 Acknowledgments
228 Picture Credits
229 Index

Map showing the countries covered in the book; the vignettes of hats and headdresses appear on the following pages: Afghanistan – head- and plait-cover (*kultapüshak*), c. 1900 (p. 61); Egypt – spangled hat, 1880s–1890s (p. 77); Iran – dervish's hat, 1890s–1940s (p. 1; for caption see p. 4); Kazakhstan – bridal headdress (*saukele*), 1850s–1890s (pp. 72–73); Kyrgyzstan – married woman's cap (*chach kep*), 1925–75 (p. 58); Oman – child's bonnet (*kulutiyya*), 2010 (p. 36); Palestine – bridal headdress (*shaṭweh*), 1920s–1940s (p. 68); Tajikistan – man's prayer cap, 1930s–1960s (p. 123); Turkey – man's fez (*ṭarbūsh*), 1900–1920s (p. 133); Uzbekistan – head- and plait-cover (*kultapüshak*), c. 1900 (p. 61); Yemen – woman's hood (*gargūsh*), 1900–1930s (p. 82).

(Modern country borders are for reference only and do not necessarily reflect actual political boundaries in existence at the time specific objects were produced. The names shown and the designations used on this map do not imply official endorsement or acceptance by the British Museum or the publisher.)

Introduction: The Fabric of Life

bīā kih rāyat-i manṣūr pādishāh rasīd
navīd-i fatḥ u bishārat bih mihr u māh rasīd

('Come, because the victorious standard of the *Pādshāh* (King) has arrived;
Good news of triumph and glad tidings have reached the sun and the moon[.]')

ay qabā-yi pādishāhī rāst bar bālā-yi tu

('O you whose height the cloak of sovereignty fits…')

Hafiz, *Dīvān*[1]

Textiles convey stories. Some are easier to read than others. This sumptuous, but fragmentary, sixteenth-century red and white silk double cloth, woven with literary characters and poetic couplets (**1**), is one of the more easily understood.[2] The Persian verses, quoted above, derive from the lyric love poetry (*ghazals*) of the celebrated Iranian master Hafiz (d. 1390).[3] The weaver's choice of verses eulogizing the victorious king implies that the textile was made for a royal context – possibly the court of Shah 'Abbas (r. 1587–1629), Safavid ruler of Iran. Moreover, the fineness of the fabric suggests that it was used for a garment, perhaps the lining of a coat, and the verses themselves include references to two courtly textiles: the ruler's banner or standard (*rāya*) and the 'cloak of sovereignty' (*qabā*).[4]

The figural imagery on this fragment evokes three of the greatest Middle Eastern love stories of all time: Layli and Majnun, Yusuf and Zulaykha, and Khusraw and Shirin.[5] The tale of the star-crossed Bedouin lovers Majnun and Layli (Layla in the original Arabic) is encapsulated in the vignette depicting a bare-chested Majnun (literally 'the mad one'), who sits in the wilderness cradling a hare and is visited by his beloved, the unattainable Layli. The story of Zulaykha's unrequited love for her irresistible slave, the biblical prophet–king Yusuf (Joseph), is condensed on this textile, with a fiery-haloed Yusuf serving his mistress a drink. A person admiring this textile would have immediately recalled the full context of this banquet scene, in which Zulaykha's female guests are totally overcome by Yusuf's beauty, and therefore exonerate her for her obsessive passion. Thirdly, the epic romance of the Sasanian king Khusraw Parviz and the Armenian princess Shirin is epitomized by a quintessential scene from the narrative, when Khusraw's 'heart catches fire and burns' at the sight of Shirin bathing

1 Textile fragment with figures from Middle Eastern epic tales and poetic verses in Persian, silk double cloth, Iran, 1580s–1620s. L 32.5 cm × W 17.5 cm, 1985,0506.1, purchased with the support of Edmund de Unger Esq.

2 Festive silk dress with silk appliqué patches outlined in metallic and cotton trim and decorated with metal paillettes, Yeshbum, Shabwa Governorate, Yemen, c. 1960. L 123 cm × W 85 cm, As2002,04.1, gift of Georgina James. Although this dress was presented to the donor by a Muslim from the 'Awlaqi tribe at Yeshbum, its style and production are also associated with Jewish communities from the neighbouring town of Habban.

in an emerald pool.[6] The iconography on this textile ultimately derives from manuscript and wall paintings – which are part of the elite context of the Safavid period – but the narratives of these epic tales of love and woe, rooted in centuries of oral literature, would have been recognized and understood by elite and ordinary viewers alike.

Stories told by the majority of textiles, however, are more enigmatic and require a more careful reading. Many textiles include visual symbols that explicitly or implicitly refer to a wide range of social and cultural factors. The fabrics used, the shapes of items of dress, dye colours, and the placement and extent of embroidery patterns all contribute to the ability of garments to communicate information about the wearer, such as gender, age, sexual maturity, marital status, occupation, wealth, tribal affiliation and religious commitment (**2**). Textiles can also indicate regional identity and a person's lifestyle – urban, pastoral or nomadic. Some textiles are markers of joyous celebrations, such as births and marriages, while others signify mourning and death.

3 Detail of a printed cotton headscarf with a design of Nokia-style mobile phones interspersed with roses, Yemen, 1990s. L 181 cm × W 85 cm, 2015,6016.1.

This volume includes more than two hundred Middle Eastern and Central Asian textiles, selected from the British Museum's renowned collection of nearly three thousand pieces from the region. There is a great variety of objects: men's, women's and children's garments, hats and headdresses, mosque curtains and prayer mats, floor-coverings, tent-hangings, hand towels and cushions, storage sacks, purses and cosmetic pouches, dolls and souvenirs, animal trappings, amulets, and modern and contemporary works of art. My choice covers as many countries and regions as possible. Thus, textiles made in Afghanistan, Bahrain, Egypt, Iran, Iraq, Jordan, Kazakhstan, Kuwait, Kyrgyzstan, Lebanon, Oman, Palestine, Saudi Arabia, Syria, Tajikistan, Turkey, Turkmenistan, UAE, Uzbekistan and Yemen are all featured, and examples from Armenia and Zanzibar (Tanzania) are also included because of their historical connections with the textile traditions of Iran and Oman respectively.[7] Most of the objects date between the late eighteenth and early twenty-first centuries, with only a handful from earlier periods; this reflects the Museum's textile holdings (**3**).[8] It is usually difficult to assign precise dates to textiles, except for those few inscribed with dates of production or connected to known individuals. However, I have made every effort to assign date ranges to the artefacts, on the basis of provenance information (where available) or comparison with other objects within and outside the collection.

The countries covered in this book are sometimes referred to collectively as a significant portion of the 'Islamic world', because these lands were historically conquered and governed by various Muslim rulers and dynasties, and the bulk of their populations adhere to Islam, in one form or another, to this day. The Arabian Peninsula was the birthplace of the Prophet Muhammad (d. 632) and of Islam, and from there a plurality of Islamic religious traditions spread to other parts of the Middle East and beyond. However, in many instances the material culture – and for our purposes specifically the textiles – produced in these countries cannot be assigned to one particular religious tradition. Garments, head-coverings and domestic furnishings were

OPPOSITE **4** Painting of a woman kneeling on a floral carpet and embroidering a textile stretched over a floor-stand frame, opaque watercolour on paper, from an album of Persian costumes, Qajar School, Iran, c. 1842. H 25.6 cm × W 18.4 cm (page), 1921,0614,0.1.13, bequest of Baroness Zouche. The bejewelled woman, whose hands are stained with henna, wears a headscarf made of fine, hand-woven striped wool called *termeh*; her embroidery floss, threaded needle and scissors rest on the frame, and a basket, envelope purse and golden pear are placed in the foreground.

ABOVE **5** Detail of the front opening and silk-embroidered button of a woman's coatdress (pp. 92–93), silk, Kirman, Iran, c. 1900, As1966,01.530.

dictated by shifting tastes in fashion, and were manufactured and used by people of all faiths (**2**). Even objects that were made explicitly for, and used within, Muslim religious contexts, such as prayer mats and prayer caps, were not necessarily produced by Muslims themselves. A number of textiles in this volume are clearly associated with Zoroastrian, Jewish, Christian and Muslim communities from specific places and time periods, but others are not so easily labelled. Taken together, the objects presented here offer a glimpse of the worlds in which the diverse peoples who made and used the textiles lived: their histories, rituals, beliefs and practices, religious identities, socio-economic positions, habitats and environments, and aesthetic tastes, and the wider political contexts – the fabric of their lives (**4**).

Western orientalist paintings, studio portraits and postcards from the nineteenth and early twentieth centuries often perpetuated the myth that dress from the Middle East and Central Asia is essentially timeless, comprising a few basic items of clothing and headgear, and often similar from one region to the next. The truth is that fashions changed everywhere through time, and the textiles in this book are products of particular historical periods and places – snapshots of when and where they were made. As a result, I have tried to avoid creating false oppositions between 'traditional' and 'modern' dress because these terms are entirely relative. Every garment was considered 'modern' when it was produced and to refer to all clothing made in earlier centuries as 'traditional' reinforces the stereotype of a timeless past when clothing styles stayed the same (**5**). In her research and the exhibitions that she has curated of the British Museum's collections of nineteenth- and early twentieth-century Palestinian textiles, the anthropologist Shelagh Weir has taken great care to counteract the impression of an unchanging past, because it was so common for the villagers and Bedouin of Palestine to be portrayed as living relics of biblical times.[9] As she explains:

> [Church] missionary societies amassed their collections [of Palestinian garments] for fund-raising and evangelical purposes, and on the mistaken but common assumption that Palestinian rural culture had hardly changed since the time of Jesus. In the 19th century they staged huge tableaux of life (as they imagined it) in Biblical times, including people dressed up as Palestinians. These shows were immensely popular in Victorian times. Special trains were laid on to transport thousands of visitors from central London to the CMJ [Church's Ministry among Jewish People] exhibitions in St Albans.[10]

BELOW, LEFT **6** Trouser-cuffs (LEFT), made of recycled printed cotton with side zips, densely embroidered in the 'Nizwa' style with a diaper pattern in silver, gold and blue metallic threads and bordered with multiple strands of metallic and cotton plaited trim (*sīm* or *tallī*), Nizwa, Interior Oman, 2010. H 10.8 cm × W 16 cm (embroidery on each cuff), 2011,6003.52.a–b. Cylindrical braid-cushion (RIGHT), with trim in progress, and six spools of golden metallic thread (*zarī*) and one spool of rainbow metallic strip thread, Nizwa, Interior Oman, 2010. L 22 cm × C 34 cm (circumference of cushion), 2011,6003.51. Gift of the Ministry of Tourism of the Sultanate of Oman (all items).

BELOW, RIGHT **7** A woman skilfully plaits *sīm* or *tallī* trim on a braid-cushion, using seven spools of black cotton and one spool of colourful metallic strip thread, Nizwa, Interior Oman, 2011; *sīm* is used as an embellishment on garments across the region (see also the Omani bonnets and face-mask on pp. 36, 113, TOP).

I have arranged the textiles presented in this book thematically, rather than by their place of origin or by category of garment. This enables cross-regional comparisons to be made of the function, significance and symbolic meaning of textiles within people's lives. Each of the first five chapters relates to a phase or facet of a person's life in which textiles feature prominently: childhood, marriage and ceremony, status and identity, religion and belief, and house and homestead. In 'Politics and Conflict', I have included a number of contemporary works of art, which grapple with both past and more recent political circumstances in the region. Together, these themes not only play to the strengths of the Museum's collection but also offer approaches to engaging with the textiles. Undoubtedly, any given object can be discussed through a number of lenses or themes. For example, many of the textiles selected for 'House and Homestead' were produced as part of bridal dowries and reflected a maker's social and economic status and regional identity, so they could also have been discussed in the chapter on marriage and ceremony or the one on status and identity.

A fundamental aspect of the textile traditions of the vast region covered in this volume is the importance of embroidery as a means of communication and expression (**6**, **7**). Until the early twentieth century, embroidered textiles were used in every sphere of life from birth to death and were prepared over several years for a girl's dowry (**8**). Whether produced at home or professionally worked and bought commercially,

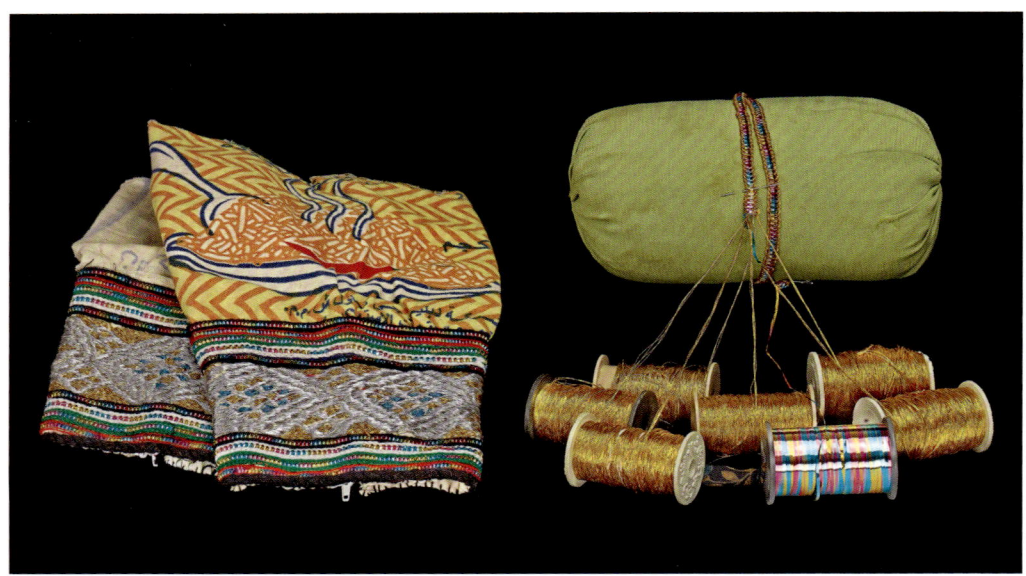

8 Detail of a woman's bridal or festive plait-cover (*kultapüshak*), made of purple velvet embellished with stylized sun and tree motifs in padded Bukharan embroidery (*zardūzī*) with metal-wrapped threads, and finished with needle-braided edging featuring blue and purple teapots and cups; silk, cotton, and gilt-metal- and silver-wrapped thread, Bukhara, Uzbekistan, c. 1900. L 52 cm × W 15 cm × D 16 cm (whole plait-cover), 2014,6039.2. (For similar examples see p. 61.)

embroidery conveyed one's marital status, regional identity, industriousness, level of upbringing and good taste, and demonstrated family wealth. In the villages of pre-1948 Palestine, girls began learning to embroider from around the age of 6.[11] Similarly, in the urban centres of the Ottoman Empire, instructors were brought to the palace and to private homes to teach girls needlework, as this skill was regarded as an important aspect of their education.[12] Stitches were often assigned memorable names, as shown on the back of a sampler from Ramallah (**9**), collected by Grace Crowfoot in the 1930s: 'old man's teeth', 'bachelor's cushion' and 'eggs in a pan', among others.[13]

Many factors have contributed to the erosion of certain textile traditions in the Middle East and Central Asia, including political destabilization, forced sedentarization of nomadic peoples, economic hardship, industrialization, changes in taste and the

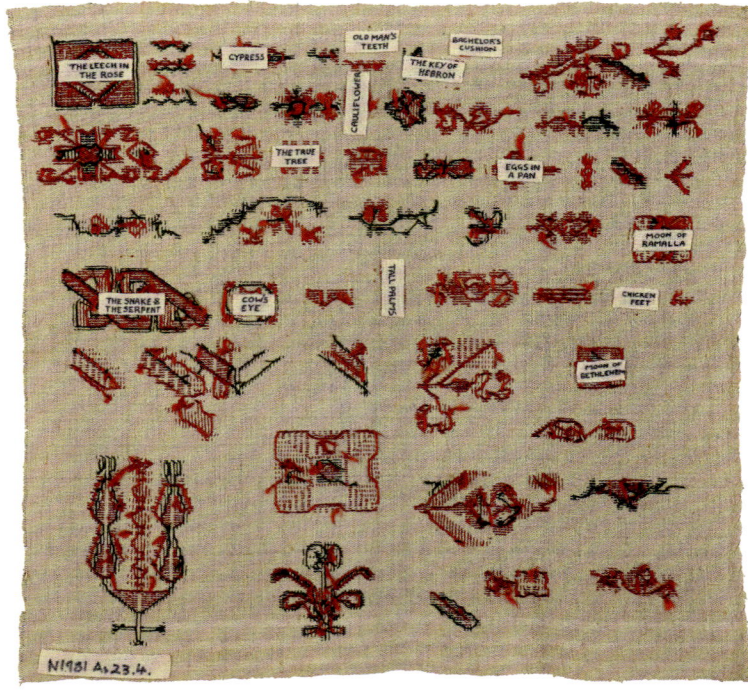

9 Front and back of an embroidery sampler collected by Grace Crowfoot in Ramallah, Palestine, in the 1930s, cotton with silk thread, Palestine, 1930–36. L 42 cm × W 45 cm, As1981,23.4, gift of Elizabeth Crowfoot. The stitches are labelled on the back of the sampler with English translations of the Arabic names: (FROM TOP LEFT) the leech in the rose; cypress; the true tree; cauliflower; old man's teeth; the key of Hebron; bachelor's cushion; eggs in a pan; moon of Ramallah; chicken feet; moon of Bethlehem; tall palms; cow's eye; and the snake and the serpent.

powerful influence of Western modes of dress. According to the textile scholars Kate Fitz Gibbon and Andrew Hale, in the countries of the former Soviet Union, 'thanks to the formidable socializing influence of women', there still remains a passion to maintain national dress styles and a tradition of handicraft production:

> In large part, this is because these traditions are so closely tied to crucial rites of passage – birth, marriage, and death. Textile production is a striking example of constancy and resilience in ethnic identity, notwithstanding changing social and political circumstances that have altered other aspects of individual and group identity.[14]

A number of cultural institutions and charitable organizations have developed within the regions themselves with the aim of preserving, and in many instances reviving, textile and embroidery traditions, while also creating opportunities for generating income. For example, the Bani Hamida Women's Weaving Project in Makawir, Jordan, was established in 1985 to revive Bedouin rug weaving; and INAASH (Association for the Development of Palestinian Camps) in Beirut, Lebanon, founded in the late 1960s, aims to revitalize Palestinian embroidery traditions as a means of providing financial and other support for refugee families living in camps.[15] In 2015 the Palestinian fashion designer OmarJoseph Nasser-Khoury (b. 1988) initiated, crowd-funded and ran, at INAASH, the 'Fifteen Stitches: Palestinian Embroidery Workshop' for fourteen women, in order to introduce fifteen additional historic stitches to their repertoire. The initiative's aim was to increase the income and skills of Palestinian refugee embroiderers so that they could expand their market by producing new and original

10 Detail of the couched embroidery on a woman's bridal or ceremonial jacket (*taqsīreh*) with colourful details worked in satin-stitch (p. 69); woollen broadcloth, silk and cotton, Bethlehem or Beit Jala, Palestine, 1900–1920s, As1966,01.6. The style and embroidery of such jackets were probably inspired by Ottoman and British military uniforms.

work, while keeping, 'the stitches, some of which are hundreds of years old, relevant and ensure their daily use amongst Palestinians wherever they are' (**10**).[16]

The practising felt artist Bita Ghezelayagh (b. 1966) has been actively researching and promoting the felt-making traditions of her native Iran since 2003. Her series of works 'Namad: A Persian Journey in Felt' is based on the humble shepherds' cloaks (*namads*) she once saw on sale in a provincial bazaar, which to her evoked the unpretentious simplicity and resilience often embodied in handmade objects (**11**). The Persian inscription on the cloak translates as: 'There is no better souvenir than that which is made by hand.' The tulip motifs, symbols of fertility, are inspired by the embroidery on nineteenth-century Turkmen women's cloaks.[17]

There are numerous private and public museums across the Middle East and Central Asia exhibiting collections of textiles and dress. Noteworthy is the Tiraz Centre in Amman, Jordan, also known as the Widad Kawar Home for Arab Dress, named for the textile expert who has collected some two thousand weavings, garments and

11 Reinterpretation of an Iranian shepherd's felt cloak (*namad*) by Bita Ghezelayagh, wool and silk, Iran and UK, 2004. L 107 cm × W 116 cm, 2011,6018.1, gift of Bita Ghezelayagh (see also p. 192). The tulip and horn motifs are inspired by 19th- and early 20th-century Turkmen embroideries (for an example see p. 59). The Persian inscription on the cloak is *Az bahr dast behtar az een yādegār nist* ('There is no better souvenir than that which is made by hand').

12 Thea Porter Couture, ʻabāya dress with colourful panels of silk ikat from India and Southeast Asia, silk-brocaded Indian sari borders, embroidered sūzanī panels from Central Asia, red cotton panels, and metallic cord tassels that hang from the sleeve ends, London, England, 1970–77. L 155 cm × W 227 cm, 2016,6045.1, gift of Venetia Porter in memory of Thea Porter (formerly in the collection of Honor Frost).

accessories from Palestine, Jordan, Syria and Sinai, a selection of which are on display there.[18] The Museum of Egyptian Textiles in Cairo exhibits a range of textiles from Coptic Egypt to the Ottoman period. The Centre for Omani Dress, within the Bait Al Zubair Museum in Muscat, is committed to the conservation, preservation and study of the dress identity of Oman. The most significant collections in Istanbul, Turkey, include the Topkapı Palace Museum's vast holdings of imperial textiles of the Ottoman sultans and their families, and the Sadberk Hanım Museum's collection of mainly Turkish garments and embroideries from the late Ottoman period. There is also a Museum of National Dress in Tashkent, Uzbekistan, and a number of ethnographic, fine arts and applied arts museums in Central Asia display regional textiles.[19]

Throughout history, Middle Eastern and Central Asian textiles and fashions have impacted Western commercial markets and tastes by means of centuries-old trade and travel networks. This is no less the case in modern times, but the context has changed significantly as a result of the relative freedom of movement of individuals and the blurring of nationalistic boundaries. Thus renowned fashion designers, originating from the so-called 'Islamic world' but trained and working in the West, have looked to Middle Eastern and Central Asian textiles for creative inspiration for their collections, among them the London-based fashion designer Thea Porter (1927–2000). Born in Jerusalem and raised in Damascus, she spent the 1950s and 1960s in Beirut; in the 1970s she introduced to Western clientele voluminous Arab-style over-garments (ʻabāyas or thawbs; **13**), incorporating vintage Middle Eastern, South Asian and Central Asian fabrics in her designs (**12**).[20] In 1990 the Tunisian-born couturier Azzedine Alaïa (b. 1940), launched a collection of knit body-suits embroidered with Arabic calligraphy in angular Kufic script, which were all the rage that year.[21] The Turkish-born designer Rıfat Özbek (b. 1953) has drawn inspiration from imperial Ottoman textiles for several of his collections. In 2011 the Musée du Quai Branly in Paris collaborated with the French couturier Christian Lacroix (b. 1951) to create an exhibition focusing on nineteenth- and early twentieth-century embroidered village and Bedouin dress from the Levant; as the artistic director, Lacroix heightened the dramatic and creative ambience of the exhibition, and the inclusion of his name in the title, 'L'Orient des femmes vu par Christian Lacroix', attracted record numbers of visitors to the show.[22]

An area of research and acquisitions that the British Museum has begun to consider is the global phenomenon referred to interchangeably as 'modest fashion'

BELOW **14** Print of a Najdi bridal *thawb al-nashal* by Safeya Binzagr (b. 1940), from her *Turāthunā* ('Our heritage') series, showing how the wide sleeve of the *thawb* is drawn over the head; coloured photogravure print on handmade paper, Saudi Arabia, 1997. H 63 cm × W 54 cm, 2015,6018.7.28.a, purchased with the support of the CaMMEA group.

ABOVE **15** Painting of a Persian woman in outdoor dress, wearing a long, all-enveloping black cloak (*chādor*) and lifting her cream face-veil (*rūband*; for an example see p. 105), opaque watercolour on paper, Qajar School, Iran, *c.* 1850. H 14.2 cm × W 10.1 cm, 2006,0314,0.22.

13 Woman's festive over-garment (*thawb al-nashal*) made of black silk brocade with a floral ground and inset panels of purple silk, worked in chain-stitch with gilt-metal threads and spangles, Riyadh, Najd, central Saudi Arabia, *c.* 1900. L 145 cm × W 231 cm, 2014,6013.13. (For an example from Bahrain see pp. 84–85.)

or 'Islamic fashion'. Defining these terms is complex. Some have expressed the phenomenon as a way of dressing in line with Islamic values, a meeting point between women's fashion and religious practice. For many women, though by no means all, this entails covering one's hair, neck and chest with a headscarf, and possibly wearing an ankle-length cloak. For others, at the opposite end of the 'modesty spectrum', it signifies wearing fashion-conscious clothing that is not clingy or revealing and sufficiently covers up the curves of the body. Scholarship on this subject has grown rapidly in recent years, much of it focused on Muslims living in the Western diaspora and expressed in discourse on Muslim identity and self-presentation in a post 9/11 world.

Covering one's head and wearing enveloping over-garments outside the home are not modern phenomena in the Middle East (**15**) and are traceable to the pre-Islamic period, when they were markers of prestige and status.[23] Until the early twentieth century, it was customary to find people of all faiths and ages and both genders in the Middle East and Central Asia covering their heads as a sign of dignity and propriety. I have included a variety of male and female headgear and female face-coverings from across the regions in this book.

Perhaps what was once considered cultural etiquette has now been reframed by some Muslims purely as a religiously driven movement. The Saudi Arabian gown (*thawb*) shown here (**13**) is a sheer, luxurious over-garment, which was worn with a

OPPOSITE **16** Runway model at the Modanisa Modesty Fashion Show held on 15 April 2017 at Olympia, London, as part of the *Muslim Lifestyle Show*. Photo: Paul Quezada-Neiman.

RIGHT **17** Demonstrators at a makeshift 'beach' outside the French embassy, London, England, on 25 August 2016, protesting against the 'burkini ban', the prohibition of full-coverage Islamic swimwear on French beaches, imposed by local authorities in thirty resort towns, including Cannes and Nice. The ban was later overturned by the French courts. The woman on the left wears a blue burkini. Photo: Raymond Tang.

colourful dress and trousers underneath; its billowing sleeves could be drawn up and over the head when the wearer wished to cover her hair (**14**). Should this festive *thawb* of c. 1900 be redefined in hindsight by contemporary scholarship as 'modest fashion'? Who defines what belongs in the category of modest or Islamic fashion? Does this imply that other forms of fashion should be characterized as immodest in some way? Why are Muslim women's clothing choices constantly pitted against Western secularist values? These and other questions have been tackled by anthropologists and cultural historians in recent years; the consensus is that modest dressing means different things to different women, and that the concept of modesty itself is mutable, changing over time and place and from person to person.[24]

What is clear is that the modest-fashion industry is big business and is here to stay (**16**).[25] In 2015 designer labels DKNY, Tommy Hilfiger and Oscar de la Renta started the trend by offering capsule 'Ramadan collections' during the Muslim holy month exclusively to clients in the Middle East. A year later Italian fashion house Dolce & Gabbana launched a range of Muslim headscarves (*ḥijābs*) and cloaks (*'abāyas*) for clients in London, Paris and the Middle East, while the renowned British department store Marks & Spencer made the move to sell Muslim swimwear, 'burkinis' (**17**), in its flagship London location. The trend continues in 2017, with the British department store Debenhams taking full advantage of the spending power of 'Generation M' (young, affluent millennial Muslims), by offering a whole range of clothing, headscarves and accessories to be sold year-round across the UK and at its international outlets in Dubai, Kuwait, Saudi Arabia, Bahrain, Iran, Indonesia and Malaysia.[26]

Childhood

Childhood

Your children are not your children.
They are the sons and daughters of Life's longing for itself.
They come through you but not from you,
And though they are with you yet they belong not to you.
You may give them your love but not your thoughts,
For they have their own thoughts.
You may house their bodies but not their souls,
For their souls dwell in the house of tomorrow, which you cannot visit,
    not even in your dreams.

Kahlil Gibran, *The Prophet*, 1923[1]

PREVIOUS PAGE Detail of a child's hat (*kulutiyya*), red silk brocade with a woollen tassel (p. 36).

18 Child's bonnet with amulets to protect the wearer from the 'evil eye' and promote well-being, cotton, fur, glass, alum and paper, Palestine, 1900–30. L 23 cm × W 22 cm, As 1966,01.329.

The value placed on children and family within the broad geographical region covered in this volume cannot be overstated. Until recent times, full adult status was conferred on both husband and wife only after the birth of their children. Women, in particular, took great pains to increase their fertility, safeguard their pregnancies and protect themselves and their children from sickness, misfortune and the dreaded 'evil eye'.[2] Textiles were essential carriers of both blessings (*baraka*) and protection, and I explore a number of examples in this chapter. Another theme considered here relates to clothing used for rites of passage, marking various stages in a child's life as she or he makes the transition to adulthood.

An imposing fertility and amuletic charm (*tumar*; **19**), to be hung inside the home and dated to the period 1925–75, is associated with the semi-nomadic Turkmen women of northern Afghanistan. It comprises several padded-cotton star shapes bound together with twisted black and white cord; the cord represents an indigenous striped snake and is used as an amulet against it.[3] In Central Asian contexts, astral symbols such as the sun, moon and stars, were believed to increase one's fertility and progeny, and thus also appear on clothing and jewellery.[4] The charm is embellished with blue glass beads, powerful prophylactic elements used in many parts of the world as a protection against illness and believed to deflect the 'evil eye' or 'eye of envy' (see also **18**). Colourful rags of silk, gold brocade, velvet and printed cotton and red woollen pompoms are attached all over the charm to ensnare and confuse wandering malevolent spirits, keeping the inhabitants of the yurt (nomadic tent) and the hopeful mother-to-be safely out of harm's way.[5]

19 Turkmen fertility charm for a yurt, cotton, silk, wool and glass, northern Afghanistan, 1925–75. H 110 cm × W 40 cm, As1993,24.25.

Some mothers may have also resorted to the use of white magic to ward off or appease intentional and unintentional evil. For example, the life of a baby during the first forty days after birth is considered especially vulnerable, and in some Central Asian contexts a mother fastened pins within the layers of her infant's swaddling clothes so that the sharp objects would pierce any malign forces at work.[6] Amuletic textiles were used for similar purposes across the Middle East and Central Asia, such as the protective over-shirts (*kurtas*) worn by Turkmen children up to the age of 4 or 5. Made and embroidered by their mothers, they were festooned with cowrie shells, mother-of-pearl, metal charms inset with carnelian, bells and other objects believed to safeguard the children. Several examples of embroidered and embellished *kurtas* are included in this volume, some incorporating a triangular-shaped amulet called a *dogha* or *tumar* (pp. 30, 39, 137). Often, small *doghas* and other amulets containing slips of paper with extracts from the Qur'an or prayers were pinned onto children's clothing (**20**); a paper triangle attached to a child's bonnet from Palestine (**18**) is folded round an inscribed amulet, and other protective objects include blue beads, coin tokens and beaded pendants containing solid crystals of alum.[7] Verses and phrases from the Qur'an and pious invocations to the Prophet or members of his family were also engraved on charms attached to children's clothing or embroidered directly onto textiles, as seen on the child's bonnet from Iran in this chapter (p. 31).

20 Three sisters from Al Hamra, Oman, 1978; the amulets pinned to the baby's dress include silver pendants with a cowrie shell and animal horn, and a religious inscription sealed inside a leather or textile pouch. Photo: Jonathan Baldock.

Among nomadic and semi-nomadic communities, amuletic coats and over-shirts were sometimes made up of silk and other textile remnants acquired from households with many healthy children. The belief that one family's prosperity could be transferred to another through the medium of textiles is discussed below, with a few examples, including a modern patchwork coat from Tajikistan (p. 33).

Other textiles served for rites of passage, such as circumcision, which in Muslim societies traditionally marks the change from babyhood to boyhood. A red felt fez with coin tokens and gilt-thread tassels from nineteenth-century Palestine is a fine example (p. 31), and was worn when the boy was paraded around the village, mounted on a horse or camel, and wearing costly garments. The tradition of parading a boy through town to announce his circumcision ceremony is still practised in modern-day Turkey, though the preferred mode of transport has changed to a luxury motorcar.

The transition from girlhood to adulthood was also marked by specific clothing. On festive occasions in Sur, eastern Oman, for example, unmarried girls once wore special head-shawls (*kimmas*) to indicate that they had reached a marriageable age.[8] Similarly, hats and headdresses were once markers of age and marital status in both Turkmen and Kyrgyz cultures in Iran and Central Asia, as embroidered skullcaps were worn only by children and unmarried girls (**21**). Once married, a woman in southern Kyrgyzstan customarily passed on her skullcap to her youngest unmarried sister or sister-in-law, and adopted for herself a cap with an embroidered back panel that covered her hair plaits (p. 58).[9]

In general, children's clothes from these regions are bright and colourful, as attested by the group of toddlers' hats from Oman (p. 36), and pastel or muted colours are not commonly favoured. Children's clothes tended to be miniature versions of what adults wore, and festive garments, such as the little boy's coat from Turkey (pp. 40–41), were made from luxurious fabrics, including patterned silks, and were painstakingly embellished with embroidery and beadwork, as seen on the girl's dress from Saudi Arabia (p. 37). Children's dress was also influenced by the tastes and fashions of the time, as illustrated by the little girl's outfit from nineteenth-century Iran (p. 34), which clearly reflects the wave of interest in ballerina-style tutu skirts at that time.

The examples of children's dress shown here represent traditions mainly from the past which are no longer produced, along with a few examples that have endured the test of time despite the powerful influence of Western modes of dress – especially the ubiquitous jeans and t-shirts – across the globe. Although styles of children's clothing have changed throughout the region, contemporary examples of a variety of amuletic pendants featuring Qur'anic verses or blue beads, sometimes in combination with hand and eye motifs, which are pinned to children's clothing or worn as jewellery, attest to parents' continued preoccupation with the safety and prosperity of their children.

21 Kyrgyz women and children, probably Tajikistan or Xinjiang, 1905–13; the children are wearing skullcaps as markers of their age, and miniature versions of adult clothing. Photo: Sir Percy Molesworth Sykes or Ella Sykes, tinted glass lantern slide, Sykes.425.

Child's over-shirt (*kurta*), Ersari Turkmen people
Northern Afghanistan, 1900–20
Silk, cotton, silver alloy, carnelian, glass and cowrie shells
(shown from the back)
Length 46.5 cm / width 50 cm
As2003.03.3, purchased with the support of the
British Museum Friends

The Turkmen are of mixed Turkic and Iranian descent, living mainly in Turkmenistan and adjacent areas of Uzbekistan, Tajikistan, Iran and Afghanistan. Once mainly nomadic, many Turkmen began to settle in cities and towns from the late 1920s, when their freedom of movement was restricted, and herdsmen were consolidated into collectivized farms under Soviet rule. Until the age of 4 or 5, Turkmen children were dressed in protective over-shirts (*kurtas*) made and embellished by their mothers to guard them against the 'eye of envy'. This talismanic *kurta*, open at the sides, is lavishly decorated on the back with embroidered starbursts, metal charms inset with carnelian and glass, a fringe of glass beads, and bell and coin pendants. The cowrie shells symbolize fertility, wealth and protection,[10] and the unfinished hem ensures the child's long life and the mother's fertility.

Circumcision cap
Palestine, 1850–1900
Felted wool, metal, gold and cotton
Height 11 cm / diameter 18 cm
As2000,08.60, gift of the Church's Ministry among Jewish People

In most Muslim societies, circumcision (*sunnat* or *khitān*) is regarded as a major milestone in a boy's life and an important social occasion on a par with a wedding.[11] This red fez (*ṭarbūsh*) embellished with tassels, coin tokens and gilded threads, was worn during a boy's circumcision parade on horseback or camel, to inform the community about his rite of passage.[12]

Child's bonnet
Iran, 1850–1900
Cotton, metal thread and cowrie shells
Height 10 cm / diameter 14 cm
As1966,01.517

This bonnet is embroidered in orange around the crown with the *shahāda*: 'There is no god but Allah, and Muhammad is His servant and messenger.'[13] Additionally, the Shi'a invocation *Yā 'Alī* ('O Imam 'Ali') is inscribed in mirror script in black on the front and in pink on the earflaps. The pious phrases work in tandem with the bird and multi-coloured eye motifs and cowries to safeguard the child against illness, misfortune or exposure to the 'evil eye'.

Child's dress (*dishdāsha* or *pashk*), Baluch people
Muscat, Oman, 1990
Cotton
Length 46.5 cm / width 69.5 cm
2011,6003.45, gift of the Ministry of Tourism of the Sultanate of Oman

This dress is gathered on either side of the waist and, like adult Baluch-style dresses, is characterized by an A-shaped pocket (*pado* or *pandohl*) stitched onto the front of the skirt.[14] It can be worn with or without matching baggy trousers (*sirwāl* or *shalwār*). The embroiderer used an inked woodblock to stamp the pattern onto the fabric before working it in colourful cross-stitched bancs. The ancestors of Baluch Omanis originated from Baluchistan, a region that today occupies areas of south-eastern Iran, western Pakistan and south-western Afghanistan.[15]

Boy's amuletic coat
Panjakent, Tajikistan, 2013–14
Cotton, silk and synthetic fibres, sequins, beads and diamantes
Length 56 cm / width 79 cm
2014,6034.12, gift of Zeina Klink-Hoppe

This patchwork (*caroq* or *kurok*) amuletic coat combines an array of brightly coloured velvet, tulle, silk brocade and synthetic strips of fabric on a white cotton base. Applied embellishments include lurex thread embroidery, golden braid, sequins, diamantes and beads. The small green pocket on the right shoulder is meant to hold a protective inscription from the Qur'an. Such coats were worn by boys born into families where a male child had previously died, and pieces of cloth belonging to people blessed with many children were incorporated whenever possible. The complexity of the patchwork, combined with the shiny elements, ensnared, confused and ultimately deflected evil forces away from the child.[16]

Girl's chemise, split skirt and leggings
Iran, 1880s–1890s
Cotton, silk and metal buttons
Chemise: length 40.5 cm / width 92 cm
Skirt: length 29 cm / width 23 cm (waistband)
Leggings: length 45 cm / width 19.5 cm (maximum, each leg)
As1981,19.12 (chemise), As1981,19.10 (skirt), As1981,19.19.a–b (leggings)

The style of this outfit reflects shifting fashion trends in Iran during the reign of the Qajar ruler Nasir al-Din Shah (r. 1848–96). Skirts, though voluminous, had become progressively shorter during the course of the nineteenth century until the shah himself introduced a modified version of the tutu skirt following his visit to a ballet in Paris in 1873.[17] This child's split skirt is made of red cotton with a pink, yellow and green floral and heart print. The cuffs of the printed chemise (*pīrāhan*) and leggings are embellished with delicate floral and blue trims and pink rickrack.

OPPOSITE **Doll in Bethlehem-style dress**
Palestine, 1880s–1920s
Ceramic, cotton, linen, felt and metal
Height 32 cm / width 23 cm
As2000,08.59.a–c, gift of the Church's Ministry among Jewish People

During the late nineteenth and early twentieth centuries, women in Bethlehem made dolls for sale as souvenirs and as gifts for tourists and pilgrims visiting the Holy Land.[18] This beautifully painted ceramic doll wears a traditional Bethlehem-style dress with winged sleeves and embroidered chest panel. The ensemble includes a removable headdress with coins (*shatweh*) and chin-chain, and a cream veil, customarily worn by married women. Both Christians and Muslims wore similar styles of dress during this period, and Christians sometimes incorporated a small cross on their embroidered chest panels.[19]

Toddlers' hats
Nizwa, Sur and Muscat, Oman, 2010
Cotton, silk and synthetic textiles, glass, metallic thread and braid
Bonnet (*kulutiyya*), from Nizwa (LEFT): height 17 cm / width 17 cm
Cap (*ṭāqiyya*), from Sur (BELOW): height 12 cm / diameter 17 cm
Hat (*kulutiyya*), from Muscat (RIGHT): height 20 cm / diameter 12 cm
2011,6003.24 (*kulutiyya*, Nizwa), 2011,6003.20 (*ṭāqiyya*, Sur), 2011,6003.21 (*kulutiyya*, Muscat). Gift of the Ministry of Tourism of the Sultanate of Oman (all pieces)

Different regions of Oman have distinct styles of headgear for children. The one similarity is that they are all brightly coloured with a variety of hand-embroidered and beaded detailing. The beaded bonnet with a colourful tassel is from Nizwa, Interior Oman. The striped cap is from Sur, north-eastern Oman, and is made of two types of starched cotton called 'Suri silk', which is imported from India for the Omani market. The red silk brocade hat is from the capital, Muscat (see also pp. 24–25).

Girl's beaded dress (*thawb* or *thob*), Bani Malik tribe
Hijaz region, Saudi Arabia, 1930s–1950s
Cotton, silk and glass beads
Length 81 cm / width 78 cm
2015,6016.2

The rectangular blocks of yellow embroidery on this cotton dress (*thawb* or *thob*) are associated with the Bani Malik tribe, who live in the lush mountains in the southern Hijaz region of Saudi Arabia. Like an adult *thawb*, the dress is cut in a T-shape with a straight skirt and close-fitted long sleeves, and is embellished with imported silk panels on the yoke. The bright yellow embroidery on the skirt, chest panel and sleeves is densely worked next to red and green threads, creating a sharp contrast against the black fabric. The chest panel and sleeves are embellished with transparent glass beads, the Hijaz being the only region in Saudi Arabia where decorative beadwork is used in rural women's garments.[20]

OPPOSITE **Triangular cloth amulet (*dogha* or *tumar*), Ersari Turkmen people**
Northern Afghanistan, 1960s
Cotton, silk and glass beads
Height 22 cm / width 13.5 cm
As2003.03.8, purchased with the support of the British Museum Friends

Embroidered triangular cloth amulets are ubiquitous in many parts of the Middle East and Central Asia.[21] Known as a *dogha* or *tumar* in Central Asia, such amulets might be decorated with additional elements that increase their protective power, including tassels, beads, bells, coins and apotropaic embroidery patterns. This cotton *dogha*, with colourful embroidery and beaded tassels, may also contain a Qur'anic inscription or prayer folded inside. Small *doghas* are sewn or pinned onto children's clothing (as shown on the over-shirt above), or worn around the neck. The amulets are also hung on domesticated animals, on doorways and on weavers' looms to keep away evil forces.[22]

ABOVE **Over-shirt (*kurta*) and bib (*kirlik*), Tekke Turkmen people; cap (*börk*), Yomut Turkmen people**
Turkmenistan, 1930s–1950s (over-shirt), and 1880–1890s (bib);
Iran, 1950s–1960s (cap)
Cotton, silk, cowrie shells, human hair, shell buttons and metal badges
Over-shirt: length 45.5 cm / width 45 cm
Bib: length 39 cm (unfolded) / width 43 cm
Cap: height 9 cm / diameter 14.5 cm
As1997,18.1 (over-shirt), gift of St John Simpson; As2003.03.2 (bib), purchased with the support of the British Museum Friends; As1975,04.20 (cap)

A Turkmen child would have worn a bib (*kirlik*) on top of an over-shirt (*kurta*) for added protection. Its hand-woven silk patchwork and long fringes served to trap the 'evil eye'. The *kurta* is replete with amulets, including triangles, beaded tassels, buttons, a cowrie shell and a lock of hair.[23] Skullcaps are worn by Turkmen children and unmarried girls. An expectant mother usually asks a woman from her family or village who has already brought up a healthy child to make a cap for her own child. A dead child's cap is never passed on; only its silver ornaments are re-used. Worked entirely in chain-stitch, the design here comprises cross motifs with pairs of rams' horns (*tirāna*) springing from each tip.[24]

Child's coat
Turkey, 1850s–1890s
Silk with cotton lining
Length 58 cm / width 66.5 cm
2015,6016.9

This coat was probably owned by a little boy from an affluent background, judging by the silk satin compound weave of the textile, with supplementary silk-weft patterning. The complete ensemble would have comprised a shift, trousers, cap and possibly a short inner waistcoat. The layering of clothing is particularly characteristic of dress styles throughout the Ottoman period, and expressed, among other things, the wearer's wealth, status and regional identity. The mid- to late nineteenth century, around the time this coat was produced, was a turning point in elite fashions in Ottoman Turkey, as the urban classes began taking up British and French modes of dress.[25] Hence, this coat may have been considered outmoded in some urban contexts within a span of a few years, and certainly by the time of Mustafa Kemal Atatürk (r. 1923–38), Turkey's first president, who actively promoted Western styles of dress.

Marriage & Ceremony

Marriage & Ceremony

Several early bridal trousseau (*jihāz*) lists have survived from medieval Egypt, which provide evidence of the variety of textiles in that period. One such list details the possessions that made up the dowry of a wealthy Jewish bride from Cairo around 1140 – an extensive inventory that amply testifies to the affluence of her family.[1] It includes a selection of textiles and furnishings, valued in gold dinars:

a cloud-coloured robe of honour (*khil'a*) comprising a robe, a head-veil and a greyish headband	50
a white head-veil with gold thread	15
a hood with stripes 'as the pen runs' and a robe, both with gold thread	10
a kerchief and skullcap of fine *Dabīqī* (Egyptian) linen	30
a blue Byzantine-style dress	6
a pomegranate-coloured robe of honour with matching head-veil	15
a robe for polo (*jūkāniyya*) with bird patterns	4
an apricot-coloured robe for polo with gold threads	10
a dressing gown of blue brocade	20
a bed cover of Byzantine brocade	10
two chameleon-coloured (i.e. shot-silk) canopies	60
a four-piece sofa and cushions of brilliant colours	15
a three-piece sofa and cushions of Byzantine brocade	40
a couch made of reeds	3

The inventory as a whole is much longer and lists many more textiles, all of the woman's jewellery, rock crystal objects, ornate mirrors, valuable pen-boxes, copper lamps and vessels – including a washbasin 'fit for a caliph' – her library of around a thousand manuscripts, two maidservants and two personal attendants. The total sum of her dowry, combined with her marriage gift ('bridewealth') from the groom's family, was valued at a hefty 2,100 gold dinars.[2] The bride was probably the daughter of a wealthy physician and was marrying another physician of similar economic standing. Although this trousseau list contains exceptionally valuable items, reflecting the high status of the bride and groom, it illustrates a feature common to wedding trousseaus throughout most of the Middle East and Central Asia from the medieval period to the early twentieth century, and among rich and poor and all religions: the high cultural

PREVIOUS PAGE Detail of a tall bridal headdress ornamented with white metal and gilded elements, coral beads and pearls (pp. 72–73).

22 Bedouin bridegroom's cotton handkerchief, Jordan, 1950s–1970s. H 38.5 cm × W 44 cm, As1975,03.13. It was embroidered by the bride for her husband, and used at the wedding for dancing.

and monetary worth placed on textiles in the form of garments, headdresses and furnishings. Second only to precious metal jewellery, textiles were appreciated for their fibres and weaves, colours and dyes, embroidery and other embellishments and their place of production.

This chapter explores a range of garments, hats, headdresses, accessories and embroideries from the late nineteenth and twentieth centuries, connected to marriage and other ceremonial and festive occasions. Although worlds apart from the medieval example discussed above, the trousseau items in this chapter reflect regional, religious and socio-economic diversity. Throughout the Middle East and Central Asia, marriages involved the exchange of material things, mainly clothing and jewellery.

23 Tajik wedding ceremony, with the bridal pair standing under a raised, block-printed wedding curtain (*chimilig* or *chimildik*) and an embroidered *sūzanī* canopy (*bolim posh*), Uzbekistan or Tajikistan, 1865–72. Note the wedding mirror held in front of the bride and groom. Reproduced from K. P. von Kaufman and A. L. Kun, *Turkestanskii Al'bom*, pt 2, vol.1 (Tashkent, 1872), pl 73, no. 227.

Money was also gifted to the bride from the groom's side of the family as part of the marriage contract (*'aqd*).[3] The custom of gift exchange and the preparation of the bridal trousseau was, and often still is, practised by people of all religious traditions and socio-economic levels, though there is a huge diversity in practices. The trousseau of a village bride in pre-1948 central and southern Palestine, for example, was divided into two categories: the *jihāz* and *kisweh*.[4] The *jihāz* comprised both festive and everyday objects and textiles, prepared at home by the bride's side of the family during the months or years leading up to her marriage and paid for by her father. In contrast, the *kisweh* was the responsibility of the bridegroom and contained only ceremonial garments bought from professional dressmakers and embroiderers, such as the richly embroidered *malak* ('royal') dress included in this chapter (pp. 66–67). Both parts of the trousseau were vital components of the exchanges preceding marriage.[5] The tasselled handkerchief shown here (**22**) was embroidered by a Bedouin bride for her bridegroom, symbolizing her commitment to the marriage, and was proudly displayed to his friends and relatives while he danced at his wedding celebrations.[6]

The trousseau was often stored in decorative bridal trunks or baskets.[7] In urban and rural Middle Eastern and Central Asian contexts, grand processions were held to escort the bride and her trousseau to her marital home following the secular wedding celebration (*arūsī*).[8] A collection of dressmaker's model garments for a bridal trousseau (pp. 48–49) represents the tastes of wealthy Armenian and Iranian urban brides in the nineteenth century. Also featured is a red silk envelope bag with amuletic embellishments, made by a Turkmen bride in the twentieth century to store her ceremonial wedding mirror (p. 70).

The significance of a bride's dowry within some urban and nomadic Central Asian contexts is aptly summarized by Kate Fitz Gibbon and Andrew Hale in their study of late nineteenth- and early twentieth-century Uzbek embroideries:

> A bride's dowry items do more than show her family's wealth and demonstrate her diligence and skill. They are understood to represent the communal endeavour of the women of her family who contribute to their preparation and, by extension, the entire network of that family.[9]

24 Detail of a Tajik wedding *sūzanī* (p. 57) with couched and chain-stitched embroidery and with an element of the drawn design left unfinished for apotropaic purposes; cotton and silk, Tajikistan or Uzbekistan, 1900–1930. 2014,6034.10, gift of Zeina Klink-Hoppe.

The preparation of a bridal trousseau was thus often a collective activity in Central Asian nomadic and sedentary cultures, requiring the participation of several women within a household. This not only ensured the timely arrangement of a girl's dowry, it also allowed mothers and grandmothers to pass on their knowledge and skills to younger generations. The rituals around the preparation of a trousseau were cemented in this way, and good wishes and blessings were transferred to the newly-weds through the textiles.

The example of a Tajik dowry textile (*sūzanī*; p. 57) illustrates this best. The designs of *sūzanīs*, thought to portray idealized gardens, were traditionally drawn by a master draughtswoman (*qalamkash*) on several loosely joined panels, which were then embroidered as separate pieces by girls and their family members and re-joined afterwards.[10] The motifs on these dowry textiles were propitious and highly symbolic, such as fruits, flowers and birds, representing fertility and love, or water vessels and teapots, reflecting purity and hospitality. A small element of the *sūzanī* was purposely left unfinished as an overt imperfection to ward off the 'eye of envy' (**24**). A *sūzanī* was presented by a bride to her husband on their wedding day and served as a cover for their nuptial bed. This *sūzanī* (**23**) was also used as a canopy (*bolim posh*) over the newly wedded couple to shield them from harm and bless them with a happy marriage.

MARRIAGE & CEREMONY 47

Model garments for a bridal trousseau
Armenia or Iran, 1850–1900
Silk, cotton and wool
Jacket (p. 49, CENTRE): length 12 cm / width 27 cm (shown at actual size)
As1934,1023.1

This collection of model garments for a bridal trousseau was once used by an Armenian seamstress as dress samples for clients.[11] It represents the tastes of wealthy urban brides, and encompasses Armenian, Iranian and Georgian fashions. The 87-piece collection comprises miniature undergarments, trousers, dresses, jackets, shawls, belts, face- and head-veils and coverlets, made of decorative silks, cottons and trims.

Armenian dress is regionally diverse, and throughout their turbulent history Armenians settled across the Ottoman and Persian empires, incorporating aspects of local dress styles.[12] The short jackets, gathered at the waist and with tight-fitting sleeves, paired with wide-legged trousers with embroidered cuffs, reflect the fashions of a wealthy urbanite living in Iran during the nineteenth century. Other pieces, showing Iranian influence, include the block-printed fringed shawl, woollen belt, and envelope pouches used for the bride's cosmetics and jewellery.[13]

OPPOSITE **Ceremonial dress (*thawb*) and headscarf**
Hadramawt, eastern Yemen, 1934–44
Silk, cotton, silver-wrapped thread, sequins, glass beads and cowrie shells
Dress: length (front) 112 cm, (back) 170 cm / width 140 cm
Headscarf: length 179 cm / width 120 cm
2011,6013.7 (dress); 2015,6013.8 (headscarf), gift of Leila Ingrams
in memory of Doreen Ingrams

This style of loosely cut dress with a long train is worn in the Hadramawt and in neighbouring Dhofar, southern Oman, where it is aptly called *abū thail* ('father of the tail'). Made of indigo-dyed silk embellished with silver thread embroidery, silk appliqué, multi-coloured sequins, red glass beads and small cowrie shells, this dress is typical of those worn by brides and on other ceremonial occasions, with matching headscarves and wide trousers embroidered around the ankle cuffs.[14]

ABOVE **Man's ceremonial outer robe ('*abāʾ* or '*abāya*)**
Hadramawt, eastern Yemen, 1930s
Silk and silver-wrapped thread with tapestry-woven decoration (shown from the back)
Length 124 cm / width 136 cm
2011,6013.2, gift of Leila Ingrams in memory of Harold Ingrams

Local Arab leaders presented the British colonial administrator Harold Ingrams (1897–1973) with this and other high-status festive robes during his posting in the former Eastern Aden Protectorate in the 1930s and 1940s.[15] In 1937 he and his wife, Doreen, helped to negotiate a truce, named 'Ingrams' Peace', with rebellious Hadrami tribes. The presentation of such 'robes of honour' as a mark of respect is an Islamic tradition dating back to the eighth century.[16]

MARRIAGE & CEREMONY

Man's ceremonial outer robe (*chapan*)
Uzbekistan, *c.* 1900
Silk-satin brocade with gilt-metal-wrapped thread, lined with silk and cotton ikat
Length 143 cm / width 205 cm
2014,6039.1

An affluent urban man, probably from Bukhara, would have worn this heavy, boldly patterned and brocaded outer *chapan* over an equally eye-catching ikat robe for his wedding ceremony or other important occasion. The trend-setting city of Bukhara has been described as 'the Paris of Russian Turkestan', and by the 1880s velvets and silk brocades (*parcha*) of Russian manufacture dominated the market in luxury textiles there, alongside locally woven silks and cheaper Russian cottons.[17] The robe is finished on the edges and sleeve-cuffs with needle-braided pink and green trim.[18]

Woman's ceremonial robe (*chapan*)
Bukhara, Uzbekistan, 1880s–1890s
Silk brocade with gilt-metal-wrapped thread and cotton lining
Length 130 cm / width 158 cm
2014,6013.3

This woman's ceremonial robe, gathered under the arms, is made of gold and salmon-pink brocaded silk with an Indian paisley pattern, lined with printed Russian cotton and silk ikat. Although Russian mills manufactured excellent imitations of Chinese and Indian silks, this brocade may have come directly from India.[19] The edging on Central Asian textiles is an art in itself and serves both amuletic and decorative purposes. Trims can be woven on tablet looms or embroidered onto fabric and then stitched to the garment. They can also be simultaneously woven and attached to a robe using the complex loop-manipulation technique, requiring two or three people.[20]

ABOVE **Wedding dress (*kurta chakan*)**
Kulob, Tajikistan, 1960s–1970s
Silk with silk embroidery
Length 99 cm / width 151 cm
As1996,12.1, purchased with the support of the British Museum Friends

Traditional bridal or festive garments worn in southern Tajikistan consisted of a red silk shift dress with matching trousers and head-shawl, all silk-embroidered with bold floral and vegetal patterns.[21] In cold weather and on festive occasions women layered as many as seven dresses with sleeves of graduated lengths, allowing the various embroidered patterns to show.[22]

OPPOSITE **Wedding *sūzanī* (*bolim posh*)**
Tajikistan or Uzbekistan, 1900–30
Cotton with silk embroidery
Length 173 cm / width 174 cm
2014,6034.10, gift of Zeina Klink-Hoppe

The stylized sliced melons or flowers in deep purple, pink and red, surrounded by black meandering vine-scrolls, on this wedding *sūzanī* are symbols of fertility and abundance.[23] During the ceremony, the *bolim posh* is used as a canopy over the bridal pair to shield them from the 'eye of envy' and bless them with a happy marriage (see **23** and **24**).[24]

LEFT **Married woman's cap (*chach kep*)**
Southern Kyrgyzstan, 1925–75
Cotton with silk embroidery and silver pendants
Length 75 cm / width 25 cm
As1997,29.1, purchased with the support of the British Museum Friends[25]

Hairstyles and headdress were once markers of age and marital status in Kyrgyz culture. In southern Kyrgyzstan, girls wore embroidered skullcaps or scarves and arranged their long hair in up to twelve plaits. A bride wore her hair in four plaits under a tall headdress. Once married, she made two thick plaits and hid them within the back panel of the superbly embroidered *chach kep*. This one is ornamented with spherical silver pendants along the earflaps; the crown, left plain, was covered with a white turban.[26]

ABOVE **Bridal headdress**
Iran, 1890s–1930s
Cotton, silk and foiled paper
Length 23 cm / width 16 cm
As1966,01.529

This hand-embroidered and embellished bridal headdress is probably from the Turkmen people of Iran. It is replete with protective elements against the 'evil eye' or the 'eye of envy'. These include tassels made up of foiled paper and fabric triangles, and indigo-dyed cotton ruffles embroidered along the edges to resemble snakes.[27] There is also a liberal use of red, symbolizing good fortune, life force, fertility and passion.[28]

Ceremonial mantle or cloak (*chyrpy*), Tekke Turkmen people
Turkmenistan, 1880s–1920s
Silk and cotton (shown from the back)
Length 119 cm (including fringe) / width 65 cm
As1993,27.16

A woman's *chyrpy* or mantle with false vestigial sleeves is draped over the shoulders or head, and a heavily embroidered one such as this was worn at weddings and on other special occasions. Young women wore dark colours, including blue, black and red. Middle-aged married women wore yellow *chyrpys*, while white ones were a prerogative of the elderly. The red tulip (*lāla*) and horn motifs are worked in silk-thread *kesdi* lacing or ladder-stitch, much favoured by Turkmen embroiderers.[29] Wild tulips are native to the remote mountains and barren steppes of Central Asia and bloom in profusion at the start of spring, thus symbolizing abundance, fertility and life. Persian poets likened tulips to goblets of red wine, red-capped beloveds and fiery flames.[30]

Marriage canopy and textile cover (*bugjama* or *bugzhoma*), Lakai Uzbek people
Northern Afghanistan, 1890s–1930s
Napped wool flannel, silk and metal grips
Length 173 cm / width 158 cm
As2002,03.42, purchased with the support of the British Museum Friends and the Art Fund

The once semi-nomadic Lakai Uzbek tribes were forced to sedentarize in the regions of southern Tajikistan and south-eastern Uzbekistan under Soviet rule.[31] Embroidered textiles of a Lakai household were a source of familial prestige, and reinforced tribal identity. This marriage canopy portrays two lovebirds amid abstract solar motifs. It is further embellished with a cross-stitched border, silk edging and tasselled netting with metal grips.[32] A multi-purpose bridal dowry textile, it was later used to wrap clothes and bedding in her new home.[33]

Head- and plait-covers (*kultapüshak* or *kallapüshak*)
Afghanistan, and Bukhara, Uzbekistan, c. 1900
Silk, cotton, gilt-metal- and silver-wrapped thread and silver spangles
Brocade (LEFT): length 121 cm / width 22 cm / diameter 18 cm
Velvet (CENTRE): length 49 cm / width 17 cm / diameter 18 cm
Ikat (RIGHT): length 51 cm / width 23 cm / diameter 19 cm
As1986,11.1 (brocade), 2014,6039.4 (velvet), 2014,6039.6 (ikat)

Both Jewish and Islamic codes of dress required married women to cover their hair as a sign of modesty and piety. Uzbek and Tajik women of both faiths wore head- and plait-covers that conformed to that dictate and also provided a myriad of creative opportunities. The *kultapüshak* (LEFT) is made of silk brocade with silver-wrapped thread, and is lined with ikat and finished with handmade edging.[34] It also features trails of twisted black silk threads (imitating hair), which terminate in bobbles wrapped in gilt thread. The *kultapüshak* (CENTRE), from a Jewish context, is made of sumptuous velvet embellished with padded Bukharan embroidery in gilt thread with silver spangles. The apple and tree motifs, made of appliqué velvet, are symbols of female beauty in Persian poetry.[35] In contrast to these high-status hair-covers, the one made with a striking pattern of silk ikat and lined with printed cotton (RIGHT) is for everyday wear. The beauty of these hair-covers was probably admired indoors, as women covered them with scarves when outside.

MARRIAGE & CEREMONY

Jewish bridal outfit
Baghdad, Iraq, 1860 – 65
Silk, cotton and gilt lace
Coatdress (*daghya qaṣṣa*): length 131 cm / width 147 cm
Bodice (*angia*): length 29 cm / width 55 cm
As1971,09.2–3, gift of Mrs R. E. Rea

Esther Manassah wore this silk brocade coatdress and richly embroidered bodice in Baghdad for her Sephardic Jewish wedding ceremony in around 1865. She also wore a pair of wide, loose trousers and a long, semi-transparent white chemise (*qamīsa*) over the bodice.[36] A striking feature of her expensive wedding outfit, with its pleated bustle, deep décolleté and lavishly ornamented slashed sleeves, is its combination of nineteenth-century Ottoman–Iraqi and Indian fashions. Many Baghdadi Jews were wealthy entrepreneurs, involved in worldwide trade networks through the East India Company, and established communities in the trading ports of Surat, Bombay and Calcutta. This style of festive dress, incorporating a sari blouse, was adapted by the Baghdadi Jewish communities of Calcutta.[37] Esther must have placed a special order for her wedding ensemble and would have turned many heads at the ceremony.

Bride's silk handkerchief or kerchief (*mandīl*)
Mosul, Iraq, c. 1890
Silk with silver-strip embroidery
Length 25 cm / width 54 cm
As1973,03.9, gift of Fakhria Shasha in memory of Faheema Kassir Shasha

This silk handkerchief once belonged to the donor's Iraqi Christian grandmother, who was born in 1871 and came from a land-owning family from Mosul. It is expertly inscribed in Arabic in silver-strip embroidery:

إِكْلِيلُ الْهَنَاءِ وَالسُّرُورِ سَلِيم

Iklīlu'l-hanā'i wa'l-surūr Salīm
('Wreath of bliss and happiness [signed] Salim')

This inscription suggests that her bridegroom presented her with the *mandīl* for their wedding. As *iklīl* can mean 'crown', 'diadem' or 'wreath', the bride may have also worn the scarf to cover her head during the ceremony.[38] The technique of silver- or gold-strip embroidery (*badla* or *tallī*), worked here as polka dots, an elaborate floral spray and borders, originated from Mughal India and spread across the Middle East during the eighteenth and nineteenth centuries.[39]

LEFT **Two kohl holders (*mukḥula*), ʿAwlaqi tribe**
Southern Yemen (former Aden Protectorate), 1947–62
Silk, cotton, glass, silver and copper alloy, and plastic
Blue: length 11 cm / width 7 cm / depth 4 cm
Green: length 12 cm / width 6 cm / depth 3.5 cm
As2002,04.12 (blue), As2002,04.13 (green),
gift of Georgina James (both pieces)

Although comparatively small in size, these velvet kohl holders are replete with decorative trims, metallic and plastic pendants, tinkling bells, sequins, pearly beads and amuletic imitation-coral beads. Their metal spout-applicators are attached with chains.

BELOW **Two kohl holders (*mukḥula*)**
Galilee, Palestine, 1920–48
Silk, cotton, glass, coins, feathers and wood
Larger (RIGHT): length 47 cm / width 26 cm
Smaller (LEFT): length 20 cm / width 23 cm
As1968,05.7 (larger), gift of Sheikh Abdullah Khayr;
As1971,01.119 (smaller)

Decorative kohl containers were important components of bridal trousseaus in the Middle East and Central Asia. These lavish examples from Palestine, made from striped satin (*aṭlas*) and taffeta (*heremzi*) silks and decorated with Ottoman coins, glass beads, silk tassels and ostrich feathers, would have also hung as wall ornaments. The larger one holds two vessels and a carved wooden applicator stick (*mirwad*) in the middle.[42]

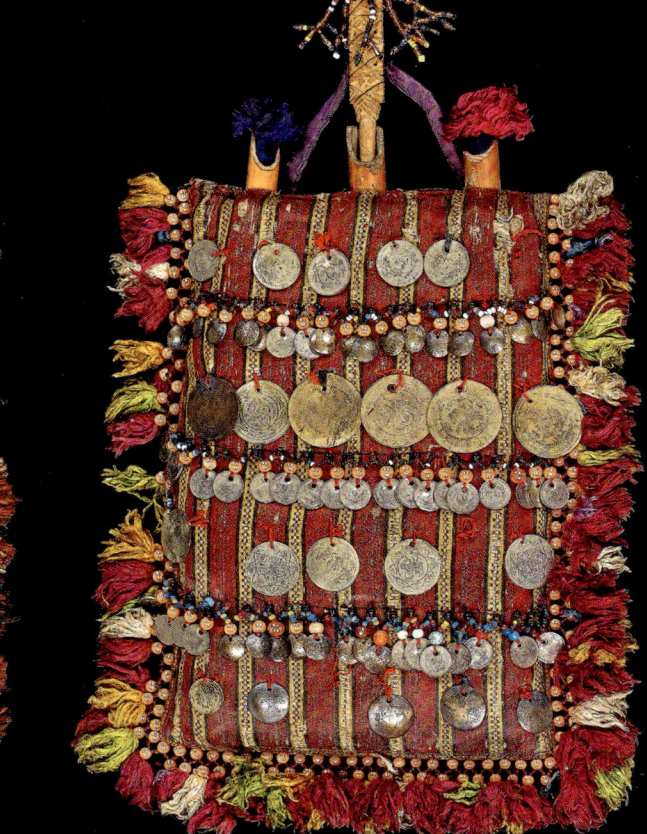

ABOVE LEFT **Kohl holder (*sormadān*), Baluch people**
Ghazni province, south-eastern Afghanistan, 1950s–1960s
Brass, cotton, silk, wool and cowrie shells
Length 70 cm / width 39 cm
As1973,07.8

The composition of kohl varies, but it is used to make the eyes look darker, shinier and more attractive. Applied to the outer and inner eyelids, it was also thought to enhance sight, cure cataracts and avert the 'evil eye'.[40] This brass kohl container is draped in a finely embroidered cotton cover with silk tassels with protective cowrie shells.[41] A long strip of embellished cloth adorning the applicator stick is used to suspend the object on a wall.

Wedding dress (*thawb malak*) and head-veil (*khirqa*)
Bethlehem area, Palestine, 1880s–1920s (dress), 1880s (veil)
Linen, silk and gilt-metal-wrapped cord (dress); linen and silk (veil)
Dress: length 133 cm / width 146 cm
Veil: length 250 cm / width 96 cm
As1967,02.11 (dress), gift of the Jerusalem and the East Mission;
As1992,08.68 (veil)

Shelagh Weir has dubbed Bethlehem the 'Paris' of Palestinian village fashions because of the widespread popularity of these distinctive dresses, which were produced for trousseaus throughout southern Palestine in the first half of the twentieth century. The fabric was woven in Palestine from linen with silk stripes, and the dress was completed with colourful Syrian taffeta inserts on the sleeves and side skirt panels. Both the fabric and dress are called *malak* ('royal'). A distinguishing feature of embroidery from the Bethlehem area is the use of silk, silver and gilt cord, couched down with tiny stitches in scrolling floral patterns that are filled in with vibrant hues of silk satin-stitch.[43] The embroidery on the chest panel of this *thawb malak* is so dense and intricate that it completely obscures the ground fabric.[44] The finely embroidered head-veil was probably first worn, concealed under an all-enveloping coat, on the wedding day when the bride was transported on horse or camel to her marital home, and on important occasions thereafter.

OPPOSITE **Bridal headdresses (*wuqāyat al-darāhim* and *shaṭweh*)**
Samu'a, southern Palestine, c. 1840s, with later additions (*wuqāyat al-darāhim*);
Bethlehem or Beit Jala, 1920s–1940s (*shatweh*)
Cotton, wool, silk, gilt-metal-wrapped cord, coins, coin tokens, metal and glass, and plastic beads and pendants
Wuqāyat al-darāhim: height 60 cm / diameter 20 cm
Shatweh: height 18 cm (36 cm with chain) / width 16 cm
As1968,04.5 (*wuqāyat al-darāhim*), As1966,01.27 (*shatweh*)

In the nineteenth and early twentieth centuries, brides in various parts of southern Palestine wore special ceremonial headdresses during their wedding ceremonies.[45] The money hat (*wuqāyat al-darāhim*) has densely packed rows of coins, beads, charms and pendants, which shielded the bride from the 'eye of envy' when she was most vulnerable – on procession to her new home and at her second public appearance, celebrating the consummation of the marriage.[46] The *shatweh*, with chin-chain (*iznāq*), was worn by brides, married women and widows in Bethlehem, Jerusalem and the surrounding villages until the 1940s, first during the wedding ceremonies, and thereafter as a symbol of married status.[47] Like other valuable coin headdresses and jewellery, these were a woman's personal assets to do with as she pleased.

ABOVE **Woman's ceremonial jacket (*taqṣīreh*)**
Bethlehem or Beit Jala, Palestine, 1900–1920s
Woollen broadcloth, silk and cotton
Length 54 cm / width 98 cm
As1966,01.6

Bethlehem and Beit Jala were mainly Christian villages, and gold- and silver-embroidered and brocaded church vestments were major sources of inspiration for the embroidery traditions in this region. So, too, were the highly decorative braided and couched uniforms of Ottoman and British military personnel, which probably inspired the waist-length *taqṣīreh* jacket. Worn over a wedding or ceremonial dress by pulling the long pointed dress sleeves through the jacket's short fitted ones, the *taqṣīreh* was a garment staple in a wedding trousseau (*jihāz*). Made of woollen broadcloth or velvet and lined with European cotton, *taqṣīreh* were produced by women in the Bethlehem area for sale to neighbouring villages. This jacket may have been commissioned for a woman in Lifta, north of Jerusalem.[48]

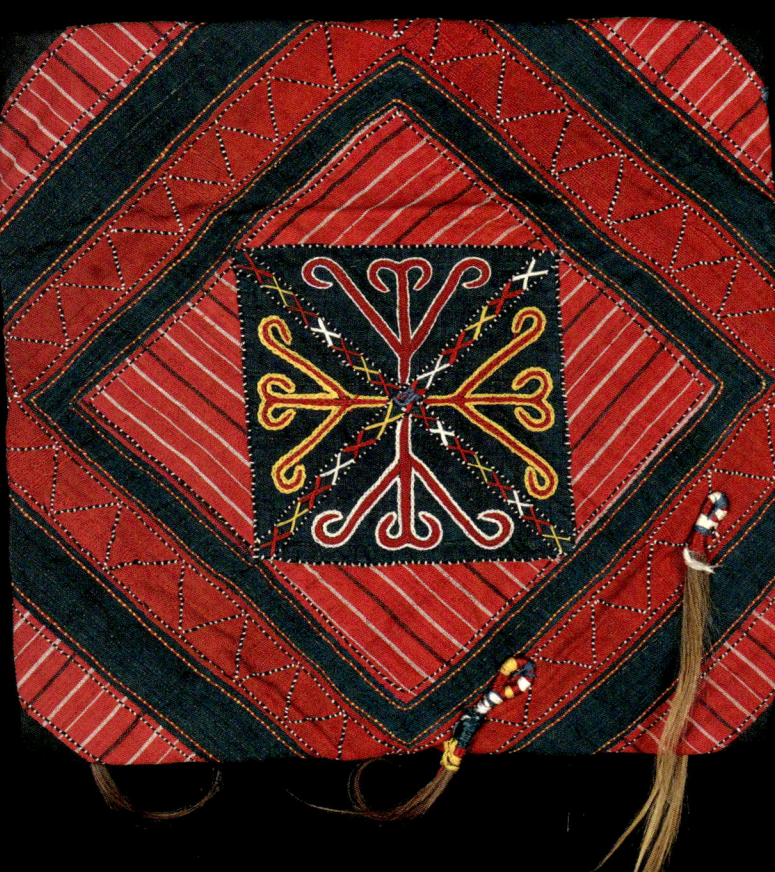

Wedding mirror bag (ā'īna bokche)
Iran, 1900–1960s
Silk, cotton, feathers and hair (front and back shown)
Length 32 cm / width 32 cm
As1975,04.15

Despite regional variations, a mirror is a key element in Iraqi, Iranian and Central Asian wedding ceremonies. A tradition that goes back centuries, it is known in Persian as the 'mirror of fortune' (ā'īna-ye bakht).[49] Once the contractual ceremony has taken place, the bride's veil is drawn back and the couple are finally permitted to gaze at each other in the mirror. A nomadic Turkmen bride used costly silk off-cuts to make this mirror bag. She decorated it with embroidered rams' horns (tirāna) and triangular motifs, feathers and locks of human hair to protect her new family and ensure her fertility.[50] The mirror should be the first object moved into the couple's new home.

Tent wall-hanging (*tus ki'iz*)
Kazakhstan, 1925–75
Cotton and silk
Length 178 cm / width 50 cm
As2002,01.3, purchased with the support of the British Museum Friends

A Kazakh yurt is replete with embroidered textiles and felts made by the women of the household during their spare time. This type of elaborate hanging, worked in chain-stitch with a hooked needle, was traditionally made by a grandmother or elder of the family, or passed down from mother to daughter.[51] During her wedding ceremony, the bride would sit in front of the propitious *tus ki'iz* in a curtained-off area. It was later hung over the marital bed or along the back wall of the yurt, facing the entrance, for all to admire.[52] The deliberately unfinished hem along the bottom edge was believed to ensure a long, happy and prosperous married life.

A Kazakh bride wearing a *saukele* headdress, Semirechenskaya district, Kazakhstan, 1880s–1890s. Photo: Konstantin Nikolaevich de Lazari (1838–1903).

Bridal headdress (*saukele*)
Kazakhstan, 1850s–1890s
Cotton, silk, wool, pearls, coral, turquoise, glass, gold and metal
Height 175 cm / width 15 cm / diameter 17 cm
As1926,0610.2, gift of Mrs T. Kallin

Saukele means 'beautiful head',[53] and a Kyrgyz or Kazakh bride wore this tall, elaborate headdress on her wedding day and on important occasions during the first year of marriage, until the birth of her first child (see the inset image). The conical structure is wrapped in red fulled wool and ornamented with stamped and engraved white metal and gilded elements stitched directly onto the fabric and as pendants hanging from chains. Many of the metal pieces are inset with amuletic coral and green beads.[54] The front of the headdress (OPPOSITE) is decorated with a net of seed pearls bordered with coral beads and a fringe of gilded pendants, while long strands of pearl, coral, silver and gold beads and silver tassels fall on the sides. Colourful silk ikat lines the inner embroidered panel and padded earflaps. The outer embroidered panel (LEFT) conceals the bride's hair plaits. Usually, a white veil is draped from the gilded finial, covering the bride's back.

ABOVE AND RIGHT **Ceremonial dress (*jillāyeh*)**
Southern plain, Palestine, 1920s
Cotton and silk
Length 137 cm / width 126 cm
As1971,10.1

Palestinian village trousseaus comprised garments purchased by the groom's side, and clothing made by the bride and her relatives, the costly materials paid for by her father or guardian. A girl began making garments for her trousseau (*jihāz*) as soon as she could embroider.[55] The *jillāyeh* was the most sumptuously embroidered and embellished dress that she produced. This one, made of indigo-dyed cotton, is heavily worked in cross-stitch on the chest and skirt panels. The satin yoke, embroidered taffeta inserts, and sleeves woven with silk stripes demonstrate that no expense was spared. The bride first wore her *jillāyeh* for the ritual of 'going out to the well' among a crowd of singing and clapping women, celebrating her newly married status.[56]

OPPOSITE **Bedouin dress (*thawb*)**
Bir Saba' region, Negev Desert, Palestine, c. 1935
Cotton and silk
Length 129 cm / width 125 cm
2011,6038.1, gift of Emma Playfair

Embroidery patterns on garments and the choice of thread colour were significant markers of Palestinian regional identity and, in some cases, marital status. The predominant use of blue on this Bedouin dress indicates that the owner was an unmarried girl or a widow. However, upon closer inspection, the lower back panel (*shinyār*) of the skirt reveals a scattering of reddish-orange triangles, and touches of gold thread have also been incorporated on the front and back, suggesting that she might have added these subtle details after marriage, or possibly remarriage.[57]

74 TEXTILES OF THE MIDDLE EAST AND CENTRAL ASIA

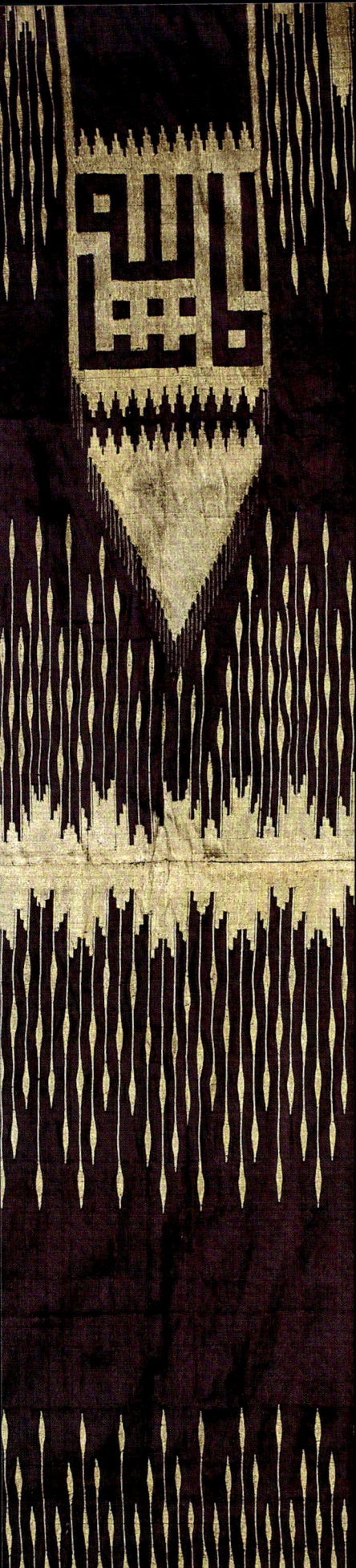

Man's ceremonial outer robe ('*abā*' or '*abāya*)
Syria or Egypt, 1880s–1890s
Silk, silver-wrapped thread and gilt-metal-wrapped thread (shown from the back)
Length 135 cm / width 130 cm
Af1994,03.1

This man's outer robe would have made a fitting garment for a groom on his wedding day. The silk, indigo-dyed in a deep purple, is richly decorated with tapestry-woven, silver-wrapped silk thread and edged in gold-dipped silver thread. It is inscribed in square Kufic script on the back with the Qur'anic phrase '*māshā' Allāh*' ('What God has willed [is good]'). This ubiquitous Muslim expression is used to convey admiration for anything good or beautiful, while guarding it from the 'eye of envy'. *Māshā' Allāh* is often found on amulets for women, children, domestic animals, cars and trucks.[58]

TOP **Embroidered skullcap**
Turkey or Egypt, 1880s–1890s
Silk, wool, cotton, gilt-metal-wrapped thread and gilt-metal spangles
Height 14 cm / diameter 19 cm
As1974,14.6, gift of Miss J. M. Watson

In the late Ottoman period, expensive velvets and metallic threads became readily available to a prospering middle class, and were no longer exclusive to the aristocracy. This festive skullcap, made of green satin silk edged with red broadcloth, is couched all over with metal-wrapped silk thread, with a repeating pattern of concentric circles framed with delicate looped borders and finished with a central spangle.[59]

CENTRE **Embroidered cap**
Turkey or Egypt, 1880s–1890s
Silk, silver-wrapped and gilt-metal-wrapped thread, gilt-metal spangles and silver and gilt-silver wire check purl
Height 4 cm / diameter 16 cm
As1974,14.5, gift of Miss J. M. Watson

A child or woman would have worn this tasselled velvet cap on special occasions. It is embroidered using the *dival* or *bindalli* technique, in which gilded threads are couched over card cut into floral shapes. The *māshā' Allāh* inscription on the front is similarly executed in silver thread and the cap is embellished all over with gilded spangles.[60]

BELOW **Spangled hat**
Turkey or Egypt, 1880s–1890s
Silk, wool, cotton, silver-wrapped thread and silver spangles
Height 10 cm / diameter 17 cm
As1974,14.4, gift of Miss J. M. Watson

Ottoman embroiderers were exceptionally skilled in working with silk and metal threads, and employed a number of techniques to transfer their designs onto the fabric, including the use of pricked stencils and printed blocks.[61] The regularity and precision of the designs on this spangled hat, using couched twisted silver-wrapped thread, were achieved in this way.

Status & Identity

In the mid-nineteenth century, at the palace of the Ottoman princess Adile Sultan, the *üçetek* ('triple-skirt') *entari* robe was worn in this way:

> the lower edges of the two front panels used to be passed between the feet, which were hidden by the folds of the *şalvar* (baggy trousers), and tucked up beneath the back panel of the skirt, so that only the back panel trailed on the ground. My mother and my elder sister immediately tucked the hems of their skirts into their narrow cashmere waistbands and walked on… Some people held the corner of their skirts in their hand as they proceeded. *Cariyes* (female servants) were not permitted to let their skirts trail, but always went around with the hems tucked in at the waist.[1]

This evocative account, from the memoirs of the Turkish poet and author Leyla Saz (d. 1936), describes the customs and etiquette within the Ottoman harem, in which dress was a clear indicator of one's status and position, in line with the established social hierarchy. Leyla's father was a highly respected court physician, and hence his

PREVIOUS PAGE Detail of velvet trousers embroidered with gilt-wrapped cord and flower motifs of silver and gilt purl with pearl centres (pp. 98–99).

RIGHT **25** Zoroastrian women wearing green and red festive attire at a ceremony to celebrate the mid-winter festival of Sadeh in the city of Shahriyar, west of Tehran, January 2010. Photo: Abedin Taherkenareh.

OPPOSITE **26** Bedouin face-cover (*burqa'*), cotton, glass, stone and resin beads, silver chains and bells, and Ottoman coins, Palestine, 1880s–1920s. L 72 cm × W 33 cm, As1982,14.1.

80 TEXTILES OF THE MIDDLE EAST AND CENTRAL ASIA

27 Woman's hood (gargūsh), cotton velvet, metal and silk cord, silver chains, gilt silver pendants, pearls, garnets, carnelians and coin pendants, Sana'a, Yemen, 1900–1930s. L 49 cm × W 46 cm, 2015,6051.1.

wife and daughters were frequent guests at the royal harem. As outsiders, they learned swiftly to adapt to shifting trends within the palace in order to assert and maintain their standing and the physician's rank in Ottoman royal circles. Palace fashions dictated changes in dress styles in Istanbul society, which, in turn, influenced shifts in taste in other urban regions of the Ottoman Empire. Several examples in this chapter from Ottoman Turkey (pp. 86–88, 98–99) and Iraq (pp. 89, 118–19) and from neighbouring Qajar Iran (pp. 92–93, 101, 104–05) explore textiles as symbols of wealth and status. Integral to these discussions is the influence exerted by courtly fashions, and the impact of Western-style garments in the nineteenth and early twentieth centuries with the increased presence of European travellers, merchants, dressmakers and products in these regions.

The choice of fabrics and the extent of embroidery and embellishment on garments not only reflected economic and social status but often indicated regional and ethnic identities. A richly appliquéd and embroidered coat (jillāyeh) produced in Ottoman Palestine (pp. 114–15) undoubtedly attests to the owner's wealth and needlework talent. However, it is also uniquely associated with the northern region of Galilee, close to Syria, which accounts for several varieties of costly Syrian silk appliquéd patches. Similarly, the cut and embroidery of particular garments in this chapter relate to specific ethnic groups, such as the Baluch people (p. 94), or religious communities, including the followers of the Druze faith (pp. 106, 116).

The Zoroastrians living in Qajar Iran (1794–1925), like other religious minorities, were required to identify themselves through dress. In particular, Zoroastrian men were permitted to wear only yellow, brown and tan-coloured clothing, trousers that were narrow and not baggy, and twisted rather than folded turbans.[2] The women also dressed in distinctive clothing, as exemplified in this chapter by the colourful and intricately embroidered Zoroastrian garments made from multiple bands of silk (pp. 90–91), worn at weddings and other special occasions. Their characteristic multi-panelled designs resulted from the restrictions on members of the community, who were not allowed to buy full widths of fabric. Notably, some Zoroastrian women in present-day Iran continue to wear tunics made from alternating panels of red and green silk on religious holidays as expressions of their dress identity (**25**).

This chapter also explores a variety of female face-coverings from the nineteenth to the twenty-first centuries that span several regions of the Arabian Peninsula (**26**, and pp. 104, 110–13) and Iran (pp. 104–05, 113). Face- and

28 Postcard entitled 'A Yemenite Beauty', showing a woman wearing a *gargūsh* made of Indian silk brocade. Published by Jamal Brothers, Jerusalem, 1921, EPH-ME.1548.

head-coverings in the Islamic world cannot be considered in isolation, or as modern political phenomena, but are 'parts of the total structure of personal appearance…[that are] consciously manipulated to assert and demarcate differences in status, identity, and commitment'.[3] Many men and women in the Islamic world customarily cover their heads, regardless of religious persuasion. This was particularly true in the nineteenth and early twentieth centuries. A group of eighteen model hats from Palestine (p. 107) highlight the complexity and diversity of headgear worn by urban and rural men in this region until the 1930s. In this context, the variations of male headgear acted as markers of age, religious affiliation, social class and occupation.

This was no less the case for female head-coverings from the Middle East and Central Asia. A compelling example is the *gargūsh* (*qarqūsh*), or woman's hood, which was the most characteristic article of clothing worn by married Jewish women and unmarried Muslim girls in Sana'a, Yemen, and was a marker of religious and social identity. An example dating from the early twentieth century is made of black velvet and is adorned with metal and silk cord, freshwater pearls, garnets, silver chains, gilded filigree plaques inset with carnelians, and gilded silver coin pendants featuring Austrian thalers and Ottoman coins (**27**). After marriage, Muslim women in Sana'a generally wore headscarves and veiled their faces (pp. 110–11), but Jewish women were permitted to wear the *gargūsh* as it complied with the legal requirement of married women to cover the head, neck, throat and shoulders, leaving only the face below the forehead exposed. After the menopause, Jewish women replaced the *gargūsh* with a black scarf.[4]

Women's hoods were also markers of economic status and varied in their material and ornamentation depending on the wearer's wealth, geographical location and the occasions on which they were worn. The gilded coins and jewellery attached to a *gargūsh* constituted the owner's personal wealth, which she could choose to sell individually in times of need, or augment when income allowed. The most lavish of all hoods was made of gold brocade imported from India (**28**), which was similarly festooned with gilded coins, filigree plaques, chains and semi-precious stones.

Over-dress (*thawb al-nashal*)
Bahrain, 1866–1900
Silk, cotton, gilt-metal- and silver-wrapped thread and gilt-metal spangles
Length 200 cm / width 310 cm
As1975,Loan01.55

This green and purple silk over-dress was expertly worked in gold- and silver-wrapped threads and gilded spangles by a professional embroiderer in Gujarat, India. The *thawb's* round, uncut neckline includes the Gujarati letters પરા (*pa-rā*, 'best'), referring to the quality of workmanship.[5] This high-status garment was presented as a gift to Prince Alfred Ernest Albert, second son of Queen Victoria and Prince Albert, between 1866 and 1900 in Bahrain.[6] The *thawb al-nashal* has been described as the 'queen of thawbs' for its densely worked panels of metal-thread embroidery.[7]

Woman's triple-skirt robe (*üçetek entari*) and chemise (*gömlek*)
Kütahya, Turkey, 1880s – 1910
Silk, cotton and gilt-metal-wrapped cord
Robe: length 135 cm / width 152 cm
Chemise: length 81 cm / width 82 cm
Belt: length 74.5 cm / width 15 cm
As1968,10.23 (robe); As1997,24.12 (chemise), gift of Ken Ward; As1968,10.50 (belt)

Until the widespread adoption of European garments in Turkey in the late Ottoman period, urban women and men of all faiths and social classes usually dressed in three basic garments: a floor- or ankle-length *entari* or kaftan robe with long sleeves, worn over a chemise (*gömlek*) and baggy trousers (*şalvar*). Further layers were added, depending on the weather and the occasion, such as waistcoats (*yeleks*), extra *entaris*, short jackets (*cepkens*) and overcoats of varying lengths. Belts with elaborate buckles and embroidered sashes created shape around the bust, waist and hips. This *üçetek* ('triple-skirt') *entari* has a front opening and deep side slits, dividing the skirt into three segments. The flowering tree embroidered in silk and silver-wrapped threads on the *gömlek* (OPPOSITE) subtly peeps through the *entari*.[8]

Woman's triple-skirt robe (üçetek entari)
Istanbul, Turkey, 1789–1807
Silk, cotton and gilt-copper-wrapped thread
Length 134 cm / width 212 cm
As1974,16.2

This *üçetek* ('triple-skirt') *entari*, with long, slit sleeves and scalloped edges, has royal associations. It is made from a richly woven silk fabric called *Selimiye*, which is patterned with stripes, floral sprigs and bands of gilt-copper threads (*kılabdan*). The fabric was named in honour of the Ottoman sultan Selim III (r. 1789–1807), who established weaving workshops in Istanbul's Üsküdar district and engaged expert weavers from France to create new fabrics with a European flavour.[9] This *entari* is said to have been worn at the court of Selim III.

Woman's triple-skirt robe (*üçetek entari*)
Mosul, Iraq, 1890s–1920s
Silk and cotton
Length 143 cm / width 277 cm
2014,6001.1, gift of Ann Searight

Iraq, bordering Turkey to the north, was part of the Ottoman Empire for almost four hundred years (1534–1918). Modes of dress in the northern Ottoman province of Mosul were greatly influenced by the latest fashions from Istanbul.[10] This ankle-length *entari*, made from locally woven taffeta silk, with scalloped edges embellished with black cord, is based on fashions from the empire's capital. The extreme length of the *entari*'s slit sleeves (277 cm, sleeve to sleeve) was a marker of wealth and social standing. By the 1930s, the elites of Baghdad and urban Christian and Jewish communities had completely abandoned Ottoman dress in favour of European-style clothing. However, among urban Muslim elites and middle classes, the adoption of Westernized clothing was a more gradual process.[11]

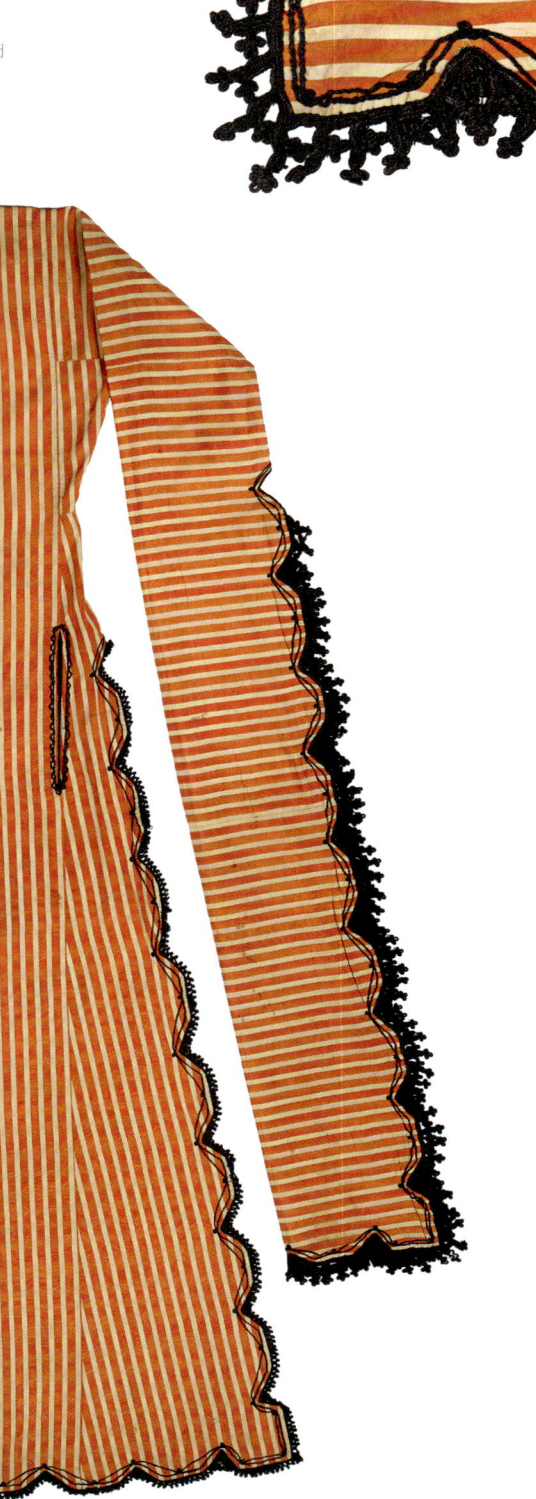

STATUS & IDENTITY

Zoroastrian garments and accessories
Yazd or Kirman, Iran, 1850s–1900
Silk and cotton
Tunic (*qamīṣ*): length 100 cm / width 97 cm
Trousers (*shalvār*): length 92 cm / width 63 cm (each leg)
Cap (*lachak*): height 19 cm / width 26 cm
Purse: length 22 cm / width 13 cm
As1966,01.556 (tunic), As1966,01.559 (trousers),
As1966,01.518 (cap), As1966,01.521 (purse)

Zoroastrian textiles from nineteenth-century Iran are instantly recognizable in terms of both their construction and fine embroidery (*zartoshtī dūzī*, 'Zoroastrian needlework'). As members of the community were not permitted, under Iranian law, to purchase cloth by the yard, they sewed their garments using narrow remnants of fabrics in contrasting colours. It was customary for young girls to embroider strips of cloth in preparation for their bridal trousseaus.[12]

This wedding ensemble comprises a loose-fitting tunic, embroidered with multi-coloured roundels in zigzag patterns, and a pair of baggy trousers made up of seven different colours of silk. The trousers are worked in dainty motifs featuring stylized suns and cats with upturned tails, thought to symbolize the male and female principles, respectively.[13] The tunic colours in *sabz-o-sorkh* ('green and red') silk were considered auspicious and continue to be worn by Zoroastrian women on special occasions in present-day Iran (see **25**).[14]

The outfit is completed with an embroidered cap tightly fitted over the head and ears and fastened under the chin, which is covered with embroidered or tie-dyed scarves (not shown) to create a layered headdress. The motifs on the cap and draw-string purse include suns, cypress trees, flowers, fish and birds, symbolizing strength, fertility, abundance and life.

Woman's coatdress
Kirman, Iran, c. 1900
Silk
Length 156 cm / width 145 cm
As1966,01.530

The cut and embroidery of this dress encapsulate both Eastern and Western influences on Qajar fashions in Iran at the turn of the nineteenth century. The Kirmani embroiderer has taken full advantage of the sandy-coloured tussah silk,[15] choosing silk floss in vivid reds and pinks to execute intricate, curling *boteh* motifs, outlined in black with highlights in green, purple and yellow. The patterns derive from Kashmiri shawls, imported into Iran from the 1780s. In contrast, the dress is cut in a Western-influenced style with tailored shoulders, sleeves and waist.[16]

LEFT **Baluchi woman's attire**
Muscat, Oman, 1990
Silk
Dress (*dishdāsha* or *pashk*): length 106 cm / width 146 cm
Trousers (*sirwāl* or *shalwār*): length 93 cm / width 46 cm (waist)
Head-shawl (*shādar* or *chādar*): length 198 cm / width 118 cm
2011,6003.44.a–c, gift of the Ministry of Tourism of the Sultanate of Oman

This satin silk, calf-length dress with matching loose trousers and head-shawl represents a style of dress worn by nomadic and urban Baluchis across the world. Its recognizable feature is the large, richly embroidered A-shaped pocket (*pado* or *pandohl*) stitched down the front of the skirt.[17] Worked mainly in box-stitch, the embroidery is concentrated on the chest panel (*jīg*), front skirt, sleeve-cuffs and ankles. Generations of Baluchis have lived and prospered in Oman over centuries, but many maintain their distinctive dress style as a marker of their ethnic identity.[18]

OPPOSITE **Over-dress (*thawb*)**
Kuwait, 1930s–1980s
Silk
Length 152 cm / width 163 cm
As2000,05.4, gift of Victoria R. Koymans

Although similar in cut to the *thawb al-nashal* (pp. 84–85), this *thawb* is made from a sheer, netted silk and has subtle embroidery around its neckline imitating a necklace. Its characteristic feature, however, is the use of contrasting bands of appliquéd jacquard silk, creating a style of *thawb* that is also worn in Bahrain and central Saudi Arabia. This one was made for the British author Violet Dickson (d. 1991), who lived in Kuwait for more than sixty years and was recognized for her intimate knowledge of Bedouin customs and the country's natural history.[19]

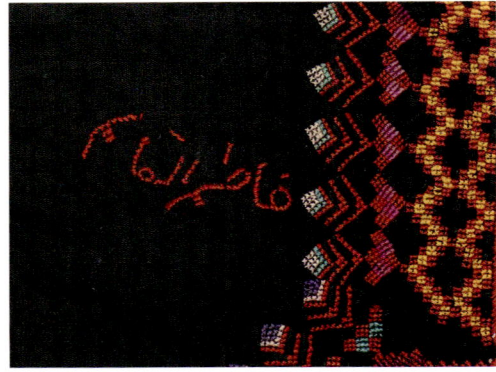

Woman's wedding coat and dress
Al-Sukhnah (coat, LEFT) and Saraqib (dress, RIGHT), Syria, 1930s–1950s
Silk and cotton
Coat: length 130 cm / width 142 cm
Dress: length 134 cm / width 143 cm
As1994,13.1 (coat), 2014,6035.1 (dress)

During the Ottoman and Mandate periods, Damascus, Aleppo and Homs were great producers and exporters of textiles. From the 1930s onwards, however, imported machine-made fabrics, including cotton sateen (*tubayt*) and satins, became increasingly popular, and were embroidered using waste canvas and newly introduced DMC mercerized cotton thread. Waste canvas provided a removable grid for cross-stitching on closely woven fabrics, and remnants of canvas thread are detected on the wedding coat from central Syria (visible in the centre of the detail opposite). Although restrained in comparison, the embroidery on the dress, from north-western Syria, uniquely includes the name of the embroiderer, Fatima al-Qasim, on the left shoulder (see detail above).[20]

Woman's şalvar and cepken outfit
Turkey, 1900–20
Silk, cotton, silver wire check purl, gilt-metal-wrapped cord, gilt-metal spangles and pearls
Trousers (şalvar): length 155.5 cm / width 156 cm
Outer jacket (cepken): length 41 cm / width 136 cm
Inner jacket (cepken): length 46 cm / width 154 cm
Chemise (gömlek): length 82 cm / width 148 cm
Sash (uçkur): length 185 cm / width 21 cm
As1968,10.21 (trousers); As1968,10.20 (outer jacket); As1968,10.22 (inner jacket); As1968,10.30 (chemise); 2011,6007.7 (sash), gift of Dominique Collon

The style of this five-piece ensemble originated from the Balkans region, once part of the Ottoman Empire. It comprises voluminous draw-string velvet trousers, two matching long-sleeved, cropped jackets, edged in gilt braid, a silk crepe chemise and an embroidered sash. The longer cuts of the chemise (gömlek) and inner jacket (cepken) create a layered effect under the cropped outer jacket. The velvet garments are embroidered with couched gilt-metal-wrapped cord in swirling patterns embellished with gilt-metal spangles, and the trousers additionally include pearls set within flowers (see pp. 78–79). Şalvar and cepken outfits were popular in Turkey in the late nineteenth and early twentieth centuries, particularly in the north-western provinces, which had significant settled populations from the Balkans.[21]

RIGHT **Woman's coat (çabūt) and trousers (çulvar), Yomut Turkmen people**
Iran, 1930s–1950s
Silk, cotton, rayon and gilt-metal braid
Coat: length 107 cm / width 86 cm
Trousers: length 78 cm / width 78 cm
As1973,09.199 (coat), As1973,09.197 (trousers)

The Anatolian adage *Türkün gözü aldadır* ('A Turk has his eye on the red') also relates to the Turkmen peoples' strong preference for the colour, as reflected in their textile traditions.[22] The striped silks used for the coat and trousers would have been locally woven by Yomut Turkmen women, who sometimes cultivated their own mulberry trees on which the silkworms fed. A long-sleeved, baggy red dress was worn over the trousers and under the short-sleeved coat, which allowed the heavily embroidered trouser-cuffs to show. The coat is bordered with gilt braid and has inner facings of colourful machine-embroidered panels. The embroidered motifs on the trousers are called *gülledi* or *gül yaydı* ('opened flower').[23]

OPPOSITE **Woman's jacket (arkhāloq or nīm-tana) and hat (kolāh)**
Mashhad, Iran, 1880s–1920
Silk, cotton, gilt-silver-wrapped cord, silver strip and mother-of-pearl
Jacket: length 63 cm / width 147 cm
Hat: height 6 cm / diameter 15 cm
2014,6013.5 (jacket), 2014,6013.6 (hat)

This velvet bridal or festive jacket is couched in gilt-silver-wrapped braided cord with pomegranates, tulips, large paisleys (*boteh*) and swirly open-work patterns, associated with the embroiderers of Mashhad. With mother-of-pearl buttons and lined in lime green taffeta, it was worn with a matching pillbox hat with silver-strip embroidery. The complete outfit comprised a long-sleeved chemise (*pīrāhan*), a short gathered skirt (*shalīta*) and cotton trousers (*shalvār*), each worked with borders of gilt-metal-wrapped cord.[24] The jacket's notched collar and flap pockets reflect the shift towards Europeanized fashions in urban Iran, which began in the 1870s under Nasir al-Din Shah (r. 1848–96). Reza Shah Pahlavi (r. 1925–41) abolished all forms of non-European-style dress in the 1930s.[25]

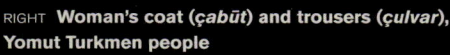

Set of dolls in Palestinian dress
Jericho, Palestine, 1950s–1960s
Silk, cotton, polyester, sequins, card and metal wire
Height 19–20 cm
2012,6014.75–83, gift of the Jerusalem and Middle East Church Association

At the turn of the nineteenth to the twentieth century, women in Bethlehem made dolls wearing regional attire for sale as souvenirs for pilgrims visiting the Holy Land (see pp. 34–35). This set of seven dolls, dressed in a variety of Palestinian garments, was made in very different circumstances – at the World's YWCA School at the Aqabat Jaber Refugee Camp in Jericho, which sheltered 30,000 refugees between 1948 and 1967. The YWCA established programmes to provide income and to help meet the basic needs of the inhabitants. Made of textile over a wired metal frame, the dolls are identified as representing the following styles of dress (LEFT TO RIGHT): Bethlehem (a married woman), Bethany or al-'Azariya, Al-Salt (a Bedouin), Nazareth, an urban Muslim in outdoor veils, Jerusalem (Bait Mahsir district) and Jericho.[26]

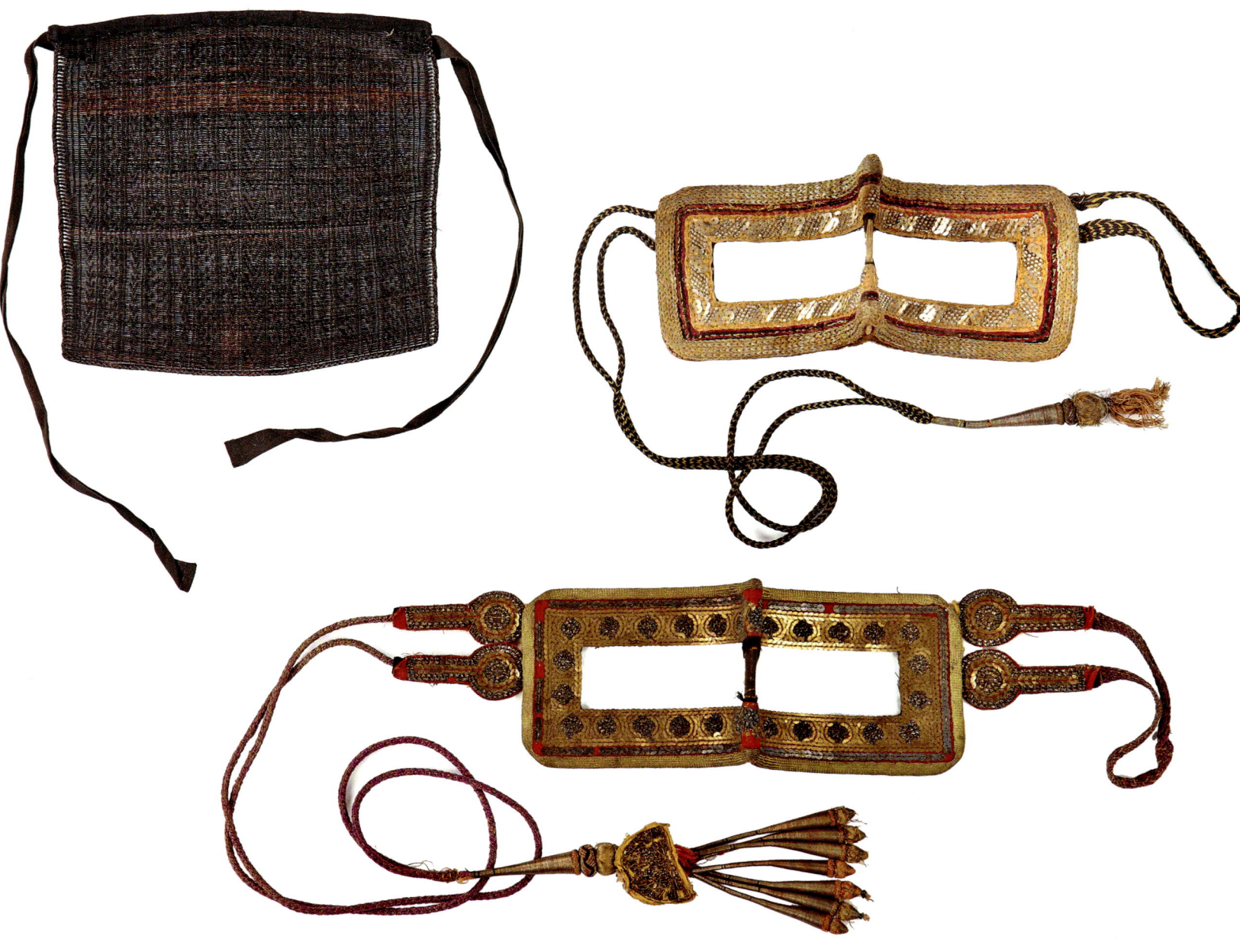

ABOVE, LEFT **Woman's face-cover (pīcha)**
Iran, 1870s–1910
Horsehair and cotton
Length 23 cm / width 22.5 cm
As1966,01.106

The square, stiff face-cover (pīcha), made of finely woven horsehair, has a long history in the Iranian world and is depicted in Persian miniatures from the fifteenth century. Worn by upper-class women as an amulet, it was a short visor (chashmāvīz), which covered the lower forehead while casting a shadow over the rest of the face.[27] The nineteenth-century example here was held in place with cotton ties and covered the entire face. The pīcha went out of fashion at the beginning of the seventeenth century, only to be revived by the urban classes in the late nineteenth century in Iran and Ottoman Turkey. Cooler and more comfortable than cloth veils, pīchas were made in both shorter and longer lengths.[28]

ABOVE **Woman's face-masks (saif malik and barakoa)**
Muscat, Oman, 1890s (saif malik); Zanzibar (barakoa), 1900–1920s
Cotton, silk, silver-wrapped thread, silver strip and gilt-silver spangles
Saif malik (ABOVE, RIGHT): length 32 cm / height 11 cm
Barakoa (BELOW): length 40 cm / height 11 cm
2010,6003.7 (saif malik), gift of Carl Phillips; 2012,6030.61 (barakoa), gift of Leila Ingrams

Face-masks of these kinds were worn by elite urban women of Muscat and Zanzibar as markers of wealth and status until the early twentieth century. They are made of sturdy cotton, embroidered with silver strip and embellished with gilt-silver spangles, ornamental tassels and braided loops and ties. Referred to as a saif malik in Oman and a barakoa in Zanzibar, the mask has a raised centre with a wooden spine that rests on the bridge of the nose. According to Princess Salme of Zanzibar (d. 1924), a bride concealed her face behind her costly mask until her bridegroom presented her with a gift.[29]

TEXTILES OF THE MIDDLE EAST AND CENTRAL ASIA

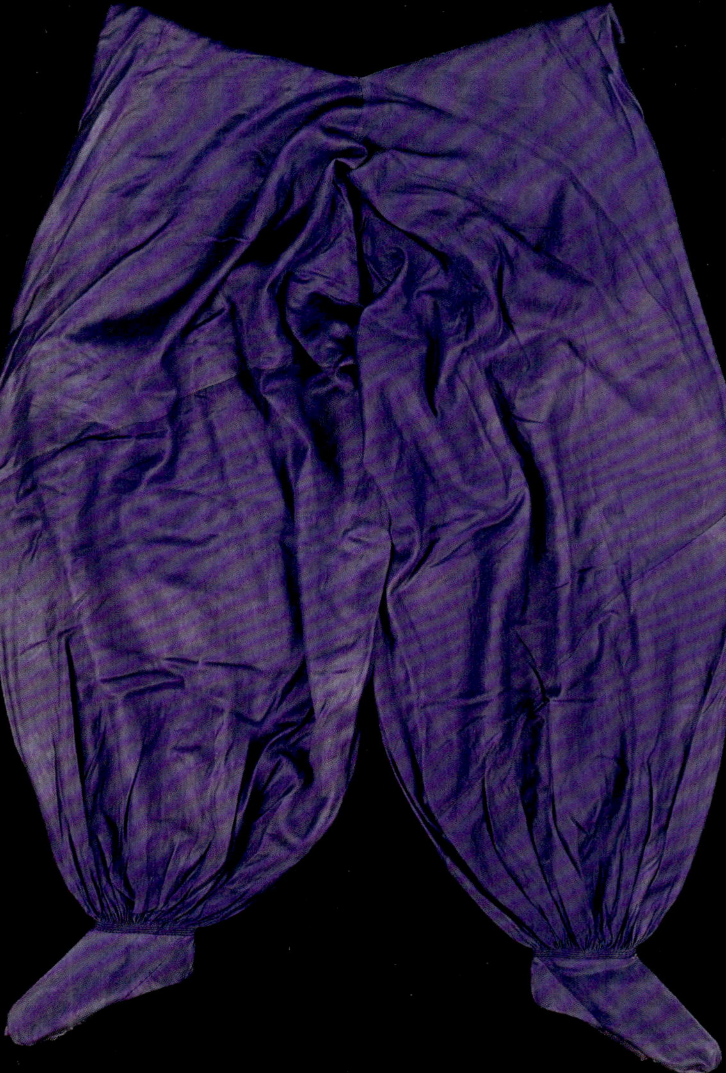

Outdoor face-veil (*rūband*) and trousers (*chāqchūr* or *chāqshūr*)
Iran, 1850s–1900
Cotton and silk
Face-veil: length 112 cm / width 47 cm
Trousers: length 141 cm / width 64 cm (maximum, each l
As 1981,19.2 (veil), As 1981,19.1 (trousers)

This type of outdoor face-veil (*rūband*), made of fi
cotton, developed from earlier models dating from
seventeenth century.[30] The grille around the eye a
is executed using pulled threadwork, in which sma
sections of thread on the cotton ground are pulle
bound tightly together using a needle and silk thr
forming a lattice pattern of holes.[31] Some women
wore voluminous *chāqchūr* trousers gathered at th
ankles, with integral slippers, allowing them to tuc
their skirts and other garments inside. The outdoo
outfit was completed with a *chādor* (*chādar*), an al
enveloping sleeveless outer garment, over which t
rūband was tied.[32] By the late Qajar period, *chāqc
trousers were considered old-fashioned and were
seldom worn by upper-class women.[33]

ABOVE **Set of model Palestinian hats**
Palestine, 1890s–1920s
Silk, wool, fur, cotton, wood and paper
Peg-board: length 43 cm / width 20.5 cm
Hats: height 3.5–8.5 cm / diameter 5–5.5 cm
As1987,07.6.a–s (peg-board and hats);
As1987,07.7.a–r (pegs). Gift of the Jerusalem and Middle East Church Association (all items)

In most parts of the Islamic world, men and women customarily cover their heads, regardless of religious persuasion. The practice of wearing some form of headgear is driven by cultural etiquette and, for Jews and Muslims, by religious requirement during prayer. As Shelagh Weir explains in the context of pre-1948 Palestine, 'The head was the locus of a man's honour and reputation, and it was proper and dignified that it should be covered, and shameful ('ayb) to leave it uncovered (as it was also for women).'[36] This set of eighteen model hats was made for tourists, pilgrims and church missions, and represents the variety of adult male headgear worn in Palestinian towns and villages until the 1930s. The model hats reflect the importance of headgear as markers of age and experience, religious affiliation, social hierarchies and occupation.

The hats are identified as follows (BACK ROW, LEFT TO RIGHT): urban man's tall fez (*ṭarbūsh isṭambūlī*), Armenian priest's pointed cowl (*veghar*), Bedouin's or villager's head-cloth (*kūfīya* or *ḥaṭṭa*) with head-rope ('*aqāl* or '*iqāl*),[37] Ethiopian priest's hat, Greek Orthodox bishop's headdress;[38] (MIDDLE ROW): Spanish Rabbi's *ṭarbūsh* wrapped in a black turban (*laffeh* or *laffa*), Hasidic Jew's velvet and fur hat (*shtrayml*),[39] Coptic priest's *ṭarbūsh* wrapped in black cloth, Armenian theological student's hat, Greek priest's hat (*kalimavkion*), town porter's felt cap with yellow head-cloth;[40] (FRONT ROW): villager's *ṭarbūsh*, wrapped in a green turban to signify that the wearer is a follower of the Qadariyya Sufi order,[41] turban-wrapped felt cap (*libda* or *libbada*) worn by porters and lower-class urban workers, Muslim religious specialist's multi-coloured *ṭarbūsh* wrapped in a green turban,[42] conical hat of a caretaker of Muslim holy sites and mosques,[43] Muslim scholar's *ṭarbūsh* smoothly wrapped in a white turban,[44] *ṭarbūsh* of a Christian or Muslim villager from the Bethlehem region,[45] village elder's or notable's *ṭarbūsh* wrapped in a silk-embroidered *ghabānī* cloth with an indigo-dyed tassel. The *ṭarbūsh isṭambūlī* is a direct reference to the tall, urban style of fez fashionable in the Ottoman Empire's capital.

OPPOSITE **Man's coat (*bisht*), Druze people**
Syria or Palestine, 1900–1930s
Wool (shown from the back)
Length 79 cm / width 86 cm
As1966,01.198

The thick, hand-woven woollen fabric (*busht*) of this short-sleeved coat lends the garment its name. Tapestry-woven with multi-coloured stripes, this style of *bisht* is associated with the Muslim Druze communities living in the mountainous terrains of northern Palestine, Syria and Lebanon. Their tight-fitting *bishts* sometimes feature intricate brocaded patterns on the back.[34] Although the Druzes are a minority and follow a closed, esoteric interpretation of Islam, they maintained considerable autonomy under the Ottoman Empire and often rebelled against it. This relative independence allowed them to develop some distinctive forms of male and female dress and headdress.[35]

STATUS & IDENTITY   107

Woman's festive dress (*korta*)
Bayt al-Faqih, Tihama, Yemen, 1950s–1970s
Cotton, silver strip, lurex and synthetic fabrics
Length 119 cm / width 131 cm
As2002,06.6, gift of Carl Phillips

This is a distinctive style of festive dress (*korta*) from Bayt al-Faqih in the southern Tihama region along the Red Sea coast of Yemen. These narrow, black cotton dresses with stand-up collars are densely worked in couched white and silver braid, and recall late Ottoman military uniforms. At one time, they were made from indigo-dyed cotton and worn as wedding dresses. The patterns, worked by professional embroiderers, are couched in precise rows forming geometric blocks, which possibly refer to the sorghum and millet fields cultivated in the region. In fact, such dresses are associated with Bayt al-Faqih's farming communities.[46] The silver-wrapped cotton bands applied on the chest and side panels were hand-plaited using cushions and pins. Some say that the complexity of the patterns, with flashes of red and green, protect the most vulnerable parts of the body from the 'evil eye'.[47]

**Woman's face-veil with head-piece
(*maghmūq* with *ra's maghmūq*)**
Sana'a, Yemen, 1960s–1970s
Silk, cotton, silver, brass and ceramic beads
Length 108.5 cm / width 54 cm
As1979,01.7

The *maghmūq*, a black face-veil with large red and white tie-dyed motifs, used to deflect the 'evil eye' and unwanted male gazes, was worn by older girls and women in Sana'a during the twentieth century.[48]

Its elaborately embroidered (optional) head-piece is densely worked in silver-wrapped white and yellow cotton threads to create both silver and gold effects. Once worn to indicate marital status, the head-piece (*ra's*, 'head') is embellished with amuletic brass chains and imitation coral beads. The *maghmūq* was worn under a colourful draped head-shawl (*sitāra*) and covered the entire face; it was worn in public as a sign of modesty and social status, and provided freedom of movement for Sana'ani women within the city's deeply conservative environment.[49]

Dolls in UAE dress
Sharjah, UAE, 1980s
Cotton, wood, plastic and synthetic fibres
Height 18 cm / width 5 cm
2011,6009.40 (woman), 2011,6009.41 (man).
Gift of Wilhelmina van de Weg and Joan Elliot

These locally made dolls may have provided a desirable alternative to Western models as children's toys. Conversely, they may have been produced for the tourist market as idealized representations of local inhabitants. The female doll is dressed in an ankle-length, loose-fitting printed dress with narrow sleeves (kandūra) and metallic trims. She also wears a black cotton face-mask (niqāb or burqa') of a kind worn mainly by Bedouin women in the north and north-east of the Arabian Peninsula, which covers the whole face except the eyes. A black head-cover (shayla) conceals her hair.[50] Her fingernails and toenails are painted red and both dolls are depicted with long-lashed, attractive eyes. The bearded male doll wears an ankle-length white tunic (thawb, dishdāsha or kandūra), and a white head-cloth (ghuṭra) held in place with a black head-rope ('iqāl). Together, they challenge Western notions of beauty, body proportions and dress, as represented in dolls such as Barbie and Ken.

LEFT **Festive Bedouin face-mask (*burqa'*)**
Dhofar, southern Oman, 1990s
Cotton, wood and metallic and synthetic trims
Height 20.5 cm / width 25.5 cm
2011,6003.58, gift of the Ministry of Tourism
of the Sultanate of Oman

Embroiderers of Oman's southernmost region, Dhofar, are renowned for their use of colourful, decorative stitching and appliqué work. Bedouin women in the region wear vibrant and glittering hand-stitched *burqa's* for special occasions, embellished with shiny trims and sequins. This example made of black cotton, with its characteristic nose-pleat stiffened with wood, is decorated with chain-stitched embroidery in coloured and metallic threads around the oblong-shaped eye-slits. The *burqa'* is framed with several borders of metallic and hand-plaited trims in pink, green, silver and gold.[51] Such masks were not only worn to uphold religious beliefs, but were objects of adornment and fashion accessories.

RIGHT **Indigo-dyed face-mask (*burqa'* or *baṭṭūla*)**
Al Ain, UAE, 2011
Cotton, wood and synthetic fibre
Height 9.5 cm / width 18 cm
2012,6004.8

This modern, urban *baṭṭūla* was made by a Bedouin woman from Al Ain from imported indigo-dyed cotton that is burnished with a stone or other hard surface to make it gleam like gold. Variations in shape, size and ornamentation in such face-masks often revealed the wearer's age and marital and economic status. Their popularity has declined in recent years among younger generations.[52]

LEFT **Face-mask (*burqa'* or *baṭṭūla*)**
Minab, Persian Gulf, Iran, 1990–92
Cotton, wood and acrylic
Height 9 cm / width 22.8 cm
2008,6025.4

Shi'a women living in the towns of Sirik and Minab along the Iranian shores of the Persian Gulf wear a distinctive *burqa'*, densely machine-embroidered in shades of red, and having a pronounced central nose-pleat; their Sunni Baluch counterparts living in the region prefer orange versions.[53]

RIGHT **Indigo-dyed Bedouin face-mask (*burqa'*)**
Central Oman, 1950s
Cotton, wood and synthetic fibre
Height 16 cm / width 20.5 cm
2011,6003.54, gift of the Ministry of Tourism of the Sultanate of Oman

The face-masks (*burqa's*) of the Bedouin women living in the desert regions of Oman are emblems of sexual modesty and moral excellence, and are essential elements of a woman's attire. Worn from the onset of menstruation, they are made by pre-pubescent girls in anticipation of their transition to womanhood. They also offer protection against the desert's harsh weather conditions.[54]

STATUS & IDENTITY

Woman's festive or wedding coat (*jillāyeh*)
Upper Galilee, Palestine, 1830s–1890s
Cotton and silk (shown from the back and inside out)
Length 121 cm / width 89 cm
As1966,01.65

The style of this high-status coat, which would have been worn for weddings and other special occasions, was unique to the villages of Upper Galilee. A glorious feast for the eyes, it is made from hand-woven, indigo-dyed cotton and features nine types of plain and patterned appliquéd Syrian silks along the front. Patches of green, yellow and red taffeta (*heremzi*) and striped and ikat-dyed satin (*atlas*) are cut into squares, triangles and slashed irregular shapes, which are carefully arranged and basted down before stitching. The appliqué stitches themselves become decorative features, as these coats were often worn inside out (ABOVE) on sombre occasions. The coat's densely embroidered back panel is another triumph of colour and pattern, worked mainly in red silks with touches of blue, yellow, white and green, and with a band of drawn-threadwork.[55]

Woman's festive coat (durāʿa), Druze people

Galilee, Palestine, 1880s–1920s
Silk and cotton
Length 124 cm / width 91 cm
As1968,05.2, gift of Sheikh ʿAbdullah Khayr

Until the early twentieth century, the main over-garment for village women in the Galilee region was a short-sleeved coat called a durāʿa, which was made from locally woven cotton. This sumptuous durāʿa, associated with the Druze community, is constructed mainly from imported luxury fabrics and trims from Syria or possibly Europe, including a fuchsia-pink silk satin, with a contrasting turquoise silk brocade. The brown sleeves and green lining are made from fine, locally woven cotton, and the decorative cord edging betrays Ottoman influence. A striped effect is created by the stitches attaching the brocade panels.[56]

Woman's festive coat (*durāʿa* or *qumbāz*)
Syria, 1930s–1950s
Cotton and silk
Length 123.5 cm / width 138 cm
2014,6051.3

The cities of Aleppo and Damascus continued to be renowned centres of production for luxury silk fabrics throughout the twentieth century. Several costly satins (*atlas*), woven with silk warps and cotton wefts, are applied as facings to this indigo-dyed cotton coat, including a yellow and orange ikat-patterned *atlas*, sometimes referred to as 'birds' tongues' (*lisān al-ʿaṣfūr*). The embroidery is worked on the front and sleeves mainly in cross-stitch with multi-coloured mercerized or perlé cotton threads, which were introduced from France around the 1930s and gradually displaced silk-floss threads produced in Homs and Lebanon.

Woman's embroidered plastron
Mosul, Iraq, 1880–90
Cotton with gilt-silver strip
Length 57 cm / width 30 cm
As1973,03.4, gift of Fakhria Shasha in memory of Faheema Kassir Shasha

A plastron is an ornamental panel worn under a gown to adorn a woman's bodice, and it can be made of luxurious materials embellished with lace or embroidery. Plastrons were fashionable in Europe in the late nineteenth century and this Iraqi example combines European design with Ottoman embroidery techniques. Gilt-silver strip is folded over the open weave of the cotton ground, creating a dense pattern of floral vine-scrolls.

Woman's festive or wedding attire
Mosul, Iraq, 1880–90
Silk, cotton, gilt-silver-wrapped thread and
gilt-silver strip
Trousers: length 84 cm / width 78 cm
Dress: length 134 cm / width 138 cm
Chemise: length 118 cm / width 168 cm
Jacket: length 45 cm / width 138 cm
Waistcoat: length 39 cm / width 46 cm
Sash: length 200 cm / width 16 cm
As 1973,03.1 (trousers), As 1973,03.6 (dress), As 1973,03.3 (chemise),
As 1973,03.7 (jacket), As 1973,03.5 (waistcoat), As 1973,03.4 (plastron),
As 1973,03.2 (sash). Gift of Fakhria Shasha (all items)

This seven-piece ensemble, comprising draw-string trousers (not visible), chemise, dress, waistcoat, jacket, plastron (opposite) and sash, belonged to a Christian woman from Mosul.[57] The European-style dress, with narrow sleeves and a gathered waist, is made from Syrian or European silk and is trimmed with blue ribbon and lace. By the late nineteenth century, in the urban centres of the Ottoman Empire, the taste for *entari* robes with trousers was changing in favour of European-style dresses, skirts and blouses. One of the greatest catalysts for the change in fashions was the increased presence of European travellers, tailors, dressmakers, merchants and missionaries.[58] French Dominican and Carmelite missionaries also set up schools in Mosul and Baghdad where they taught girls embroidery as a formal subject from the age of 7.[59]

Religion & Belief

Religion & Belief

> O children of Adam! We have bestowed upon you clothing (*libās*) to conceal your private parts and as adornment. But the garb of piety (*libās al-taqwā*) – that is best. That is from the signs of Allah that perhaps they will remember.
>
> Qur'an 7:26

The holy Qur'an, believed by Muslims to be the Word of God revealed in Arabic to the Prophet Muhammad (d. 632) through the Angel Gabriel, refers to clothing twenty-three times, both explicitly and metaphorically. One of the most symbolically charged garments mentioned is the shirt (*qamīṣ*) of the prophet Yusuf (Joseph), which served time and again to establish truth and validate Joseph's position as God's chosen prophet–king.¹ Analogously, the historical account in which the Prophet wrapped his cloak (*kisā'*) around the four people dearest to him – his daughter Fatima, his cousin and son-in-law 'Ali, and their sons, al-Hasan and al-Husayn – established the pre-eminence of these five individuals, known collectively as the 'People of the Cloak'. For Shi'a Muslims, the cloak is a metaphor for the temporal and spiritual authority that was transferred by the Prophet to his immediate family and their descendants.²

Undoubtedly, the most famous religious textile in an Islamic context is the *kiswa*, the fabric covering of the holy *Ka'ba*, the cube-like stone structure in the centre of the Great Mosque (*al-masjid al-ḥarām*) in Mecca (**29**).³ Although it was a venerated structure before Islam, the Prophet sanctioned the Muslim annual pilgrimage (*ḥajj*) to the *Ka'ba*, the sevenfold ritual circumambulation (*ṭawāf*) around the structure and the dressing of the *Ka'ba*. The privilege of presenting sacred textiles to the sanctuaries at Mecca and Medina was highly coveted by Muslim rulers throughout history. Inscribed with

PREVIOUS PAGE Detail of a child's over-shirt made of silk, with a protective cotton triangle and amulets of black and white cord and human hair stitched to the back (p. 137).

29 Postcard from Mecca showing the Ka'ba covered in the *kiswa*; the minarets of the Great Mosque appear in the background. Published by Sarawat Printers & Designers, Saudi Arabia, 2010–2011, 2011,6043.22, purchased with the support of the Modern Museum Fund.

30 Man's ikat-dyed quilted and embroidered conical cap for daily use (including prayer), cotton, silk and glass beads, Tajikistan, 1930s–1960s. H 13 cm × D 20 cm, 2014,6034.15, gift of Zeina Klink-Hoppe.

the patron's name and date and made in imperial workshops primarily in Egypt and Turkey (and since 1926 in Mecca), these textiles and their associated ceremonies publicly legitimized a ruler's religious and political authority.[4] The *kiswa's* main outer covering is made up of several pieces of black silk, which are inscribed with woven and embroidered Qur'anic verses. Equally splendid are the belt (*ḥizam*) encircling the Ka'ba and the elaborate curtain (*sitāra* or *burqu'*, 'veil') for the external door, which are inscribed with verses from the holy scripture couched over padding with gold and silver thread.[5]

This chapter includes a curtain commissioned by the Ottoman sultan Selim III (r. 1789–1807) for the Prophet's Mosque at Medina (pp. 126–27). As the first residence of the Prophet after he left Mecca, his burial place and that of members of his family, Medina is held in the highest regard, together with Mecca and Jerusalem, and is also visited by Muslim pilgrims. The positioning of the sultan's name on the richly embroidered curtain, alongside the names of the four rightly guided caliphs of Islam (Abu Bakr, 'Umar, 'Uthman and 'Ali), and the choice of Qur'anic verses alluding to God's promised rewards for the pious substantiate Selim's political and spiritual ambitions.

From the majestic textiles for the holy sanctuaries to the humble child's bonnet we encountered in 'Childhood' (p. 31), for centuries Muslims have been inspired to draw on the Qur'anic text, sayings of the Prophet and other pious invocations to sanctify and ornament buildings and objects of all media as expressions of their piety and faith.[6] Many Muslims also have faith in the power of God's Word and in

RELIGION & BELIEF

OPPOSITE **32** Special bags and pouches were made to store personal copies of the Qur'an. This cotton Qur'an bag, decorated in silk cross-stitched embroidery by a nomadic Uzbek woman, features silk tassels with glass beads; Afghanistan, 1880s–1890s. L 60 cm × W 42 cm, As1997,03.5.

31 Painting of a Mevlevi Sufi dervish performing his ritual dance (*samā'*) and wearing a tall *sikke* hat, opaque watercolour on paper, from an album of late Ottoman-period costumes, Turkey, *c.* 1790 ('Costumes turcs', vol. 2, fol. 50r). H 37 cm × W 22 cm (sheet), 1974,0617,0.12.2.50.

other inscribed prayers and blessings to protect them from harm. The belief in the potency of non-Qur'anic pious invocations is attested by the inscriptions woven on a woman's jacket from Syria in this chapter (p. 136); the recurring expression of wishes for good health reflect a well-established tradition of inscribing benedictory phrases on objects of daily life to procure divine blessings for the owner. The written word is used for an entirely different purpose on a cloak from Iraq or Iran, embroidered with the age-old proverb 'If speech is silver, silence is golden' (p. 132). One can only speculate on the original purpose and context of this enigmatic garment.

Several textiles in this chapter can be grouped under the general theme of amuletic objects, believed to protect their owners against the 'evil eye' and other malevolent forces (pp. 140–41). Some are inherently protective, such as the shimmering indigo-dyed and burnished cotton garments from Yemen (pp. 134–35). The deep indigo blue transfers to skin and hair, and is considered not only attractive but also defensive against illness and misfortune. Other examples have amuletic components sewn onto them, including human hair, cowrie shells or textile elements in the shape of snakes or triangles (pp. 120–21, 137, 141). We have already seen examples of how Qur'anic and other inscriptions on paper are worn enclosed within textile amulets or pinned onto textiles as jewellery (see 'Childhood', pp. 26, 28, 33). The present chapter also features articles of clothing made for Muslim funerary rituals (pp. 138–39), in contrast with textiles used for day-to-day religious practices, such as prayer caps (**30**), prayer mats (p. 130), and decorative bags used for storing copies of the holy Qur'an (**32**).

Finally, this chapter includes a selection of objects associated with specific religious groups, including an embroidered prayer mat for Shi'a Muslims from Qajar Iran (pp. 128–29) and a prayer cloth with a distinctive function and iconography, made for the Shi'a Hazara communities of Afghanistan (p. 130). In simplest terms, Shi'as believe that the Prophet entrusted the political and spiritual leadership of the Muslim community to his cousin and son-in-law 'Ali ibn Abi Talib (d. 661), the first Shi'a imam ('leader') and fourth Muslim caliph. This authority was passed on to 'Ali's descendants through the Prophet's daughter, Fatima. Shi'a material culture and ritual thus reflect a deep reverence for the Prophet and members of his family.[7] Also included in this chapter are tall felt hats (*sikke*; p. 133) associated with the Mevlevi Sufi order, popularly known as the whirling dervishes (**31**).

Curtain (*sitāra*) for the Prophet's Mosque at Medina
Medina, Saudi Arabia, 1204 AH (1789–90)
Silk, silver and silver-gilt wire, and cotton padding
Length 252 cm / width 150 cm
2016,6030.1, gift of the Khalili Family Trust [8]

This sumptuously embroidered curtain, featuring a mosque lamp and candlesticks within an arch, was presented to the Prophet's Mosque by the Ottoman sultan Selim III (r. 1789–1807) in 1790 as part of the ceremonies for the annual pilgrimage (*ḥajj*) to Mecca. Inscribed with Qur'anic verses and a saying of the Prophet Muhammad (d. 632) – 'He who prays for me once shall be blessed by God tenfold' – the *sitāra* asserted Selim's position as the custodian of Islam's holiest cities.[9]

Prayer mat (*sajjāda*) and prayer-stone (*mohr* or *turba*)

Iran, 1790–1850 (prayer mat); Karbala, Iraq, 1900–17 (prayer-stone)
Silk, wool, cotton and silver-wrapped thread (prayer mat)
Prayer mat: height 49 cm / width 34.5 cm
Prayer-stone: height 0.8 cm / diameter 3 cm
2014,6013.8 (prayer mat); 1917,0414.11 (prayer-stone), gift of R. Fleming Crooks

This prayer mat (*sajjāda*) of satin silk, backed with red cotton, is designed with a pointed prayer arch (*miḥrāb*), which is oriented towards the *qibla* (Mecca) during prayer. It is embroidered with floral sprigs, outlined in couched silver-wrapped yellow thread and filled with shades of blue and yellow silk floss, and edged in woven *termeh* striped wool. A sunburst motif worked in couched silver-wrapped thread marks the placement of a circular tablet (the prayer-stone) made of compressed earth from Karbala, the sacred site in Iraq where the Prophet's grandson and Shi'a imam, Husayn ibn 'Ali, and his family members were martyred in the year 680.[10] Following a tradition dating back to at least the tenth century, some Shi'a Muslims prostrate their foreheads upon a *mohr* during ritual prayers.[11]

Prayer cloth (*mohr posh*) and prayer-stone (*mohr-e-namāz*), Hazara people

Ghazni, Afghanistan, 1950s–1960s
Cotton and silk (prayer cloth)
Prayer cloth: height 33 cm / width 29 cm
Prayer-stone: height 3 cm / width 4.5 cm
As1973,10.1.a–b

The Hazara are the third-largest ethnic group of Afghanistan, representing nearly a fifth of the total population, and originally occupied the central part of the country, a mountainous zone called the Hazarajat.[12] Unlike the majority of Afghans, most Hazaras are Twelver Shi'a Muslims, and they developed a tradition of textiles that reflected their religious beliefs and practices. This cotton prayer cloth, worked in brightly coloured silk satin-stitch, is associated with the Hazaras of Ghazni and was used to wrap and position the prayer-stone (*mohr-e-namāz*) made from pressed soil from the holy city of Karbala. The two hands flanking the prayer-stone are a reference to Hazrat 'Abbas, Imam Husayn's flag-bearer, whose hands were severed by the enemy at Karbala when he went to fetch water for his camp.[13]

130 TEXTILES OF THE MIDDLE EAST AND CENTRAL ASIA

Prayer rug (*sajjāda*) with *qibla* compass
Mecca, Saudi Arabia, 2010
Polyester, plastic and metal
Height 107 cm / width 67 cm
2011,6043.55.a, purchased with the support
of the Modern Museum Fund

This modern prayer rug, printed with an image of the holy Kaʿba and fitted with a *qibla* compass, was sold as part of a souvenir gift set to pilgrims on *ḥajj*.[14] Magnetic *qibla* compasses, used to establish the direction of prayer towards the Kaʿba, are mentioned in textual sources from the thirteenth century.[15] Today, paraphernalia and souvenirs intended for *ḥajj* pilgrims, from prescribed clothing (*iḥrām*) and headgear to prayer beads, rugs and toys, are designed with Islamic iconography and are imported from the Far East and elsewhere.

Hooded cloak
Iraq or Iran, 1880s–1900
Wool and silk
Length 167 cm / width 186 cm
As1967,02.24, gift of the Jerusalem
and the East Mission

This circular, hooded cloak of cream-coloured wool is embroidered in cream silk along its borders with an ancient adage in Arabic:

إِنْ كَانَ الْكَلَامُ فِضَّةً كَانَ السُّكُوتُ ذَهَبًا

In kāna'l-kalāmu fiḍḍatan kāna'l-sukūtu dhahaban
('If speech is silver, silence is gold')

A version of this proverb can be traced back to ancient Egypt, but it appears in this form in a Hebrew rabbinical text from fifth-century Palestine. Not much is known about this cloak, though the *basmala* (the Qur'anic formula translated as: 'In the name of God, the Merciful, the Compassionate'), inscribed on each corner, suggests a Muslim religious context. Perhaps it was used by the head of a mystical Sufi order.[16]

BEHIND, LEFT AND RIGHT **Dervish hats by Mehmet Girgiç**
Konya, Turkey, 2001
Felted camel hair and wool
Brown: height 42 cm / diameter 21 cm
White: height 28 cm / diameter 20 cm
As2001,07.49, As2001,07.48

Although relatively modern, the brown conical hat (*sikke*) and the flat-topped white hat (*arakıye*) are based on headgear worn from at least the fifteenth century by the whirling dervishes of the Mevlevi mystical order,[17] named after the world-renowned Persian Sufi and poet Mawlana (Mevlana) Jalal al-Din Rumi (d. 1273). An initiate received a *sikke* ('seal' or 'symbol') as the very first garment upon joining the order, and it was sometimes worn with a turban cloth (*destar*) tied around it. A mystic kissed his *sikke* as a sign of respect and was even buried with it.[18] The finest examples were once made in Konya and Bursa by the hatters' guild (*Arakıyeci*), and today Mehmet Girgiç is the last felt-maker in Konya to make *sikkes* in the traditional way.[19]

FRONT **Man's fez (*ṭarbūsh*)**
Turkey, 1900–1920s
Felted wool
Height 14 cm / diameter 20 cm
As1968,10.51

In 1826 Sultan Mahmud II (r. 1808–39) carried out a dramatic restructuring of the Ottoman army and government, as part of which he instituted a Europeanized dress code. The turban was abolished and replaced with a fez. This modern headgear still permitted Muslim men to bow their heads to the floor while in prayer, unlike the less popular brimmed hat introduced in 1925.[20]

Indigo-dyed dress (*zanna* or *zinna*) and trouser-cuffs
Jabal Haraz, Yemen, 1970s–1980s
Cotton, silk, mother-of-pearl, brass sequins and chains
Dress: length 120 cm / width 144 cm
Trouser-cuffs: length 38.5 cm / width 15.5 cm (maximum, each leg)
As2002,06.11 (dress), gift of Carl Phillips; 2015,6004.2.a–b (trouser-cuffs), gift of Rosalind Wade-Haddon

The women of the mountainous region of Jabal Haraz, south-west of Sana'a, wore festive dresses and trousers made of indigo-dyed cotton, which was hammered with wooden mallets or burnished with smooth stones to produce a shimmering iridescence. Indigo is believed to possess talismanic and medicinal properties and has been highly coveted for more than five thousand years.[21] Several triangular-shaped amuletic elements embellish the dress, including small pouches of herbs, pieces of mother-of-pearl, brass chains and embroidered motifs.

Woman's inscribed jacket
Syria, 1880s – 1920s
Silk and cotton
Length 64 cm / width 180 cm
As1966,01.314

The Arabic benedictory phrase

مَلْبُوسُ الْعَافِيَة

malbūs al-'āfiya
('Worn for health/well-being')

is woven in repetition on alternate stripes of this jacket. The tradition of inscribing good wishes for the owner on everyday objects dates back to at least the eighth century in the Muslim Middle East.[22]

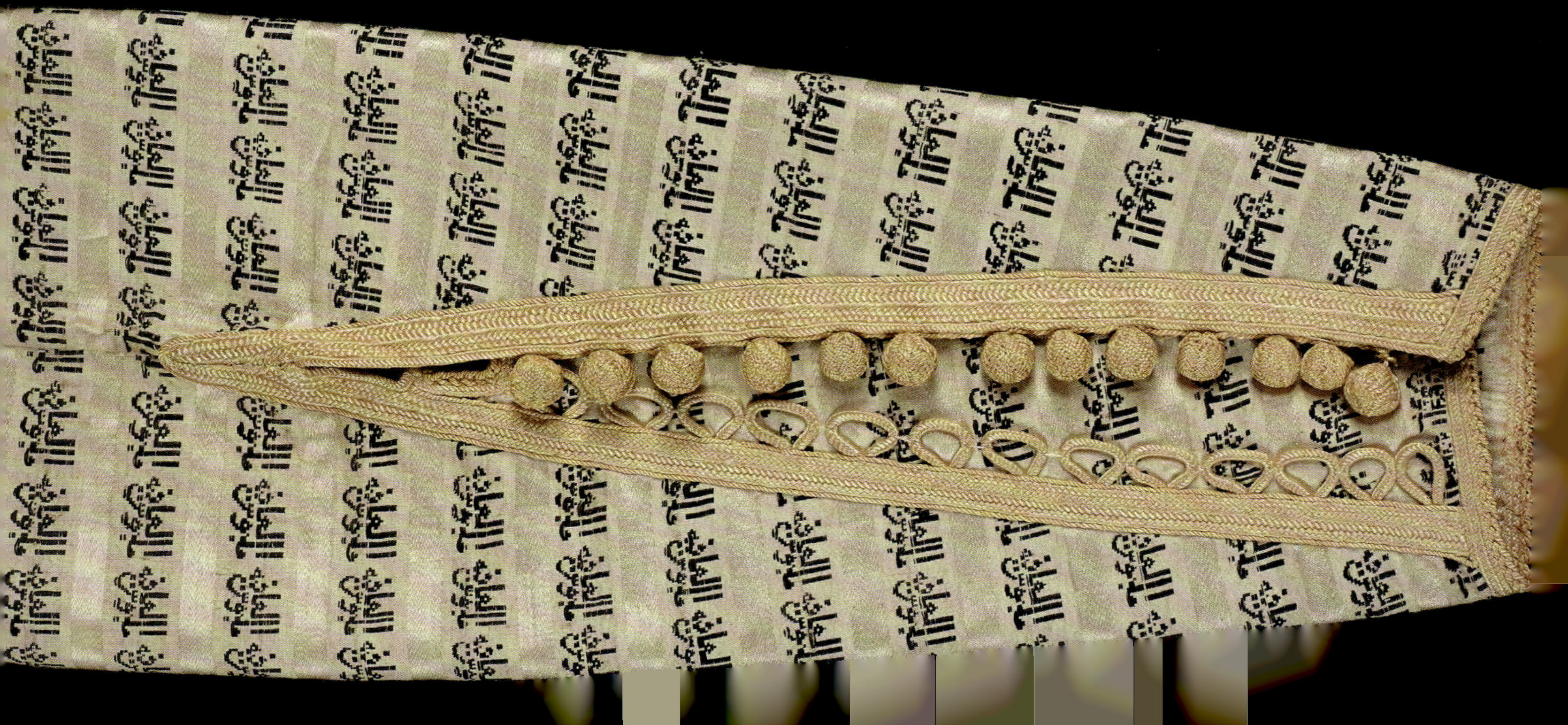

Child's over-shirt (*kurta*), Tekke Turkmen people
Turkmenistan, 1930s–1940s
Silk, cotton and human hair (shown from the back)
Length 37.5 cm / width 43 cm
2008.6025.22

The twisted black and white cotton cord stitched onto the back of this Tekke Turkmen child's over-shirt (*kurta*) represents a type of snake native to the Karakum Desert of Turkmenistan. These textile snakes served as charms against snakebite, and the protective cotton triangle (*dogha*) was a defence against the 'evil eye' or 'eye of envy' (see detail, pp. 120–21). The matted human hair stitched alongside also serves an amuletic purpose, as hair embodies the power of growth and symbolizes the life force of a person. Similarly, matted or plaited human hair stitched onto Turkmen headdresses and the textile covers for camels in wedding processions signifies fertility and protection.[23]

Take your cup and your comb in your hand!
In the afternoon are your bath and your feast.
O graveyard, a bride is coming to you in a green dress.
And she is gilded, adorned with gold.
She is white, and dyed with henna.[24]

Model funerary garments and accessories
Artas, Palestine, 1927
Cotton, loofah sponge, gold leaf and wood
Dress: length 50 cm / width 51 cm
2011,6035.1–11, gift of the family of Hilma Granqvist

These small-scale female burial garments and accessories were collected in 1927 by the Finnish anthropologist Hilma Granqvist (1890–1972) as part of her research on death and funerary rituals in the village of Artas, south of Bethlehem. Grave-clothes were traditionally hand-stitched from new fabric in green and white cotton – symbolizing Islam, purity and righteousness – by women who were considered ritually pure (that is, post-menopausal). This sample set consists of eleven items: a green dress, a white dress (not shown), trousers, head- and face-coverings (OPPOSITE, ABOVE), a shroud (not shown), items used to prepare the body – loin-cloth (OPPOSITE, RIGHT), loofah, towel and comb – and a fragment of gold leaf.[25] For their burials, unmarried virgins were adorned as brides with make-up and gold leaf on their faces, and their bodies were dusted with henna powder and sprinkled with perfume.[26]

ABOVE **Talismanic goat's skull, Yomut Turkmen people**
Turkmenistan, 1960s–1980s
Goat's skull and horns, cotton, wool and seeds
Height 31 cm / width 48 cm
2008,6025.23

This protective goat's skull is covered with embroidered cotton and plaited yarn, and features embroidered eyes and ears and a tasselled beard with seeds. It would have hung at the entrance of a Yomut Turkmen yurt or house to safeguard the inhabitants. The belief in the protective power of horns dates back thousands of years, and amuletic rams' horns appear as motifs on carpets, felts and embroidered textiles throughout Central Asia. Horns also denote wealth, status and the hunter's skill, and their sharp points are capable of piercing a passing 'evil eye'.[27]

OPPOSITE **Felt amulet (*nazarlık*) by Ramazan Recep**
Balıkesir, Turkey, 2001
Wool, cotton, silk, cowrie shells, glass and plastic
Length 59 cm / width 38 cm
As2001,07.44

This modern amulet in the shape of an eagle was made by Ramazan Recep, a contemporary Yörük felt-maker from north-western Turkey. He decorates his amulets with an array of beads, buttons, cowries and fragments of older embroideries, which are meant to confuse and deflect the 'evil eye' (Turkish *nazar*).[28] Another of his felt amulets, in the shape of a whirling dervish, features two interlocked wedding bands to protect a married couple. He also produces ex-voto felts in the form of body parts (e.g. hands, legs and breasts) for healing purposes.[29]

House & Homestead

Keregem saga aitam, kelinim sen uk,
U'ugum saga aitam, u'ulum sen uk.

('I say to you, if I speak to my *kerege* (yurt wall), my *kelin* (daughter-in-law)
 will listen to me.
I say to you, if I speak to the *u'uk* (yurt roof poles), my son will listen to me.')

Kyrgyz proverb[1]

There are many Middle Eastern and Central Asian proverbs relating to the home and domestic settings. This one, though derived from a Kyrgyz nomadic context, has widespread relevance. It encapsulates the notion that sometimes it is better not to advise people directly (particularly your children), but to offer your counsel indirectly 'to the walls' (that is, through someone else), and then it is more likely that you will be listened to. Similarly, the messages from the Arabic adage 'The stingy have large porches and little morality' (*al-bakhīl ʿaẓīm al-riwāq wa ṣaghīr al-akhlāq*), and the Turkish saying 'Stretch your foot according to your blanket' (that is, spend within your means, *ayağını yorganına göre uzat*) also have universal resonances.[2] The home is thus, by extension, a reflection of human behaviour and a locus for family and other social dynamics. The textiles in this chapter, dating mainly from the nineteenth and early twentieth centuries, derive from both nomadic and sedentary contexts. The construction, decoration and function of the objects from nomadic societies, such as the vibrant Uzbek and Turkmen tent- and animal-hangings (pp. 148–49, 160–61, 172–73), are in stark contrast to those produced in urban settings – for example, the embroidered Turkish hand towels and a sumptuous Afghan floor-spread (pp. 150–51, 152–53). The two spheres, however, have a number of characteristics in common.

Firstly, during the period under discussion, the domestic world in general was considered the female domain and most of the soft furnishings for the home were made by women, often as part of their marriage trousseaus. Within the nomadic societies of Iran and Central Asia, women were also in charge of assembling and dismantling the external structures of entire yurts (*üy* or *öy*; **33**) as part of the regular cycle of seasonal migration. The chapter includes a pair of tent-pole bags used to cover roof poles when they were transported on pack animals from one site to

PREVIOUS PAGE Detail of a cotton napkin, embroidered in silk with silver-wrapped thread and silver strip (p. 151, TOP).

33 A Tekke Turkmen girl, dressed in her finery, stands on a carpet at the entrance to her family yurt; Turkmenistan, c. 1911. Photo: S. M. Prokudin-Gorskii.

another (p. 156). These and other textiles, such as the purely decorative embroidered tent-hangings (pp. 157–59), were made by Uzbek women for their dowries in the months leading up to their marriage. Dowry textiles were a source of familial prestige, and their embroidered and woven designs often reinforced tribal identities. An early twentieth-century photograph by Sergei Prokudin-Gorskii (d. 1934) of a Tekke Turkmen family, seated inside their circular yurt and wearing their finest clothing, jewellery and headdresses, illustrates this point (**34**). They are surrounded by the hand-knotted carpets and storage bags, featuring their tribal medallion or emblem (*göl*) patterns, that were made by the women of the household. Colourful patchwork trappings, also displayed in the background, were once used to decorate the Tekke woman's camel on her wedding procession to her new home. A comparative example of a camel-hanging from a Yomut Turkmen context is included in this chapter (pp. 174–75).

In the same way, within the towns and villages of the Ottoman Empire, young girls embroidered soft furnishings for their trousseaus, such as sheets, hand towels, napkins, quilts, cushions and other textiles, examples of which from Turkey and Palestine are included in this chapter (pp. 142–43, 150–51, 154–55). Trousseaus were displayed during wedding festivities and demonstrated the bride's skills, taste and wealth. Once married, women embroidered special bed linen to be used following the birth of a child and for circumcision ceremonies.[3] Until the late nineteenth century, Ottoman homes did not have much in the way of European-style movable furniture, but were simply equipped with storage chests, fitted cupboards, and low platforms along the walls for sitting and entertaining. Likewise, virtually any room in an Ottoman house could serve as a dining, sitting or sleeping room, with mattresses and quilts laid out on the floor at bedtime and stored away when not in use. Hence, textiles served not only decorative, but important functional purposes in the form of bedding, cushions, pillows, curtains, prayer rugs, mats, towels and multi-purpose covers and wrapping cloths.[4]

Traditional Ottoman homes (and palaces) were divided into separate courtyards or areas: some were considered more publicly accessible (*selamlık*), where visitors were received and formal entertaining of male guests took place; others were the

OPPOSITE **35** Knitted silk socks and purse, Iran, 1850s–1890s: (ABOVE, LEFT) socks with stitched leather soles, L 22 cm × W 9 cm, As1981,19.3.a–b; (ABOVE, RIGHT) socks, L 28 cm × W 10 cm, 2015,6016.4.a–b; and purse, L 17.5 cm × W 7.5 cm, 2015,6016.5; (BELOW) socks, L 31 cm × W 12 cm, 2015,6016.3.a–b.

34 A Tekke Turkmen family inside their yurt, with the sun shining through the roof-wheel; Turkmenistan, c. 1911. Photo: S. M. Prokudin-Gorskii.

private family quarters of the house (*haramlık*), where women and children lived and where entry for non-family female guests was restricted. Analogously, the interior spaces of a nomadic tent were also divided up into male and female sections. In the case of the Turkmen yurt, the women's side included the kitchen area, utensils, woven storage packs for clothing (p. 162), and the bedding pile with floor felts, quilts and mattresses. The men's side contained the sacks of food provisions such as grain, rice or salt, and the women's loom. A similar separation of public and private spaces was implemented in the Bedouin tents of the Arab world, using a dividing wall.[5] The Lakai Uzbeks also divided their yurts into male and female spaces, but the area opposite the door was designated as the place of honour (*tör*), where guests and the elderly would sit, and where the family's textile wealth was stored in elaborately constructed stacks of bedding, quilts and blankets. This bedding pile (*jük* or *chuk*) was decorated with finely embroidered hangings and bands (pp. 157–61).

A third and final shared feature between sedentary and nomadic domestic settings in the regions across the Middle East and Central Asia was the practice of taking off one's shoes when entering a home or mosque. This custom, still maintained today, must have played a role in the development of knitted socks (*jurāb*), the earliest examples of which date from twelfth- or thirteenth-century Egypt.[6] The finely knitted, patterned silk socks from nineteenth-century Iran illustrated here (**35**) were produced using the same 'Eastern' technique as the medieval examples, starting from the toe and working upwards.[7] The heels, made last and attached to the completed body of the sock, were easily replaced when they wore out. The custom of removing one's shoes while indoors may also have spurred the production of soft floor-coverings, such as carpets, rugs and felts.[8] Despite the radical changes in nomadic lifestyles over the course of the twentieth century, the art of felt-making has managed to survive in some regions of Turkey, Iran, Afghanistan and Central Asia. Many people living in village houses and city apartments in Kyrgyzstan still use felt floor-coverings which continue to be made almost exclusively by women.[9] This chapter also features modern Central Asian felts, including a butterfly felt made by one of Kyrgyzstan's most famous masters (pp. 168–69).

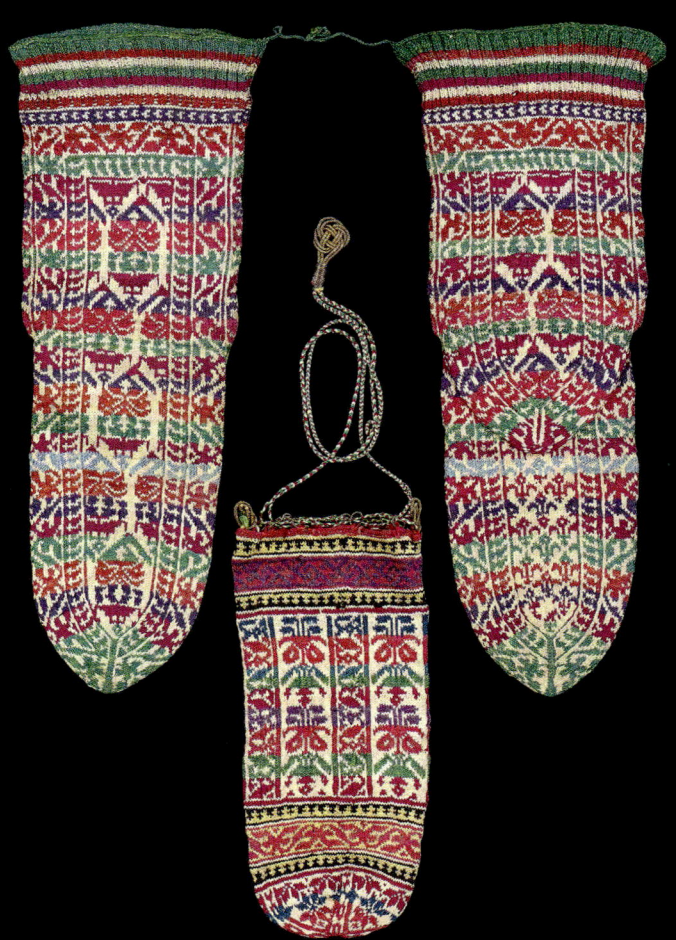

Door- or tent-hanging
Tajikistan, 1920s–1940s
Silk, cotton, glass beads, and metal spangles and grips
Length 207 cm / width 134 cm
2008,6025.17

This finely embroidered door-hanging may also have served to embellish the place of honour (tör) inside the yurt, on the wall opposite the door. Here, stacks of colourful bedding and textiles were piled high and decorated with embroidered bands to protect and cherish the household's textile wealth. The embroidered motifs, with curled and serrated edges, are used throughout Central Asia, their ancient antecedents relating to the horned animals of the steppe. The minute, multi-coloured cross-stitching, the braided netting and the beaded tassels are hallmarks of Uzbek and Tajik embroidery.[10]

RIGHT **Stilted clogs (*nalın* or *qabqab*)**
Turkey, 1800–50
Wood, pewter, mother-of-pearl, leather, silk velvet, gilt-metal-wrapped thread and spangles
Height 26 cm / length 24.5 cm
As.1553.a–b, gift of Henry Christy

These wooden bath clogs, inlaid with pewter and mother-of-pearl, have leather straps covered in gold-embroidered velvet with gilded spangles. Although they raised a woman's feet off the wet floor of the ḥammām (public bathhouse), she required the support of a personal attendant to walk in them owing to their towering height. Together with her embroidered towels, kerchiefs and bathing accoutrements, the clogs elevated her status within the ḥammām. The Arabic word *qabqab* derives from the clacking noise they made on marble floors.

BELOW **Hand towel (*peşkir*)**
Turkey, 1850s–1860s
Cotton, silk, silver-wrapped silk thread and gilt-metal-strip thread
Length 153 cm / width 47.5 cm
2011,6007.6, gift of Dominique Collon

Embroiderers were accorded professional status in the Ottoman world, producing pieces on a massive scale in commercial workshops during the nineteenth century. At the same time, qualified teachers taught embroidery to girls in their homes, and pattern templates based on those produced at the palace were sold commercially. New motifs introduced during this period included flower baskets and vases, sunbursts, imperial ciphers (*tughra*), inscriptions and figures.[11]

OPPOSITE, ABOVE **Napkin (*yağlık*)**
Turkey, 1800–50
Cotton, silk, silver-wrapped thread and silver strip
Length 122 cm / width 51.5 cm
2013,6037.1, bequest of Christopher Lennox-Boyd

Embroidered napkins were laid on the knees during meals, and used for drying the hands when washing before and after eating.[12] The small buildings set within a landscape of flowers, cypress trees and fountains derive from Western-style mural paintings on nineteenth-century Ottoman architecture. The buildings may represent mosques or tombs adjoining stylized public water fountains (*sabīl*; see detail, pp. 142–43), suggesting that the napkin was used for ritual ablutions.[13]

OPPOSITE, BELOW **Hand towel (*peşkir*)**
Turkey, 1830–50
Linen, silk and silver-wrapped thread
Length 163 cm / width 60 cm
2014,6013.10

Each end of this self-patterned damask linen hand towel has a panel of scrolling leafy stems, roses and other flowers, worked in double darning-stitch in shaded tones, using silk and silver-wrapped threads. The centre of each rose is filled with drawn-threadwork in silver-wrapped thread.[14] Finely worked embroideries for trousseaus and household use were made in abundance in the palace, urban workshops and homes.

Floor-spread (*dastarkhān*)
Afghanistan or Kashmir, 1817–39
Silk on a cotton ground
Length 635 cm / width 93.5 cm
2014,6010.1

At more than 6 metres in length, this *dastarkhān* was used for communal dining. The dense embroidery transforms it into an Afghan garden, with a ground of flowers and foliage, large undulating medallions echoing pools of water, and borders of upright paisleys (*boteh*) resembling trees. It is professionally executed in silk chain-stitch, using an *aari* needle (tambour hook), with the work stretched on a frame. Fit for a king's banquet, this floor-spread is associated with Dost Muhammad Khan (r. 1826–39, 1842–63), Emir of Afghanistan and founder of the Barakzay dynasty.[15]

154 TEXTILES OF THE MIDDLE EAST AND CENTRAL ASIA

Cushion covers (*wisādāt*)
Hebron area, 1920s–1930s
Silk and cotton
Length 80 cm (average) / width 43 cm (average)
(FRONT TO BACK) As1971.01.31, As1971.01.131, As1968.04.30.a, As1968.12.6

The fronts of these silk cushions are decorated in a variety of very fine cross-stitched patterns on silk taffeta panels and patches. The cushion in the foreground, with silk tassels, has a large motif repeated three times in each section, possibly representing candlesticks (*sham'addānāt*) in mirror image (see detail), which are densely surrounded by rows of diamond shapes called 'slices' (*shaqahāt*).[16] Cushion covers were expensive and laborious to make, and a bride prepared between six and twelve of them for her new home.[17]

OPPOSITE **Tent-pole bags (*okbash*), Uzbek people**
Uzbekistan, 1890s–1930s
Wool, horsehair and cotton
Length 120 cm (including tassels) / width 35 cm (each)
As1997,04.7, As1997,04.8: purchased with the support of the British Museum
Society Eastern European Purchase Grant

A Central Asian yurt is a portable, circular tent, made up of expanding lattice walls, a door-frame, bent roof poles and a crown, which are covered and furnished with skins and felts (see p. 145). Once dismantled, the parts are transported by pack animals to be rebuilt on another site. These felt bags covered and secured the ends of roof poles in transit. Made in pairs for the bridal dowry, they are embroidered in black and white wool with patterns recalling animal horns, and embellished with horsehair tassels.[18]

ABOVE **Tent-hanging (*at torba ilgitsh* or *at torba ilgich*), Lakai Uzbek people**
Northern Afghanistan, 1890s–1930s
Wool, cotton and silk
Length 57 cm / width 59 cm
As2002,03.9, purchased with the support of the British Museum Friends
and the Art Fund

This finely embroidered wool panel is a purely decorative tent-hanging, made by a Lakai Uzbek bride during the months leading up to her marriage. Usually made in pairs, these embroideries were prestige items for her dowry, and demonstrated her technical and artistic skills to her in-laws. The silk-embroidered motifs are stylized representations of insects and powerful elements of nature, which echo the steppe environment and the Lakai's shamanistic past. The panel is finished with cross-stitched borders and netted and fringed edging.[19]

Tent-hanging (*at torba ilgitsh* or *at torba ilgich*), Lakai Uzbek People
Northern Afghanistan, 1890s–1930s
Wool, cotton and silk
Length 57 cm / width 61 cm
As2002,03.14, purchased with the support of the British Museum Friends and the Art Fund

Embroidered textiles of a Lakai Uzbek household were vital elements of the bridal dowry and a source of familial prestige that reinforced tribal identities. Lakai women produced a range of purely decorative pieces to hang on either side of the bedding pile (*jük*) to adorn and emphasize the family's textile wealth.[20] The whirling circles on this panel, perhaps symbolizing the sun, alternate with animal-horn motifs. The abstract designs on Lakai embroideries, featuring scorpions, spiders, horned creatures and elements of nature, are described as exuding a magical or electric energy and possessing a primal quality.[21] Older women, working as pattern designers, outlined the designs in chalk or stitches and a well-to-do Lakai bride embroidered three to four pairs of *ilgitsh* for her dowry.[22]

Bedding-pile hanging (*segusha* or *saye qosha*), Lakai Uzbek people
Northern Afghanistan or Uzbekistan, 1920s–1940s
Cotton, silk and glass beads
Length 110 cm (side to side) / width 67 cm (centre, including tassels)
As1997,02.7, purchased with the support of the British Museum Society Eastern European Purchase Grant

The bedding pile (*jük*), consisting of a stack of rolled-up quilts, blankets and other textiles, was placed along the back wall of the yurt, opposite the door – the highest place of honour (*tör*), reserved for guests and elders of the family. Many Uzbek tribeswomen, including the Lakai, produced silk-embroidered, V-shaped hangings (*segushas*) that were tucked in the middle of the *jük* as embellishments. This *segusha*, worked in complex cross-stitched geometric patterns, has a fringe of twisted silk with beaded ends. A few amuletic seed beads are stitched into the main design to protect the household and its contents.[23]

Storage bag (*karçín*), Yomut Atabay Turkmen people
North-eastern Iran, 1940s–1960s
Wool and cotton
Length 126 cm / width 78 cm
As1973,09.125

The inside of a Turkmen yurt was divided into several sections, with the western portion allocated to cooking pots, crockery, tea supplies and the household's wardrobe. At least six flat-woven bags such as this were used to store clothing and finery. They were laced up and stacked flat in pairs on top of wooden trestles.[24] This one was produced using the countered soumak weaving technique, creating embroidery-like patterns of stepped geometric lozenges outlined with hooked edges – the tribal emblem (*göl*) of the Atabay Turkmen.[25]

Storage sack (*çuval*), Yörük people
Taurus Mountains, Turkey, 1940s–1960s
Wool
Length 120 cm / width 61 cm
As1968.10.1

Despite centuries of forced sedentarization during the Ottoman and post-Ottoman periods, a census in the mid-1990s confirmed that around ten thousand fully nomadic Yörük people still live in the mountainous regions of southern Turkey. Dwelling in tents made from goat hair, Yörük are known for their textile arts, including brocaded flatweaves like this colourful storage sack.[26] Often mistaken for embroidery, brocaded designs are produced entirely on the loom.[27] This sack probably contained grain, though sacks were also used to store clothing and other possessions.

Tent-wall felt (*tus ki'iz*), Kazakh people
Republic of Karakalpakstan, Uzbekistan, 2003
Wool, velvet and silk brocade
Length 368 cm / width 192 cm
As2003,22.1

This huge, modern Kazakh wall felt is decorated entirely in appliqué work, incorporating fine felts, velvets and brocade-patterned pieces, on a thick felt backing. The multiplying rams' horn motifs (*tört müyüz*) associated with protection, well-being and fertility, are couched down with colourful twisted cords, creating an endless pattern.[28] Kazakh *tus ki'iz* are hung along the back wall of the yurt facing the entrance – the highest place of honour within the tent. Embroidered versions on cloth were introduced much later, in the late nineteenth-century (see p. 71).[29]

Kitchen utensil bag, Uzbek people
Turkmenistan, 1940s–1960s (bag); 1990s (ladle);
Central Asia, 1890s (spoons)
Wool, cotton, cowrie shells, metal, glass and plastic, and wooden utensils
Height 113 cm / width 45 cm
As1997,02.4 (bag), purchased with the support of the British Museum Society Eastern European Purchase Grant; As1997,42.24 (ladle), gift of St John Simpson; As1883,0132.46.a–b (spoons), gift of Sir Augustus Wollaston Franks

Ornamented bags of all shapes and sizes hung from the lattice walls of nomadic tents, storing an array of household necessities from kitchenwares, tea supplies and foodstuffs to scissors, mirrors and combs. This plaited mesh bag, made by a nomadic Uzbek woman, housed her long wooden cooking spoons and other utensils. It is constructed from interlaced woollen plaits that form a dense net, with a tasselled fringe. The decorative and amuletic applied embellishments include colourful tassels and pompoms, assorted buttons, metal discs and amuletic mirrors and cowries.[30]

166 TEXTILES OF THE MIDDLE EAST AND CENTRAL ASIA

Pot holders (*tutaç*), Yomut Atabay Turkmen people
North-eastern Iran, 1940s–1960s
Wool and cotton
(ABOVE) Length 69 cm / width 23 cm
(BELOW) Length 66 cm / width 19 cm
As1973,09.180, As1973,09.181

The Turkmen of Iran live in the north-east of the country and share many customs, including diet, with fellow Turkmen in neighbouring Turkmenistan. Families gather around a floor-spread or table-cloth (*sofra*) to partake of hearty soups, meat or fish pilaf, cheeses, home-baked bread and grilled sturgeon or stewed mullet, freshly caught from the Caspian Sea and flavoured with pomegranate syrup. Embroidered and appliquéd felt pot holders, made by a bride for her dowry, displayed her creative needlework skills while assisting in her cooking duties.[31]

Mosaic floor-felt (*shyrdak*) by Jangyl Alibekova
At-Bashi, Naryn region, Kyrgyzstan, 1990s
Wool
Length 265 cm / width 145 cm
As1996,13.35, purchased with the support of the British Museum Friends

High-quality mosaic felts (*shyrdaks*) are still produced by women in the villages and mountain areas of Kyrgyzstan. A large *shyrdak* may take several women a winter or two to make, but it will last for up to thirty years.[32] Jangyl Alibekova was a renowned master (*usta*), and drew inspiration from Russian embroideries for her finely cut and quilted butterfly (*köpölök*) *shyrdaks*. Her uniquely designed felts were in great demand and she was also invited to draw patterns for other felt-makers.[33]

ABOVE **Bicycle saddlebag (*çarkh horcin* or *khorjīn*), Yomut Atabay Turkmen people**
North-eastern Iran, 1950s–1960s
Wool and silk (edging and tassels)
Length 64 cm / width 31 cm
As1973,09.142

The form of a double-pouched saddlebag, traditionally laid across the backs of horses or pack animals, is adapted here to suit modern transportation needs. This knotted-pile bicycle saddlebag, woven predominantly in red, blue, ivory and orange, features stylized rosettes and horn motifs favoured by Turkmen carpet weavers. With the exception of sheep-shearing, the entire process of carpet production fell within the female sphere. Floor-coverings, sacks, pouches and saddlebags were woven exclusively for domestic use until the mid-1960s, when weavers began making products for urban markets.[34]

OPPOSITE **Spindle bag (*ig serk* or *ig torba*) and spindles (*ig*), Yomut Turkmen people**
North-eastern Iran, 1960s
Wool and cotton, and wooden spindles
Length 45 cm (including tassels) / width 25 cm
As1973,09.138 (bag), As1973,09.93–95 (spindles)

Spindles are used to spin fibres such as wool, silk and cotton into twisted yarn and thread. The spiked spindle shafts are usually made of wood and are often weighted with a spherical whorl, like the Turkmen examples here. This tapestry woven and brocaded bag carried spindles and yarn, and was made by a bride as part of her dowry. Turkmen women carried out tasks such as washing wool, carding, spinning and dyeing during the course of their day, alongside child-rearing and food preparation.[35]

OPPOSITE **Horse headdress, Lakai Uzbek people**
Northern Afghanistan, 1890s–1930s
Wool, silk and goat hair
Length 95 cm / width 40 cm
As2002,03.49, purchased with the support of the British Museum Friends and the Art Fund

Lakai Uzbeks specialized in horse breeding and training, and both men and women rode stallions, as it was considered shameful to ride mares. Women's saddles and trappings were more ornate than those of men. This horse headdress is finely embroidered in silk Bukhara couching, and has padded hangings finished with tufts of goat hair. It would have been used on ceremonial and festive occasions, such as weddings and important religious holidays.[36]

ABOVE **Horse blanket (*daour* or *dauri*), Lakai Uzbek people**
Northern Afghanistan, 1890s–1930s
Wool, cotton and silk
Length 114 cm / width 156 cm
As2002,03.43, purchased with the support of the British Museum Friends and the Art Fund

Horses were essential during rites of passage in a Lakai man's life, from the time he attained maturity, when he was gifted his first horse, to his wedding, and finally his funeral, when his clothing was flung across his stallion's saddle as his family performed a ritual circumambulation around his horse.[37] Horses were used for hunting, racing and *buzkashī* tournaments, and decorating them in fine trappings and silk-embroidered blankets like this one was perceived as a source of prestige in Central Asian society.[38] This blanket features insects and horned motifs, signifying power and tribal identity.

HOUSE & HOMESTEAD

Camel neck-hanging (*duye bashlyk*), Yomut Atabay Turkmen people
North-eastern Iran, 1920s–1940s
Silk, wool, cotton, carnelian, metal, glass, mother-of-pearl and feathers
Length 168 cm / width 137 cm
As1973,09.176

This elaborate hanging decorated the neck and back of a bedecked camel, bearing a Turkmen bride on the wedding procession to her new home. Produced with matching trappings for the animal's flanks and forelegs, it is made of locally woven silk, indigo-dyed and plain cotton, and Russian printed cotton pieces. Added embellishments include silk embroidery, carnelian amulets, Bohemian glass beads, buttons, feathers, silk tassels and a fringe of indigo-dyed cotton. These elements honoured and protected the bride sitting inside her covered palanquin (*kejebe*).[39]

Politics & Conflict

Politics & Conflict

> After the death of the Umayyad caliph Hisham b. 'Abd al-Malik, found among his possessions were a vast quantity of garments and textiles that required seven hundred camels to carry them…He had curtains, clothing and textiles with the inscription of his name embroidered or woven on them (ṭirāz), something that no other ruler before him had done. He was the first to adopt the ṭirāz in the year AH 108/AD 727, and he wrote to all parts of the world to make for him something in the same manner with regard to every type of textile, furniture, vessel, and equipment. Hisham and all the descendants of the Banu Marwan used to clothe people in silk of various colours except for yellow and red, which they kept for themselves.
>
> *Book of Gifts and Rarities*[1]

This account attests to the long-standing and inextricable link between textiles and politics in the Islamic world. As elsewhere, luxury textiles have been used as conspicuous emblems of imperial power and status throughout history. However, Caliph Hisham's introduction of woven and embroidered borders with Arabic inscriptions on royal fabrics inaugurated a new genre of politically charged textiles, firmly rooted in the Muslim world. The term ṭirāz derives from the Persian word for 'embroidery' or 'decorative work', but it came to denote medieval textiles and garments with Arabic inscriptions, as well as the state-sponsored and regulated workshops that produced them for the caliph. Borders of complete pieces usually included the ruler's name and titles, pious phrases and the place and date of production. The fragmentary ṭirāz shown here (**36**), made in the twelfth century towards the end of the Fatimid dynasty in Egypt, is inscribed with the Qur'anic phrase and Fatimid motto *naṣr min Allāh* ('Help from God'), in repeated succession. The textile also features stylized birds and hares and the Arabic word *ghibṭa* ('happiness'), set within interlaced bands. On religious holidays and other ceremonial occasions the caliphs distributed ṭirāz fabrics as robes of honour, and turban cloths to court officials and family members.[2]

The politically motivated use of Qur'anic inscriptions on textiles was not limited to the medieval period. A nineteenth-century silk curtain commissioned by the Ottoman sultan Mahmud II (r. 1808–39), is embroidered with several carefully selected Qur'anic verses for public display at the Prophet's Mosque at Medina (pp. 182–83). The political messaging on this curtain was intended not only for Mahmud's enemies,

PREVIOUS PAGE Detail of an Afghan war rug featuring boats, a mountain range and a sky full of military helicopters and planes dropping star shells; the border includes a variety of tanks and armoured vehicles. Afghanistan, 1979–85. L 135 cm × W 133.5 cm, 2010,6013.14, gift of Graham Gower.

OPPOSITE **36** Tapestry-woven silk and linen ṭirāz, with hares, birds and Arabic inscriptions, Egypt, 12th century. L 43.5 cm × W 33 cm, 1893,0514.189.

37 The Palestinian leader Yasser 'Arafat, wearing the black and white keffiyeh that was strongly associated with him from the 1960s; Ramallah, Palestine, 2002. Photo: Chris Hondros.

who succeeded in seizing Mecca and Medina from the Ottomans for a period of time. It was also aimed at everyone visiting the sacred mosque at Medina, so they too would appreciate that God, through the holy words of the Qur'an, legitimized the sultan's position as the rightful caliph of all Muslims and the guardian of Islam's two holiest cities.

Textiles continue to be central elements of political discourse in recent times. A well-known example is the black and white checked keffiyeh, or man's head-cloth, which became a symbol of Palestinian national identity in the late 1930s, and later was strongly associated with Yasser 'Arafat (1929–2004), who became president of the Palestinian National Authority and chairman of the Palestine Liberation Organization (PLO) (**37**). This chapter includes several examples of the head-cloth, which has developed multi-layered meanings and associations since its origins as a Bedouin head-covering (pp. 204–05).

Another recent example of a textile that is immediately identifiable with a political figure is the green and blue striped coat (*chapan*) adopted by former Afghan president Hamid Karzai (r. 2001–14) (**38**). Karzai created his signature style by wearing this silk-woven garment at all public gatherings, along with his lamb's fleece hat (*qarākulī*) – both symbols of wealth, high culture and social status (**39**). The historian Willem Vogelsang argues that Karzai's dress choice was a deliberate attempt to create a national dress of Afghanistan, a country with a multitude of ethnic groups, and to style himself as leader of all Afghan peoples.[3] There are several examples in this chapter of textiles used as vehicles for expressing national identities and allegiances, such as the portrait rugs of iconic figures (pp. 190–91), and a printed silk scarf produced in the 1960s to commemorate the creation of a pan-Arab union (pp. 188–89). Meanwhile, the American flags assembled as collages of Western and Eastern textiles by the artist Sara Rahbar (b. 1976) challenge notions of national identity and belonging (pp. 198–201).

This chapter also explores a diverse range of Middle Eastern and Central Asian textiles from the nineteenth to the twenty-first centuries connected to specific periods and events in history. A number of objects produced by contemporary artists and designers reference the conflict in Palestine, the Iranian Revolution and the Iran–Iraq War (pp. 185, 192, 202–04). The Soviet invasion of Afghanistan (1979) and ten-year occupation of the country triggered decades of war and civil unrest, which is documented by female carpet weavers on pictorial 'war rugs' (pp. 194–97). Other pieces show the impact of foreign industrialization on the textile industries of the Middle East and Central Asia (pp. 184, 206–09), and the effect of the introduction of European embroidery pattern books by missionaries in the late nineteenth century (pp. 186–87).

LEFT **38** *Chapan*, previously owned by Hamid Karzai, former president of Afghanistan, silk and cotton, Afghanistan, 2001–14.
H 133 cm × W 269 cm, 2015,6014.1, gift of Hamid Karzai.

BELOW **39** President Hamid Karzai, pictured at the NATO summit in Lisbon, 2010, wearing his signature chapan and holding his *qarākulī* hat. Photo: Peter Macdiarmid.

POLITICS & CONFLICT 181

Curtain (*sitāra*) for the Prophet's Mosque at Medina
Medina, Saudi Arabia, 1813–1839
Silk, silver wire, gilt-silver wire and cotton padding
Length 253 cm / width 206 cm
2016,6030.2, gift of the Khalili Family Trust[4]

The Arabic inscriptions on this sumptuous, silk-appliquéd curtain, worked in silver and gilt-silver wire, reflect the politics of its time. It was commissioned for the mosque of the Prophet Muhammad (d. 632) at Medina by the Ottoman sultan Mahmud II (r. 1808–39), who upheld the tradition of presenting luxe textiles to Mecca and Medina in his role as the Caliph of Islam.[5] During the early years of his reign (1812–13), he reconquered the two holy cities from the emirs of the First Saudi State.[6] Thus, Mahmud's insignia (*tughra*) and his sobriquet, '*adlī* ('just'), are embroidered between two Qur'anic verses near the bottom of the curtain: 'If God assists you, then there is none that can overcome you' (Q.3:160) and 'Indeed, God's help is [always] near!' (Q.2:214).[7] The Baroque-style floral scrolls, ribbons and wreaths reflect Mahmud II's purported modernizing reforms and his penchant for all things European.[8]

POLITICS & CONFLICT

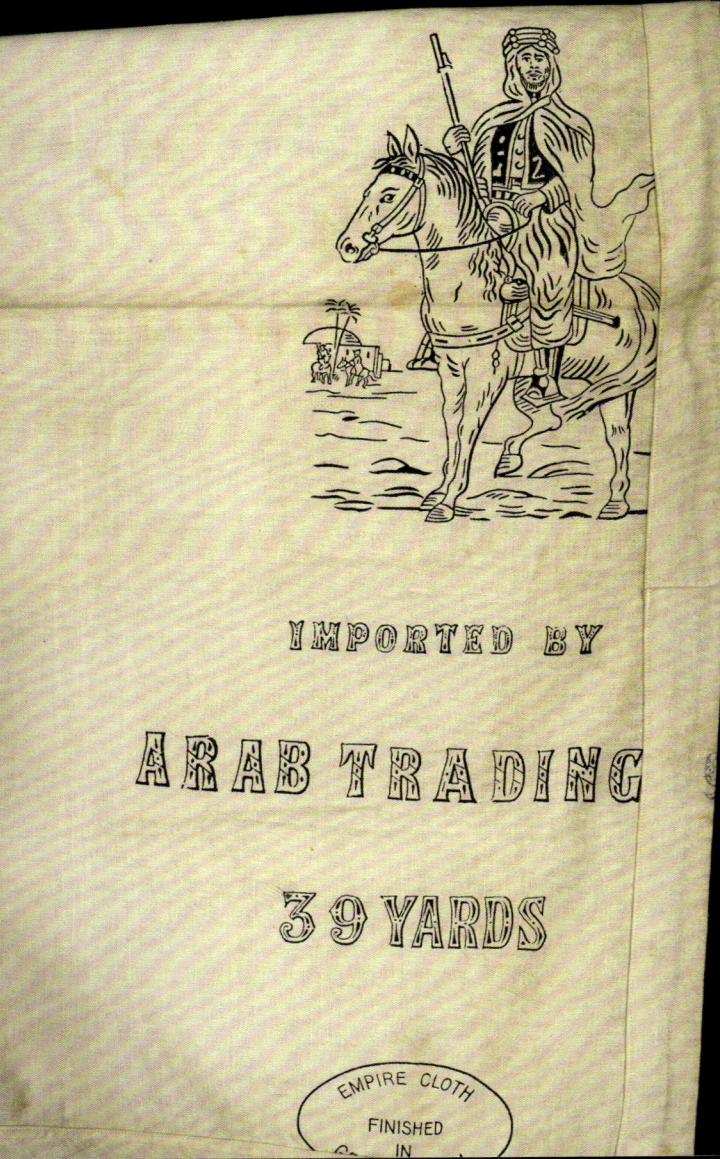

THIS PAGE **Men's trousers (*sirwāl*, *libās* or *elbās*)**
Palestine, 1850s–1900
Cotton
Length 82.5 cm / width 86 cm
As1967,02.9, gift of the Jerusalem and the East Mission

These trousers are a product of the Industrial Revolution, and attest to cotton's importance as a trade commodity for the British Empire in the nineteenth century. By the mid-1830s, cotton accounted for more than half the total value of all British foreign exports to Africa, the Middle East, India, China and Japan.[9] Each bolt of fabric was stamped with a company's mark that was visually appealing and familiar to its intended buyers.[10] These trousers bear an iconic image of a Bedouin Arab on horseback, and the British mark inscribed on one of the legs would have augmented the owner's display of his wealth and prestige: 'Imported by Arab Trading 39 Yards / Empire Cloth Finished in Great Britain / EXTRA [FINE]'.[11]

OPPOSITE **Dress (*thawb*)**
Majdal (Mejdel) area, Palestine, 1960s or earlier
Cotton and silk
Length 134 cm / width 133 cm
As1968,12.8

The southern village of Majdal was once the largest weaving centre in Palestine, boasting five hundred looms in operation by professional male weavers in 1909.[12] This dress, featuring an embroidered necklace (*qilāda*) design, is made of indigo-dyed cotton, woven with multi-coloured silk warp stripes in hot pink, red, orange and green. The fabric, known as *abū mitayn*, was one of many Majdal textiles worn across the southern coastal plain of Palestine. Majdal's textile industry was decimated, along with the village, in 1948, following the First Arab–Israeli War, when most inhabitants fled to the Gaza Strip. Some Majdal weavers continued working into the 1960s, providing fabrics for women in the refugee camps, who chose to maintain their dress identity despite their desperate circumstances.[13]

Dress (*thawb*)
Ramallah area, Palestine, c. 1900
Linen and silk
Length 136 cm / width 146 cm
As1981,23.3, gift of Elizabeth Crowfoot

Between 1869 and 1889, Quaker missionaries opened a number of girls' schools in and around Ramallah. The curriculum included embroidery from Quaker pattern books, which, alongside officers' uniforms and church vestments, offered fresh ideas for the constantly expanding repertoire of Palestinian embroidery.[14] This dress is worked in naturally dyed red silk, with injections of brilliant, chemically dyed pink and green silks, which were growing in popularity.[15] Some of the motifs express local identity, others reflect daily life or show the influence of European pattern books. Their names include: snowflake, palm of the hand, snapdragon, tall palm, Roman rose, pitchfork, stick, feathers, geese/swans, kohl-pot, harp, hoopoe bird, tree of scorpions, turning around and lilies.[16]

Scarf with political portraits
Yemen or Egypt, 1963–64
Length 80 cm / width 76 cm
As1997,01.9

This scarf was designed to promote the creation of a pan-Arab union in the 1960s.[17] It features a map of thirteen countries of the Middle East and North Africa, with their respective flags, surrounded by political portraits captioned in Arabic. Pan-Arabism is based on the principle that all Arabs share a common language, culture and history, and should unite as one nation or state. The idea was conceived by Arab intellectuals as a result of the growing resentment against Ottoman Turkish rule and, after the First World War, in response to the Western imperialist partition of the Ottoman Empire's Arab provinces. By the 1940s, younger generations had embraced the pan-Arab nationalist agenda, instigating political movements, including the Ba'th Party. In 1958 this culminated in the union of Egypt and Syria as the United Arab Republic, a single sovereign state, which lasted until 1961.[18] After the Ba'thist coup in 1963, Syria and Iraq adopted similar flags (as shown) with three stars symbolizing the proposed union of Syria, Egypt and Iraq; however, these ambitions were never realized.[19]

The scarf depicts leaders who were lauded as heroes of Arab nationalism (ANTICLOCKWISE, FROM TOP LEFT): Field-Marshal 'Abdullah Al-Sallal (r. 1962–67, North Yemen); President Amin Al-Hafiz (r. 1963–66, Syria); General Ibrahim 'Abboud (r. 1958–64, Sudan); President Habib Bourguiba (r. 1957–87, Tunisia); King Hussein (r. 1952–99, Jordan); President 'Abdel Nasser (r. 1956–70, Egypt); King Sa'ud (r. 1953–64, Saudi Arabia); General Fu'ad Chehab (r. 1958–64, Lebanon); Field-Marshal 'Abdul Salam 'Arif (r. 1963–66, Iraq); President Ahmed Ben Bella (r. 1963–65, Algeria); Emir 'Abdullah Al-Sabah (r. 1961–65, Kuwait); King Idris Al-Senussi (r. 1951–69, Libya); and King Hassan II (r. 1961–99, Morocco).[20]

OPPOSITE, FAR LEFT **Portrait rug of Imam-Caliph 'Ali, Yörük people**
Şanlıurfa (Urfa), Turkey, c. 2000
Felted wool
Length 97 cm / width 64 cm
As2001,07.19

This depiction of 'Ali ibn Abi Talib (d. 661), the fourth Muslim caliph and first Shi'a imam, on a felt mat is clearly derived from the Byzantine tradition of portraying Christ with an angel, as often seen on church mosaics or portable icons. It was made by female felt-makers of the semi-nomadic Yörük tribe from the mountainous regions of south-eastern Turkey, and may indicate the maker's Alevi leanings.[21]

OPPOSITE, ABOVE **Portrait rug of Ayatollah Khomeini**
Iran, 2000–11
Wool and cotton
Length 63 cm / width 43 cm
2011,6012.1, gift of John E. Curtis

Ayatollah Khomeini (1900–89), the Shi'a Muslim cleric and political revolutionary who made Iran the world's first Islamic republic in 1979, has been memorialized in numerous posters, photographs and examples of graffiti art, and on rugs. Although this rug is not inscribed and is of lesser quality than other portrait rugs, Khomeini's long, white beard and characteristic black turban are unmistakable. Such mass-produced tools of visual propaganda allowed the widest possible dissemination of political and religious ideologies in both private and public spaces.

OPPOSITE, BELOW **Portrait rug of Lenin**
Turkmenistan, 1970
Wool and cotton
Length 75.5 cm / width 48 cm
As2002,01.4, purchased with the support of the British Museum Friends

This knotted-pile rug was probably produced in 1970 to mark the hundredth anniversary of the birth of Lenin (1870–1924), and it combines the traditions of Russian portraiture with Turkmen carpet weaving.[22] Before the collapse of the USSR in 1991, Soviet authorities strongly encouraged carpet weavers, artists, musicians and writers to glorify communist heroes and socialist ideologies in their works, as a way of portraying a consolidated Soviet identity across a vast region.[23]

RIGHT **Portrait rug of al-Farabi**
Almaty, Kazakhstan, 1991–95
Wool
Length 100 cm / width 65 cm
As1995,13.1, gift of Professor Kopzhasar Naribaevich Naribaev

This rug from the Al-Farabi Kazakh State University exemplifies the continued popularity of portrait rugs in post-Soviet Central Asia.[24] In place of a Soviet icon, however, the rug depicts the renowned Muslim philosopher and polymath Abu Nasr Muhammad al-Farabi (d. 950). Formerly named after the Bolshevik leader Sergei Mironovich Kirov (d. 1934), the university purged its association with its Soviet past after the country's independence in 1991. Portrait rugs continue to be produced across Central Asia in honour of state leaders, poets and heroes.[25]

Shepherd's cloak (*namad*) by Bita Ghezelayagh
Iran and UK, 2009
Wool, silk and metal
Length 102 cm / width 116 cm
2009,6029.1

This reinterpretation of a shepherd's cloak by Bita Ghezelayagh (b. 1966) is inspired by the tradition of talismanic tunics worn by soldiers to protect them during warfare. The cloak is inscribed with a Persian slogan from the Iran–Iraq War (1980–88), 'Martyrdom is the key to Paradise', and is covered in 1,001 metal keys symbolizing those carried into battle by young Iranian soldiers. Although the work reflects on her painful memories of war, the artist celebrates the resilience embodied within the felt and in the people of her homeland.[26]

Veiled Threats by Maliheh Afnan
London, UK, 2005
Ink on paper, overlaid with gauze
Length 60 cm / width 42 cm
2005,0712,0.1, purchased with the support of the Brooke Sewell Permanent Fund

The works of Maliheh Afnan (1935–2016) reflect her multi-faceted identity and her experiences of political upheaval as a Palestinian-born artist of Persian Baha'i descent. She uses Arabic, English and even imaginary scripts as starting points for her pieces, though the words are unreadable and meaningless. *Veiled Threats* is a response to the excessive post-9/11 media debate on the veiling of Muslim women as a threat to social integration. The gauze symbolizes other forms of veiling – the concealment not of hair or bodies, but of truths, intolerances, agendas and feelings.[27]

Garden war rug
Afghanistan, 1979–89
Wool and cotton
Length 207 cm / width 99 cm
2010,6013.17, gift of Graham Gower

At first glance, one might mistake this hand-knotted rug for a typical garden carpet, reflecting a long-standing Persianate tradition. But upon closer inspection, amid the repeating pattern of large floral medallions against a peach ground, one discerns the transformation of the dark blue *boteh* or paisley motifs into helicopters. The impact of the 1979 Soviet invasion of Afghanistan on the country's carpet-making tradition was felt almost immediately, as female weavers began subtly – and later overtly – to incorporate complex war imagery into their designs.[28]

ABOVE The hero Rustam slaying the evil White Div, or demon, from the *Shāhnāma* of Firdawsi. Iran, 1576–77
1937,0710,0.327. [29]

LEFT **War rug with demons**
Afghanistan, 1980–89
Wool and cotton
Length 158 cm / width 101 cm
2010,6013.12, gift of Graham Gower

The iconography of this war rug derives from an episode of the *Shāhnāma*, the Persian national epic composed by the medieval poet Firdawsi (d. 1020) (SEE ABOVE). In parallel, the four Russian soldiers on the rug are depicted as horned, white demons, while an Afghan soldier prepares to slay his enemy in combat, echoing Rustam's heroics. The central ground includes camels, helicopters and Afghan soldiers, and the wide border comprises a convoy of tanks with machine guns.[30]

Texas Flowers by Sara Rahbar
USA and Iran, 2008
Silk and cotton
Length 183 cm / width 122 cm
2015,6005.2, purchased with the support
of the Brooke Sewell Permanent Fund,
CaMMEA and Maryam and Edward Eisler

Sara Rahbar (b. 1976) began her Flag Series in the aftermath of 9/11, when Americans felt compelled to display their flag as a visible sign of solidarity and identity. Having migrated to the USA as a child, following the Iranian Revolution of 1979, she grapples in her work with the entangled relationship between her adopted country and her native Iran. In *Texas Flowers* she assembles brightly coloured floral motifs from Central Asian *sūzanī* textiles onto a vintage American flag. Traditionally embroidered for bridal dowries, *sūzanīs* bear symbols of love and fertility. Here, however, these motifs resemble loaded revolver chambers, surrounding an outline of the state of Texas.[31]

RIGHT AND OVERLEAF *Narcissist*
by Sara Rahbar
USA and Iran, 2014
Silk, cotton, silver and metal
Length 183 cm / width 119 cm
2015,6005.1, purchased with the support of the Brooke Sewell Permanent Fund, CaMMEA and Maryam and Edward Eisler

Narcissist, the last flag in Sara Rahbar's series, is an assemblage of textiles and amulets from Iran, South Asia and Central Asia, military buttons, patches and empty bullet cartridges from Iran and the USA, and a crucifix. This flag explores themes of national belonging and the futility of war and borders. Some of the textiles are associated with the Baluch and Lakai Uzbek peoples, groups who were historically obliged to settle within imposed national borders that were meaningless to them. Rahbar collects symbolically potent materials from across Iran and the USA and makes them into collages, reflecting her own multi-layered identity and heritage.

POLITICS & CONFLICT 199

FAR LEFT AND LEFT **Unisex bolero jacket by OmarJoseph Nasser-Khoury**
Palestine and Lebanon, 2009
Wool, silk and cotton, with copper and amber beads
Length 76 cm / width 81 cm
2011,6016.1, purchased with the support of the Modern Museum Fund

This jacket, by Palestinian fashion designer OmarJoseph Nasser-Khoury (b. 1988), is visually inspired by the politics of his homeland and its dressmaking traditions. Traditional 'star-key' (*mafātīḥ al-nujūm*) motifs are cross-stitched in shades of golden-yellow cotton, interspersed with skulls and embellished with copper and amber beads. In place of floral motifs, the ominous skulls allude to the bombs dropped over Gaza in 2009.[32] The embroiderer was Nazmieh Salem from the Mar Elias Refugee Camp in Beirut, under the aegis of INAASH (see below).

ABOVE **Cushion cover by INAASH**
Beirut, 1980s
Silk and cotton
Length 39 cm / width 37 cm
As1988,25.1

Founded in 1969 by Palestinian and Lebanese women in Beirut, INAASH (Association for the Development of Palestinian Camps) focuses on raising the quality of life of refugees in the camps, and keeping women's embroidery skills alive. Projects are funded mainly through the sale of hand-embroidered cushions, clothing and textiles. This cushion features four central 'star-keys' surrounded by other patterns.

LEFT **Woman's keffiyeh scarf**
Palestine or Jordan, 1980s
Cotton and synthetic wool
Length 152 cm / width 14 cm
As1988,06.21

The black and white keffiyeh (*kūfīya*) head-cloth became a unifying symbol of Palestinian national identity in the late 1930s, following the Arab Revolt in Palestine.[33] Although it is worn mainly by men, and was strongly associated with Yasser 'Arafat from the 1960s, many young Palestinian women living in the West Bank and refugee camps in Jordan in the 1980s appropriated this potent symbol by adapting the keffiyeh into a neck scarf, with woollen fringes modelled on the Palestinian flag.[34]

RIGHT **Bedouin man's keffiyeh**
Palestine, 1920–48
Cotton
Length 114 cm / width 121 cm
As1966,01.290

Until the 1920s, head-cloths of varying colours and patterns were worn exclusively by the Bedouin of Iraq, Arabia, Palestine, Syria and Jordan, and suited their pastoral nomadic lifestyles and harsh environments. Folded diagonally and held in place with a head-rope (*'aqāl*), the head-cloth visibly distinguished the Bedouin from sedentary villagers and townsmen, who preferred to wear the fez (*ṭarbūsh*) or turban. Head-cloths were made of cotton, silk and fine wool.[35] This cotton keffiyeh (*kūfīya*) is woven with a pattern in indigo-dyed thread; indigo is a natural dye believed to protect the wearer from misfortune.

FAR RIGHT **Man's keffiyeh and head-rope (*'aqāl* or *'iqāl*)**
Palestine or Yemen, 1950s–1980s (keffiyeh); Saudi Arabia,
1940s–1950s (head-rope)
Cotton (keffiyeh), silk, cotton and gilt-metal-wrapped thread (head-rope)
Keffiyeh: length 127 cm / width 124 cm
Head-rope: circumference 119 cm
2015,6054.1 (keffiyeh), bequest of Leila Ingrams; As1974,05.3 (head-rope), gift of Gerald de Gaury

The checked keffiyeh (*kūfīya*)[36] has a number of designations across the Arab world, including *ghuṭra*,[37] *shimāgh*[38] and *mashada*.[39] It sometimes features tassels, like this example, and can be worn with or without a white cotton skullcap (*ṭāqiyya*). Although occasionally wrapped around the head like a turban, the keffiyeh is commonly draped over the head and secured with a double-looped head-rope of dyed camel or goat hair, wool or silk. This head-rope, bound with an abundance of gilt thread, denotes the wearer's high status.[40]

OPPOSITE **Man's ikat robe (*chapan*)**
Bukhara, Uzbekistan, c. 1900
Silk and cotton
Length 129 cm / width 164 cm
2014.6013.2

Bukhara, Samarkand and Marghilan were primary centres of the Central Asian textile industry in the nineteenth century. Ikat-dyed and woven silks, called *abr* ('clouds'), were produced in numerous specialized workshops, tightly controlled by weavers' guilds.[41] High-quality silk robes served as status symbols and were worn in layers for added ostentation. This silk summer robe has watermelon and horn patterns, and is lined with blue floral cotton.[42] Everything changed, however, with the creation of the Soviet Union in 1922. Private workshops were required to form cooperatives or risk confiscation of their looms and equipment. These gradually transformed into state-run industrialized factories, engaged in mass production.[43]

ABOVE AND OVERLEAF **Woman's ikat robe (*munisak*)**
Bukhara, Uzbekistan, 1880s–1920s
Silk and cotton
Length 132 cm / width 152 cm
2014.6013.1

A woman would have worn this fitted robe over a dress and trousers during important rites of passage, from weddings to funerals.[44] It is *abr*-dyed and woven with stylized rams' horns and pomegranate flowers – symbols of strength, abundance and fertility. The panels of glazed *abr* lining and silk edging (*zeh*) add to its value.[45] By the 1870s, machine-printed cottons from Tsarist Russia, like the brilliant red lining in this coat, had flooded the bazaars and supplanted locally woven, block-printed varieties. Russian-controlled Central Asia (i.e. Turkestan) not only provided a market for these affordable factory cottons, but also supplied the raw materials to drive the industry.[46]

Tent wall-hanging (*tush kiyiz*) with communist heraldry
Kyrgyzstan, 1950s–1980s
Cotton
Length 187 cm / width 360 cm
As2001,13.1, gift of Dinara Chochunbaeva

Made in the style of a traditional tent-hanging for a Kyrgyz yurt, this enormous cotton embroidery has been transformed into a Soviet propaganda textile.[47] Judging from its size, it was probably commissioned to be hung in a public building. The chain-stitched emblems, representing fourteen Soviet Socialist Republics, are (OPPOSITE, ABOVE, FROM BOTTOM LEFT): Estonia, Tajikistan, Georgia, Russia, Uzbekistan, Ukraine, Belarus, Kazakhstan, Kyrgyzstan, Moldova, Turkmenistan, Armenia, Lithuania and Latvia. Each emblem features the communist symbols of the hammer and sickle, red star, rising sun and wreath of wheat, and the motto 'Workers of the world unite!' in Russian and the local language.[48] Detail images shown are (CLOCKWISE, FROM TOP RIGHT) Tajikistan, Kyrgyzstan, Kazakhstan and Uzbekistan.

A Note on the Collection

The British Museum's renowned collection of nearly three thousand Middle Eastern and Central Asian textiles falls under the curatorial Department of the Middle East. The objects are stored by country, and date mainly from the nineteenth century to the present day. Important exceptions to that date range include a sizeable group of archaeological textile fragments from Fatimid and Mamluk Egypt (tenth to fourteenth centuries; p. 179), one silk textile from Safavid Iran (1580s–1620s; p. 8), and several eighteenth-century Ottoman textiles (p. 88) and military banners, including two curtains made for the Prophet's Mosque at Medina, which were gifted by the Khalili Family Trust in 2012 (pp. 126–27, 182–83). Egyptian textiles from the nineteenth century to the present day (p. 76) are counted among the African department's holdings and are therefore not included in the total of three thousand items mentioned above.

Palestinian textiles form approximately one third of the Middle Eastern textile collections, and were acquired in large part from three main church missionary organizations: the Church Missionary Society (1966; pp. 26, 68–69, 106, 114–15, 204–05 (blue keffiyeh)); Jerusalem and the East Mission, later renamed the Jerusalem and Middle East Church Association (1968; pp. 66–67, 102–03, 107, 132, 184); and the Church's Ministry among Jewish People (1990s; pp. 31, 35). Shelagh Weir, the curator responsible for all of the Asian and European ethnographic collections from 1965 to 1998, expanded the Palestinian and Jordanian textile holdings (pp. 45, 154–55, 185), following extensive fieldwork in Israel, the West Bank, Gaza Strip and Jordan, and mounted several textile exhibitions, including 'Palestinian Costume' (1989–91).

The Museum acquired a rich collection of nineteenth-century Iranian textiles from the Church Missionary Society in 1966 (pp. 31 (bonnet), 58, 90–91, 92–93, 104). Between 1966 and 1975 significant portions of the collection, focusing on Turkey (pp. 86, 98–99, 133, 163) and Iran, were built up by the architect and ethnographer Peter Alford Andrews. These items included a substantial assemblage of Turkmen textiles from Iran, collected in the field for the Lake District Art Gallery Trust's travelling exhibition 'The Turcoman of Iran' (1971–72; pp. 39 (cap), 70, 100, 162, 167, 170–71, 174–75), which were purchased in 1973 by the British Museum, the Horniman Museum (London) and the Whitworth Art Gallery (Manchester).

Shelagh Weir's major exhibition 'Nomad and City', organized as part of the UK's World of Islam Festival (1976), resulted in an important acquisition of textiles from Yemen, which had been collected by the anthropologist Martha Mundy and others from the University of Cambridge in 1974–75 (pp. 110–11). The Museum's Yemeni textiles were augmented by Weir in the 1980s and through substantial donations from the archaeologist Carl Phillips (2002; pp. 108–09, 134–35) and the author Leila Ingrams (2011–12; pp. 50–51). The Museum also has noteworthy early twentieth-century collections from other parts of the Arabian Peninsula, including Harold and Violet Dickson's garments from Kuwait (2000; p. 95) and Gerald de Gaury's men's garments from Saudi Arabia (1974; p. 205). The Museum's textile holdings from Oman were expanded in 2010 through a generous donation from the Ministry of Tourism of the Sultanate of Oman for my exhibition 'Adornment and Identity: Jewellery and Costume from Oman' (pp. 14, 32, 36, 94, 113).

The Museum also has important collections of Central Asian textiles from the nineteenth century to the present day. In 1995–96 the anthropologist Stephanie Bunn collected a large number of Kyrgyz felts, a selection of which were exhibited in 'Striking Tents: Central Asian Nomad Felts from Kyrgyzstan' (1997; pp. 168–69). Several acquisitions of tent-hangings, felts, amulets and garments were made in the 1990s and early 2000s under the curatorship of Sarah Posey, including an assemblage of around sixty embroidered tent-hangings associated with the Lakai Uzbek people of Afghanistan, collected by Pip Rau in the 1970s (pp. 60–61, 156–57, 158–59, 172–73). The Museum received a generous donation of forty Afghan war rugs and kilims from Graham Gower in 2010 (pp. 176–77, 194–95, 196–97), and the Ministry of Foreign Affairs of the Republic of Tajikistan presented around fifty Tajik textiles to the Museum in 2015.

Notes

INTRODUCTION, pp. 8–23

1. Hafiz, *Dīvān*, ed. Qazvini and Ghani, pp. 216, 311; trans. Avery, *Collected Lyrics*, pp. 302, 487.
2. The design on double cloths can be seen on both sides, though the calligraphy can be read only on one side; thus the cartouches of writing on this piece appear reversed in some areas. Double cloth involves a complicated weaving technique, requiring two sets each of warp and weft threads. For other examples see Bier, *Woven from the Soul*, pp. 184–87; Ekhtiar et al., *Masterpieces*, pp. 248–49; Hillenbrand et al., *The Sarikhani Collection*, pp. 102–03.
3. The repeating text includes the first two lines (i.e. first couplet) of one *ghazal* (each line is inscribed in its own cartouche) and only the first line of another *ghazal* (in a third cartouche). I am deeply indebted to Dominic Parviz Brookshaw for identifying the poetry on this textile and for supplying me with copies of the original Persian text and English translation.
4. Although there are several examples of this type of double cloth in museum collections, they are all relatively small fragments, so their precise use remains unclear. The fragments from the Textile Museum in Washington, DC (no. 3.280), and the Metropolitan Museum of Art (no. 46.156.7) are from the same textile and also include a reference to clothing in their poetic verses, alongside images of Shirin and Farhad (the latter was another of Shirin's admirers in the tale of Khusraw and Shirin). See Bier, *Woven from the Soul*, and Ekhtiar et al., *Masterpieces*.
5. Within the Iranian context, the stories of Layli and Majnun and Khusraw and Shirin derive from the celebrated Persian retelling of the tales by the poet Nizami Ganjavi (1141–1209) in his *Khamsa* ('Quintet', or five narrative poems). The most renowned adaptation of the story of Yusuf and Zulaykha (the biblical Joseph and Potiphar's wife) in Persian was composed by the scholar and Sufi mystic 'Abd al-Rahman Jami (1414–92) in his *Haft awrang* ('Seven thrones'). Jami also composed a version of Layli and Majnun as the sixth volume of his *Haft awrang*.
6. For examples of these stories depicted on a range of Safavid textiles see Bier, *Woven from the Soul*, pp. 180–93. Dominic Brookshaw pointed out to me that the scenes on this textile and the frames around each vignette recall the fresco paintings on the walls of Pir-Nia House (now an ethnological museum), a Safavid-period building in Na'in, central Iran. I also wonder if the designs on the frames on this textile are stylized inscriptions with the words '*amal Ghiyāth* ('work of Ghiyath'), referring to a high-ranking textile designer and weaver during the reign of Shah 'Abbas (r. 1587–1629). For a discussion of Ghiyath see Bier, *Woven from the Soul*, pp. 188–89.
7. Very few objects from Egypt have been included in this volume and none from North Africa because the Museum's collections from these regions have been well published by my colleagues Christopher Spring and Julie Hudson (see the bibliography).
8. The exception to this is the vast number of archaeological textiles at the Museum from pharaonic and Coptic Egypt.
9. Personal communication, 12 May 2016. Weir, *Palestinian Costume*, pp. 14–15, 17, 20; Weir, 'Beauty and Meaning', p. 14. Weir curated three exhibitions of Palestinian textiles at the British Museum (then the Museum of Mankind in Burlington Gardens, the premises of the Museum's Department of Ethnography): 'Costumes of Palestine' (1970–71); 'Spinning and Weaving in Palestine' (1970–71); 'Palestinian Costume' (1989–91).
10. Weir, 'Beauty and Meaning', p. 14. The Palestinian collections derived from three main missionary organizations: the Church Missionary Society (1966), Jerusalem and the East Mission (1968) and the Church's Ministry among Jewish People (1990s).
11. Weir, *Palestinian Costume*, p. 101.
12. Bilgi and Zanbak, *Skill of the Hand*, p. 17.
13. Grace Crowfoot published her research on these stitches in Crowfoot and Sutton, 'Ramallah embroidery', pp. 25–37. The names of the stitches were fluid and sometimes the same stitch was referred to by different names from village to village.
14. Fitz Gibbon and Hale, *Uzbek Embroidery*, pp. 86–87. The authors also mention that textile traditions in northern Afghanistan survived up to the 1980s until war impoverished and destabilized the region.
15. The establishment of institutions such as the Mansoojat Foundation, a charity registered in the UK and based in Jeddah, and the Art of Heritage Group in Riyadh share a common objective to collect, preserve and disseminate information about the diversity of dress traditions within the Kingdom of Saudi Arabia.
16. Quoted from the workshop website <https://www.indiegogo.com/projects/palestinian-embroidery-workshop-fifteen-stitches#/>. Other commercial enterprises aimed at reviving and promoting Palestinian embroidery are burgeoning in the region, including the online shop Taita Leila, which designs and produces women's fashions that are hand-embroidered by women in the West Bank and shipped anywhere in the world (<https://www.taitaleila.com/pages/about-us>). Nasser-Khoury's own work is discussed in 'Politics and Conflict', pp. 202–03.
17. Ghezelayagh, *Namad*, pp. 1–15. The production date '1383' embroidered on the cloak refers to the *hijrī shamsī* (Islamic solar) calendar used in Iran and Afghanistan, and converts to the year 2004. See 'Politics and Conflict', p. 192, for a discussion of another of her works, and 'Marriage and Ceremony', p. 59, for an example of a Turkmen embroidered cloak with tulips. Tumar <www.tumar.com>, a Kyrgyz craft collective and retailer based in Bishkek, works with artists, designers and felt-makers throughout the country to produce contemporary felt clothing, furnishings and floor-coverings in order to preserve the tradition of Kyrgyz felt-making and disseminate it to a global audience.
18. For the Widad Kawar collection see Kawar, *Threads of Identity*, and <http://www.tirazcentre.org/en>. Selections from the Al Lulwa private collection of Middle Eastern textiles in Kuwait are published in Wearden, *Decorative Textiles*.
19. A comprehensive database of textile collections in the Middle East and Central Asia is urgently needed.
20. The vintage fabrics Thea Porter used included Syrian brocades, Indian saris, Southeast Asian ikats and Central Asian ikats and *sūzanīs*. Porter was designing '*abāyas* in the early 1970s, at a time when contemporary Middle Eastern dress was largely unknown in the West and people's perceptions were tainted by stereotypes presented in Hollywood films; Helms and Porter, *Thea Porter*, pp. 28–43. Her clients came from East and West and ranged from film stars and the wives of film stars to princesses; *ibid.*, pp. 115–23.
21. See the excellent online article by 'The Polyglot' on the use of Arabic calligraphy by Western fashion designers: <http://the-polyglot.blogspot.co.uk/2010/12/are-western-fashion-designers-ready-to.html>.

22 The show was curated by Hana Al-Banna-Chidiac, curator of the North African and Near Eastern collections at the Quai Branly. The regions covered were Jordan, Palestine, Syria, Lebanon and the Sinai Peninsula in Egypt. Many of the garments, face-veils and headdresses were borrowed from the Widad Kawar collection. Al-Banna-Chidiac, *L'Orient des femmes*, pp. 19–20.

23 Shirazi, *Veil Unveiled*, pp. 3–4.

24 Academic studies around this subject include Arthur, *Undressing Religion*; Lewis, *Modest Fashion*; Shirazi, *Veil Unveiled*; Tarlo, *Visibly Muslim*.

25 The first London Modest Fashion Week was held at the Saatchi Gallery in London in February 2017 (<http://lmfw.co.uk>). In 2015 the Second Annual Turin Islamic Economic Forum included a special round-table discussion on modest fashion, to address the challenges and opportunities in the global Islamic economy sector (<http://www.tief2015.org/modestfashion.shtml>). According to Samuel Fishwick and Lucy Tobin, the modest fashion industry is estimated to be worth $484 billion annually, while two-thirds of Generation M (young, affluent millennial Muslims, who are big spenders) are under thirty and with an annual global spend of some $2.6 trillion. See Fishwick and Tobin, 'How the Hijab Became this Week's Biggest Talking Point: From Lindsay Lohan to London Modest Fashion Week', *Evening Standard Online*, 24 February 2017 (<http://www.standard.co.uk/lifestyle/london-life/how-the-hijab-became-this-weeks-biggest-talking-point-from-lindsay-lohan-to-london-modest-fashion-a3475441.html>).

26 Kimberly Chrisman-Campbell, 'Why Western Designers are Embracing the Hijab', *The Atlantic Online*, 7 January 2016 (<https://www.theatlantic.com/entertainment/archive/2016/01/dolce-gabbana-high-fashion/423171/>); Zlata Rodionova, 'Marks & Spencer Burkini Collection Sells Out', *The Independent Online*, 23 August 2016 (<http://www.independent.co.uk/news/business/news/burkini-marks-and-spencer-sells-out-france-ban-muslim-islam-attire-a7205456.html>); Rebecca Flood, 'Debenhams Becomes First Major Department Store to Sell Hijabs', *The Independent Online*, 11 February 2017 (<http://www.independent.co.uk/news/uk/debenhams-hijab-muslim-clothing-women-uk-department-store-religion-a7575306.html>).

CHILDHOOD, pp. 24–41

1 Extract from *The Prophet* (1923) by the Lebanese–American artist and poet Kahlil Gibran (1883–1931); 86th reprint (New York, 1970), p. 17.

2 The notion of, and continued belief in, the 'evil eye' or 'eye of envy' are widely distributed among many cultures across Europe, North Africa, the Middle East and the Indian subcontinent. These are harmful forces that arise from the human emotions of jealousy and envy, and are most often associated with the contexts of marriage, female reproductive experiences and the domestic sphere (conception, pregnancy, childbirth and lactation, the nurture and care of children, protection against disease and illness, and welfare of one's livestock and motor vehicle). Special amulets are made and worn as protection against these forces, often in combination with spoken phrases and/or specific hand gestures. The 'evil eye' or 'eye of envy' has many names is Middle Eastern and Central Asian cultures (Hebrew '*ayin ha-ra*'; Arabic *al-'ayn, al-nazar, al-hasad*; Persian *bad chasm, chasm zakhm, ol*). See Dundes, ed., *The Evil Eye*.

3 Paine, *Embroidery from Afghanistan*, pp. 64–65. For an example of the use of black and white cord on Turkmen children's clothing for the same purpose see 'Religion and Belief', p. 137.

4 Arakelova and Asatrian, 'Amulets, Fortune-Telling, and Magic'.

5 In other Islamic contexts, in the Middle East and elsewhere, pilgrims often tie rags of cloth and string to the tombs of holy persons by way of supplication to the saint. The rag acts as a marker of the pilgrim's vow to a specific saint. Zimney, 'Islam: Saints and Sacred Geographies'.

6 Arakelova and Asatrian, 'Amulets, Fortune-Telling, and Magic'. The authors do not specify the countries in which this tradition was or is practised. In many Middle Eastern countries, a blue bead is customarily fastened to a child's clothing, using a safety pin in order to pierce the 'evil eye' and protect the child against illness or harm.

7 Pendants of alum (potassium aluminium sulphate) are worn as protection against the 'evil eye' and fires and to stop excessive bleeding.

8 Richardson and Dorr, *Craft Heritage*, pp. 298–99. The *kimma* is still worn in Sur but no longer holds such a connotation.

9 Vogelsang-Eastwood, 'Dress from Kyrgyzstan', pp. 395–98. For Kyrgyz headdresses and other married women's headgear see 'Marriage and Ceremony', pp. 58, 72–73.

10 Paine, *Amulets*, pp. 73–74.

11 A child is usually circumcised (the ritual removal of the foreskin) before the age of 6, and the operation is preceded by a celebration marking his formal adoption of his Muslim identity. As Weir points out, in pre-1948 rural Palestine the boy was ornamented in similar ways to a bride, and in some parts of Turkey today a boy's right hand is painted with henna before his circumcision. Weir, *Palestinian Costume*, pp. 61–63, 254–55; Vogelsang-Eastwood, 'Prince for a Day', pp. 32–33.

12 This tradition dates back to the early Ottoman period and continues to be practised in Turkey today, on horseback or by motorcar. Vogelsang-Eastwood, 'Prince for a Day'; Bulookbashi and Marnani, 'Circumcision'.

13 The *shahāda* is the Muslim profession of faith. I wish to thank Asma Hilali for deciphering this part of the inscription. The remaining portion is yet to be deciphered.

14 Stehlin-AlZadjali, *Traditional…Dress*, pp. 66–71. The pocket is called a *koptān* or *jīb* in Iran. See Firouz and Jahanbani, 'Clothing xiii'. See 'Status and Identity', p. 94, for a Baluch woman's attire.

15 Oman maintained close political ties with parts of Baluchistan from the 1780s to the 1950s, and Baluchis have lived and prospered in Oman for centuries, speaking both Arabic and their native languages.

16 Paine, *Amulets*, p. 92; Meller, *Silk and Cotton*, pp. 123, 131, 231. As this coat was acquired from an urban market shop we do not know its context of production or the source of the textiles used. The use of patchwork decoration is probably a reference to this tradition.

17 Diba, 'Clothing x'. According to the acquisition notes, the outfit was made for a girl aged 3.

18 Weir, *Palestinian Costume*, p. 136.

19 Kawar, *Threads of Identity*, pp. 140, 151–52. According to Shelagh Weir, in the late nineteenth and early twentieth centuries members of both religious traditions sometimes incorporated a small cross on their embroidered chest panels, which showed an acceptance of each other's religious symbols and a lack of religious differentiation in that context (personal communication, 12 May 2016).

20 I wish to thank Aisa Martinez for this information and for helping me to identify this dress.

21 Paine, *Amulets*, pp. 150–52, says: 'Almost no person, building or car can be seen in Central Asia without an embroidered triangle.' In *Afghan Amulet*, she gives an enthralling account of her travels in search of the meaning of the triangle, from northern Pakistan to eastern Bulgaria.

22 Paine, *Amulets*, p. 150; Meller, *Silk and Cotton*, pp. 132–33. Women wear *doghas* in the form of silver jewellery.

23 The inclusion of Soviet badges suggests that it may have been 'repackaged' for the tourist market when it was purchased in the 1990s. This may also explain why the amulets are sewn on the front of the *kurta*, rather than the back as is customary.

24 For a detailed discussion of the construction and embroidery of this skullcap see Andrews and Andrews, *Türkmen Needlework*, pp. 27–28.

25 According to Selin Ipek, this turning point in the urban sphere took place during the reign of Sultan

Abdülaziz (r. 1861–76), but European influence on Ottoman court fashions was felt much earlier. Ipek, 'Ottoman Fabrics', p. 5. For reciprocal influences see Jirousek, 'Ottoman Influences'; Inal, 'Women's Fashions'.

MARRIAGE AND CEREMONY, pp. 42–77

1. This list is extracted and adapted from a bridal trousseau list for a Jewish bride found in a *geniza* (the storage area for documents in a synagogue) and dates from the period of Fatimid-governed Cairo (979–1171). For the full translation and explanation of this and other trousseau lists see Goitein, *Mediterranean Society*, vol. 4, esp. pp. 323–24. Comparable lists from Muslim or Christian contexts in medieval Cairo have not survived.
2. According to Goitein, a modest family could live for ten years on 250 dinars. Hence, this bride came from a fabulously wealthy family. Goitein, *Mediterranean Society*, vol. 4, p. 311.
3. This money, referred to as *mahr* in the Qur'an and in Islamic law (Hebrew *mohar*), is an essential condition for a legal marriage and is referred to as 'brideprice', 'bridewealth' or 'marriage payment' by anthropologists. Spies, 'Mahr'.
4. Weir, *Palestinian Costume*, pp. 74–75.
5. A girl wore items from her trousseau for the very first time at her wedding, and her other best pieces during the days and months that followed, when she received guests at home or attended another wedding or festivity. Weir, *Palestinian Costume*, pp. 44–46, 74–76. By contrast, according to Shelagh Weir's research findings, in rural Yemen the groom's side provided everything (i.e. money, jewellery, clothes, soap, etc.) and the bride's nothing (personal communication, 7 January 2017).
6. As part of wedding ceremonies in general across this vast region, articles of clothing, money and other gifts are also customarily exchanged between various relatives of the bridal pair as overt symbols of the new social bonds formed between families. For an example see Weir, *Palestinian Costume*, p. 243.
7. The British Museum has a number of examples made of basketry and painted metal from Yemen (As1980,17.32.a–b, As1993,03.56, As1980,17.64), and examples made of wood from Mecca (As1958,05.1.a) and Palestine (As1971,02.23).
8. Such processions also occurred in the Ottoman period at various levels of society. See the wonderful description of the royal procession of Princess Mihrimah Sultan's bridal trousseau in Istanbul, 1836, by Julia Pardoe (*City of the Sultan*, pp. 495–96). The British Museum has a twentieth-century Turkish shadow puppet (As1980,11.10) of a man carrying a tray of cosmetic items as part of a wedding procession. The *'arūsī* (wedding celebration) did not always occur on the same day as the *'aqd* (religious wedding-contract ceremony). Hence, traditionally, the couple must wait for the *'arūsī* before the bride could move into her marital home. Betteridge, "Arūsī'; Betteridge and Javadi, ''Aqd'.
9. Fitz Gibbon and Hale, *Uzbek Embroidery*, p. 74.
10. This accounts for the slightly skewed pattern-matching along the joins of some *sūzanīs*, both on older nineteenth-century pieces made at home and on mid-twentieth-century commercial examples made in Soviet-established artels (cooperatives). Among the most popular stitches on Uzbek and Tajik *sūzanīs* are couching (*basma*) outlined in chain-stitch (*yurma*). For a full explanation and a range of regional examples see Meller, *Silk and Cotton*, pp. 164–91; Fitz Gibbon and Hale, *Uzbek Embroidery*, pp. 138–56.
11. These items were registered as dolls' clothes from eastern Armenia when they were acquired by the British Museum in 1934. In 2014 Marine Mkrtchyan, deputy director of the Museum of Russian Art in Yerevan, deduced that they were model garments and not dolls' clothes. I thank her for this information and for pointing out to me the connections with Georgian (Tbilisi) dress.
12. Armenian communities were concentrated in Anatolia, Iranian Azerbaijan and Isfahan. After the First World War and the 1915 Armenian massacre in Ottoman Turkey, they migrated to Arab lands and beyond.
13. The inclusion of a model outdoor face-veil (*rūband*), usually worn by Muslims in Iran (not shown in the illustration), suggests that the dressmaker had Muslim clients as well and may have been based in Isfahan, rather than in Armenia. See 'Marriage and Ceremony', p. 105, for an example of an Iranian *rūband*.
14. These pieces were gifted to Doreen Ingrams (1906–97) in Yemen. See her obituary on the British–Yemeni Society's website <http://b-ys.org.uk/journal/obituaries/ingrams-doreen>.
15. Hadramawt (sometimes spelled Hadhramaut) was then part of the Aden Protectorate in south-west Arabia and is now a province of the Republic of Yemen. Ingrams was initially posted as political officer to Aden in 1934, and then served as British resident advisor at Mukalla from 1937 to 1944.
16. The Middle Eastern custom of bestowing garments of honour is ancient, and pre-dates Islam. However, the 'Abbasid caliphs of Baghdad (750–1258) institutionalized this practice. Stillmann, 'Khil'a '; Gordon, 'Khil'a'. Harold's robe was probably imported from Syria, Egypt or Iraq – places famed for such robes. Wearden, *Decorative Textiles*, pp. 98–99, 158–59. For an Iranian example see Wearden and Baker, *Iranian Textiles*, pp. 28–29. See the Egyptian or Syrian *'abāya*, p. 76.
17. For excellent examples of the different types of robes, including ikat and *bekasab* (striped silks), see Meller, *Silk and Cotton*, pp. 36–43, 54–75, 120–21. For the reference to Paris see *ibid.*, p. 36.
18. Traditionally worn over a tunic and draw-string trousers, with a waist sash tied around the inner robe. See a Bukharan Jewish groom in Jerusalem from the 1920s wearing his brocaded *chapan* with a shirt and necktie in Juhasz, *Jewish Wardrobe*, pp. 194–95.
19. Meller, *Silk and Cotton*, pp. 74–75.
20. Warp-twining loop manipulation is explained in Meller, *Silk and Cotton*, pp. 36, 105; and by Frieda Sorber in Appendix II of Fitz Gibbon and Hale, *Uzbek Embroidery*, pp. 192–98. The trim on this robe appears to be tablet- or finger-woven with additions of cross-stitched embroidery, which were then sewn onto the edges of the garment.
21. Kulob, the third largest city in Tajikistan and a former province, is also referred to as Kulyab (Russian) and Kulab (Persian). Very little appears to be published on the symbolism of the embroidery, but its affinity with Lakai Uzbek designs is not surprising, given that many Lakai settled in the region from at least the nineteenth century, if not earlier. See the entry by Habib Borjian, 'Kulāb', *Encyclopaedia Iranica*, updated version available online at <http://www.iranicaonline.org/articles/kulab>.
22. For an image showing the layered dresses, and for further discussion see Maitdinova, 'Clothing xv'. For similar dresses see Meller, *Silk and Cotton*, p. 81.
23. The design, worked in couching (*basma*) outlined in chain-stitch (*yurma*), is characteristic of the 'Samarkand style' of *sūzanīs* produced in the early to mid-twentieth century. Meller, *Silk and Cotton*, pp. 179–81, 198–99. As Meller was told that the vine-scrolls are called 'melon vines', I suggest that the rosettes are actually melons, since Uzbekistan has over 160 varieties of the fruit and it is a source of national pride.
24. Contemporary artist Sara Rahbar subverts the symbolism of the motifs on *sūzanīs* in her work *Texas Flowers*. See 'Politics and Conflict', p. 198.
25. Specifically, the British Museum Society Eastern European Purchase Grant
26. See Vogelsang-Eastwood, 'Dress from Kyrgyzstan', pp. 395–98, for a detailed discussion of the *chach kep* (literally 'hair bag') and the turban (*ileki*) that was worn on top of it. For other examples see Meller, *Silk and Cotton*, p. 163; Gillow, *Textiles*, pp. 216–17. For the Kyrgyz wedding headdress see the *saukele*, pp. 72–73.
27. See Paine, *Amulets*, pp. 124–25, 147–52, for the significance of triangles, rags and snakes specific to Turkmen culture. For the amuletic power of indigo see 'Religion and Belief', pp. 134–35.
28. Krody, 'Tradition of the Bridal Trousseau', p. 431; Paine, *Amulets*, pp. 104–06.

29 The *chyrpy* is worn over trousers and a long tunic. For more examples and a discussion of the block-printed lining see Harvey, *Traditional Textiles*, pp. 44, 114, figs 168–69 and 211. The base fabric of this coat seems to be a silk and cotton blend, and it has an indigo-dyed and block-printed cotton lining. Published in Paine, *Embroidery from Afghanistan*, pp. 62–63.

30 Found on the hillsides of Afghanistan and Iran – hence throughout Turkmen territory – tulips were first cultivated by the Persians and Turks around the tenth or eleventh century. The flower was introduced to Western Europe and the Netherlands in the sixteenth century via Ottoman Turkey. For the poetry see Schimmel, *Two-Colored Brocade*, pp. 167–69.

31 Originating from the Central Asian steppe, the Lakai were primarily horse-breeders who traced their lineage back to Genghis Khan. Once semi-nomadic pastoralists and largely independent, the Lakai were forced into settled agriculture in the regions of southern Tajikistan and south-eastern Uzbekistan in the late nineteenth century, following brutal clashes with the armies of the Emir of Bukhara. Many fought against the Bolsheviks as anti-Soviet militant fighters (*basmachi*) in the 1920s and were defeated. As a result, Lakai lands were pacified and converted into collective farms to serve the Soviet cotton industry. Some Lakai groups moved into northern Afghanistan to escape religious and political oppression by the Soviets. For their full history see Fitz Gibbon and Hale, *Uzbek Embroidery*, pp. 27–37.

32 The main decoration is worked in slanting blanket-stitch. Published in Paine, *Embroidery from Afghanistan*, pp. 40–41.

33 To see how a similar *bugjama* is used see Meller, *Silk and Cotton*, p. 237, nos 6–7. For a description of a traditional Lakai marriage ceremony see Fitz Gibbon and Hale, *Uzbek Embroidery*, pp. 72–74.

34 I have not found a standardized name or spelling for this headgear. The alternatives (with or without the umlaut) are *kulta püsh*, *kultapüsh*, *kultapüshak*, *kulta peshak* and *kallapüshak*.

35 For example, the cypress (*sarv*) is a metaphor for the slender, elegant stature of the beloved, and her chin is likened to an apple (*sīb*). Schimmel, *Two-Colored Brocade*, pp. 163–64, 384. This *kultapüshak* is lined in red cotton and includes matt gilt-metal wire (rough purl) and couched gilt-metal-wrapped cord within the design. It is finished with needle-braided edging in a delicate floral pattern. According to some scholars, Muslims wore simple cotton *kultapüshaks* until the early twentieth century, after which time the headdress was abandoned in urban contexts. However, Jewish women wore more expensive and richly embroidered versions and continued wearing them until the 1940s. For this argument see Juhasz, *Jewish Wardrobe*, pp. 114–15, 324. The examples in Meller, *Silk and Cotton*, pp. 162–63, seem to contradict this view.

36 The term *daghya* is apparently an anglicization of the Arabic *durrāʿa* (a woman's outer coat) and *qaṣṣa* means 'cut'. The chemise shown is not part of the original outfit and has been added for illustrative purposes only. For comparative examples, including an authentic chemise, see Juhasz, *Jewish Wardrobe*, pp. 272–75.

37 The Jewish communities of Surat, Bombay and Calcutta clung to their Iraqi Jewish traditions, though most Baghdadi Jews had begun wearing English-style clothes by the early twentieth century. For a full discussion see Juhasz, *Jewish Wardrobe*, p. 277.

38 I wish to thank Mahmoud Hawari for his assistance in deciphering this inscription. The Arabic word *iklīl* refers specifically to a Christian marriage ceremony. The word *hanāʾi* also means 'happiness', 'good health' and 'well-being', and the word *surūr* also means 'joy', 'pleasure' and 'delight'. Within Eastern Christian churches in the Middle East, crowns are held over the heads of the bride and groom during the wedding ceremony. I thank Zeina Klink-Hoppe for this information (personal communication, 24 April 2017).

39 It is also called 'plate embroidery'. Vogelsang-Eastwood, *Embroidery from the Arab World*, pp. 97, 114–16.

40 Arabic *al-kuḥl*; Persian *sorma*, Turkish *sürmä*. Folk tales mention the application of kohl to turn oneself invisible and to enable the wearer to see through the earth to locate buried treasure. For its composition, use and literary references see Wiedemann and Allan, 'al-Kuḥl'; Mottahedin and Yagmaʾi, 'Cosmetics'.

41 It is worked in interlacing, herringbone-stitch and chain-stitch. Published in Paine, *Embroidery from Afghanistan*, pp. 66–67.

42 According to Weir's research on the Palestinian village of Beit Dajan in the 1920s, brides danced for their husbands on the wedding night, holding their ornamental kohl holders. These were sometimes ornamented with ostrich feathers, as was the bride. The larger of the two holders is published and discussed in Weir, *Palestinian Costume*, pp. 250–51, 264.

43 *Taḥrīrī* is silk-cord couching and *qaṣab* is silver-wrapped or gilt-metal-wrapped cord couching. According to Skinner, the central motif on this chest panel is called 'key of the heart' (*miftāḥ al-qalb*) and the two birds are named 'birds of Paradise' (*ʿaṣfūr al-janna*), but these names could vary through time. Skinner, *Palestinian Embroidery Motifs*, pp. 76, 112. According to Weir's research, a renowned Bethlehem embroiderer named Miriam Ibrahim Jadallah was said to have introduced the bird motif. The skirt panel on the back of the dress is woven with silver wire (*qaṣab*) – another feature of *malak* fabric. For a discussion of the *malak* fabric and dress and Bethlehem couching see Weir, *Palestinian Costume*, pp. 29–31, 95, 127, 130–31, 133; Munayyer, *Traditional Palestinian Costume*, pp. 190–209.

44 Bethlehem couching was mainly a commercial enterprise because the groom purchased the components of *malak* dresses for the bridal trousseau. Here, the matching high-quality chest, sleeve and skirt panels attest to the groom's wealth. If he could not afford matching pieces, the groom would have spent the majority of his funds on the chest panel and settled for less fine skirt and sleeve panels. If customers were in a hurry, ready-made dresses were available for purchase rather than as separate pieces. Weir, *Palestinian Costume*, p. 133.

45 These special ceremonial headdresses were usually family heirlooms, and were lent to families who did not own one for a few piastres or were returned filled with sweets. For fuller discussions of this headdress see Weir, *Palestinian Costume*, pp. 184–87; Stillman, *Palestinian Costume*, pp. 62–64.

46 The Arabic word *wiqāya* means 'protection' and is a general term for several types of headgear worn by women after marriage. The majority of coins are Ottoman paras (worth a fourtieth of a piastre) and such headdresses were probably made shortly after 1844 when paras were becoming obsolete but were still readily available. Weir, *Palestinian Costume*, p. 186.

47 Both these types of headdress were made commercially by professional female embroiderers in Bethlehem and nearby villages. This *shaṭweh*, featuring coin tokens, glass beads and a crude chin-chain, is less costly than others. It is also a 'newer' style of *shaṭweh*, introduced around 1918. For superlative examples with silver coins and coral beads see Weir, *Palestinian Costume*, p. 181; Kawar, *Threads of Identity*, pp. 174–75; Munayyer, *Traditional Palestinian Costume*, pp. 224–25. According to Weir, widows covered the coins on their headdresses with dark fabric as a sign of mourning. Weir, *Palestinian Costume*, pp. 178–79.

48 According to Weir, in the early twentieth century the women of Lifta were fond of large embroidered designs on the backs of their woollen *taqṣīrehs*, whereas the women of Bethlehem preferred more restrained, couched patterns. Weir, *Palestinian Costume*, pp. 127–28, 152–55.

49 *Bakht* has many meanings, including 'fortune', 'luck', 'prosperity', 'felicity' and 'happiness'. For the ceremony see Betteridge and Javadi, ''Aqd'.

50 The ubiquitous rams' horns have many names in Turkmen embroidery parlance, as discussed in Andrews and Andrews, *Türkmen Needlework*, pp. 27–29. For the amuletic power of hair and feathers see Paine, *Amulets*, pp. 119–22. For other examples see Meller, *Silk and Cotton*, pp. 224–25.

51 According to Anna Portisch, who conducted her doctoral field research on the textiles of Kazakh women of western Mongolia (and curated a subsequent exhibition), a year was the average time a woman took to complete a *tus kiʾiz* if she embroidered for a few hours each day. However,

some could produce one in under a month if they worked intensively. Portisch's website includes images and video footage of women making the *tus ki'iz*, and valuable information on the processes (<http://www.kazakhcraftswomen.co.uk/Kazakh_Craftswomen/wall_hangings.html>).

52 Both of these positions were considered a place of honour within the yurt. See Meller, *Silk and Cotton*, pp. 210–11. The difference between a Kyrgyz *tush kiyiz* and a Kazakh *tus ki'iz* is that the latter is embroidered throughout, whereas the former is left blank or cut out in the middle. See a Kyrgyz example in 'Politics and Conflict', pp. 210–11, and in Gillow, *Textiles*, p. 215. For a felt *tus ki'iz*, see 'House and Homestead', pp. 164–65.

53 From *sau* ('sunny', 'beautiful') and *kele* ('head'). The sources are rather ambiguous on the finer distinctions between Kyrgyz, Kazakh and Karakalpak *saukeles* and *shökülös*. Vogelsang-Eastwood, 'Dress from Kazakhstan', p. 387, and 'Dress from Kyrgyzstan', pp. 395–96; Meller, *Silk and Cotton*, p. 135. This *saukele* was collected in Semiryechensk, historically a province of Russian Turkestan, south of Lake Balkhash (modern-day Zhetysu in south-eastern Kazakhstan), which was predominantly Kyrgyz.

54 The silver elements deflect the 'evil eye', carnelian is believed to offer protection from illness, coral banishes poverty, and pearls are said to guard against cataracts and brighten one's sight.

55 Individual pieces of a garment (sleeves, chest panel and skirt panels) were embroidered and then sewn together after the decoration was complete. The groom's contribution to the trousseau was called the *kisweh* and included the *thawb malak* (see pp. 66–67), which was commissioned from professional embroiderers. See Weir, *Embroidery from Palestine*, pp. 10–11.

56 For a discussion of this ritual in Beit Dajan and the symbolism of the *jillāyeh* in this context see Weir, *Palestinian Costume*, pp. 265–70.

57 Kawar, *Threads of Identity*, pp. 380–81, 390–91; Weir, *Palestinian Costume*, pp. 141–42.

58 Spring and Hudson suggest an Egyptian provenance, *Silk in Africa*, p. 28. For a very similar robe, thought to be Syrian, see Wearden, *Decorative Textiles*, pp. 158–59. For a fuller discussion of this phrase see Ed., 'Māshā' Allāh'. The cap on p. 77 (centre) is also inscribed with this phrase.

59 Spangles differ from sequins. Before 1925 spangles were made from small lengths of curved metal wire that were flattened with a hammer, producing a flat circle with a central hole and a tiny notch where the two ends of the wire met. After 1925 the notch disappeared, since spangles were machine punched from large sheets of metal alloy. Although similar in appearance, technically a sequin is made out of glass, plastic or other non-metallic substance, whereas spangles are always metallic. I wish to thank Gillian Vogelsang-Eastwood for this information.

60 For remarkable examples of Ottoman padded gold-work embroidery, using card and cotton cord, see Bilgi and Zanbak, *Skill of the Hand*, pp. 106–13, 335–41; Görünür, *Women's Costume*, pp. 188–205, 268–73.

61 For a discussion of the modes of transferring patterns see Krody, 'Turkish Embroidery', pp. 121–22.

STATUS AND IDENTITY, pp. 78–119

1 Adapted from Görünür, *Women's Costume*, pp. 22–23. Adile Sultan (1826–99) was the sister of the Ottoman sultan Abdülmecid (r. 1839–61). Shortly before her death, she donated her palace, located in the Üsküdar district of Istanbul, to the state in order to build a high school for girls. It is now a cultural centre.

2 Amighi, 'Kerman xiii'.

3 Chatty, 'The Burqa', p. 147.

4 Juhasz, *Jewish Wardrobe*, pp. 108–09, 323; Mundy mentions the amuletic significance of the dangling pendants on hoods, 'Ṣan'ā' Dress', pp. 533–35. The jewellery attached to the hoods was made by Jewish silversmiths in Sana'a.

5 It is worked mainly in chain-stitch. I wish to thank Vandana Patel for the translation. She also suggested that the word may refer to a village or suburb called Para in the district of Mehsana in modern-day Gujarat, though its existence and role in Gujarat's textile industry in the nineteenth century are uncertain.

6 The *thawb* was presented to Prince Alfred as a gift between 1866 and 1900. During this period he was appointed Duke of Edinburgh and Earl of Ulster and Kent in 1866, and Duke of Saxe-Coburg and Gotha in 1893.

7 Campbell, 'Gown that Steals', p. 26. A *thawb* is usually worn over a fitted dress and trousers.

8 Scarce, *Women's Costume*, and Görünür, *Women's Costume*, provide good introductions to the subject of early and late Ottoman dress. Micklewright, 'Tracing the Transformations', discusses the changes in dress styles in nineteenth-century Istanbul. The mother-of-pearl button on this *entari* seems to have been added later.

9 Ipek, 'Ottoman Fabrics', pp. 2–4. The *entari* has fastenings of fifteen knotted buttons and loops made of green silk and concealed inside the chest area. It also has a watch pocket on each side of the bodice. For excellent examples of *entaris* from this period see Görünür, *Women's Costume*, esp. pp. 70–87.

10 Iraq is bordered by Turkey to the north, Iran to the east, Saudi Arabia and Kuwait to the south, and Syria and Jordan to the west. Between 1831 and 1920, Iraq was divided into three Ottoman provinces (*vilayets*): Mosul, Baghdad and Basra.

11 Görünür, *Women's Costume*, pp. 200–45; Ipek, 'Ottoman Fabrics', pp. 5–6; Scarce, *Women's Costume*, pp. 130–31. According to Al-Khamis and Hami, 'Iraqi Dress', p. 264, European-style clothing became more widespread among the urban Muslim populations of Iraq (outside Baghdad) around the 1950s.

12 For more examples and a fuller discussion see Wearden and Baker, *Iranian Textiles*, pp. 35–40; Nabholz-Kartaschoff and Langer, *Pfauen, Blüten & Zypressen*, pp. 92–98. For a complete outfit see the V&A website <http://collections.vam.ac.uk/item/O163643/shawl/>.

13 Kahooker, 'Zoroastrian Marriage Apron'.

14 According to Katayun Mazdapour, after the forced unveiling of women in Iran in 1936, many Zoroastrian women abandoned their traditional colourful garments. Mazdapour, 'Zoroastrian Women'.

15 Tussah or tussar silk is made from wild tussah silkworms that eat juniper leaves and oak, giving the yarn a characteristic beige colour. The silk tends to be coarser and less lustrous than mulberry silk. I wish to thank Jennifer Wearden for identifying the unusual base fabric of this dress.

16 I wish to thank Jennifer Wearden, Rosemary Crill, Jennifer Scarce, Jenny Lister and Moya Carey for their helpful comments. The dress may have been made for an Iranian woman with a taste for European fashions or a European woman living in Iran who appreciated Iranian embroidery. For the impact of European fashions in Qajar Iran see Vogelsang-Eastwood and van Doorn, *Introduction to Qajar Era Dress*, pp. 38–39. For more traditional Kirman-embroidered garments, made from wool or a cotton and silk blend with woollen or silk embroidery, see Wearden and Baker, *Iranian Textiles*, pp. 29–31; Nabholz-Kartaschoff and Langer, *Pfauen, Blüten & Zypressen*, pp. 82–83. For an explanation of the *boteh* or *būta* (paisley) motif see Wearden and Baker, *Iranian Textiles*.

17 Stehlin-AlZadjali, *Traditional…Dress*, pp. 66–71. The pocket, called a *koptān* or *jīb* in Iran, was described as a receptacle for embroidery thread, small change, snuff and medicines for older generations of Baluchis. Firouz and Jahanbani, 'Clothing xviii'; Hunte, 'Clothing xix'. Nowadays, it is used to carry a woman's keys, money and mobile phone.

18 Baluchistan is a region that today occupies areas of south-eastern Iran, western Pakistan and south-western Afghanistan, and Oman maintained close political ties with parts of Baluchistan from the 1780s to the 1950s. Baluch women in Oman have also adapted another dress style called *barka al-jig*, which is influenced by northern Omani dress. Stehlin-AlZadjali, *Traditional…Dress*, pp. 72–73.

19 Violet Penelope Dickson (1896–1991) was wife of Harold Dickson (d. 1959), author of *The Arab of the Desert: A Glimpse into Badawin Life in Kuwait and Sau'di Arabia* (1949). Her love and respect for the nomadic peoples of Kuwait earned her the local title *Umm Kuwait* ('Mother of Kuwait'). The striped *thawb* was also favoured in Bahrain and by urban and Bedouin women of the Najd, Saudi Arabia, and referred to as *thawb al-mufaḥḥa* ('with strips') or *al-mutaffat* ('with taffeta'). Campbell, 'Gown that Steals', p. 27. For an example from Saudi Arabia see Vogelsang-Eastwood, 'Saudi Arabian Dress', p. 225. This *thawb* was given to the donor by the Dickson family. See also Vogelsang-Eastwood, 'Snapshot'.

20 Weir, *Palestinian Costume*, pp. 36–43, 93; Gillow, *Islamic Textiles*, pp. 96–109; Kawar, Pio and Vogelsang-Eastwood, 'Embroidery from Syria', pp. 456–61, 465–67. The wedding coat is probably from Al-Sukhnah (sometimes called Es-Suchne), a village near Palmyra in central Syria, and the dress was probably made in Saraqib in the north-west of the country (or a nearby region). My attributions of the coat and dress to these villages are based on comparisons with similar textiles published by Gillow and Kawar *et al.* (cited above). The dress was purchased by Gustaaf H. Stöve in Aleppo, which is a short distance from Saraqib. As in Palestine, the concentration and choice of motifs on women's garments usually reflected the wearer's regional identity and social status. DMC (Dollfus-Mieg et Compagnie) also distributed pattern books in the Middle East.

21 For similar garments, described as marriage outfits from Balıkesir and Eskişehir, see Günay *et al.*, *Costumes historiques*, p. 47. Luxurious *şalvar* and *cepken* outfits are discussed in Görünür, *Women's Costume*, pp. 48–49, 112–17, 150–63. The regions where these garments were popular include Kütahya, Eskişehir and Balıkesir, all in north-western Turkey.

22 As quoted and translated from Andrews *et al.*, *Turcoman of Iran*, p. 78.

23 The women used narrow pit-treadle looms, operated with their feet. The blue rayon facings are sometimes tacked back with a few stitches to display the colourful embroidery. A more elaborate, long-sleeved coat, festooned with coins along its edges, was often worn on top of the short-sleeved coat. For an example and detailed discussions see Vogelsang-Eastwood, 'Turkmen Dress', p. 357; Andrews *et al.*, *Turcoman of Iran*, pp. 78–81, 93. For the embroidery see Andrews and Andrews, *Türkmen Needlework*, pp. 23, 50–55.

24 See Yusofi, 'Clothing xxvii', for the terms. For the complete outfit with a similar jacket, though without the Europeanized collar and pillbox cap, see Juhasz, *Jewish Wardrobe*, pp. 303, 336; she dates the outfit to the early twentieth century. Distinctions between Jewish and Muslim dress in Mashhad disappeared after 1839, when the Jews were forced to convert to Islam (though they continued to practise their Jewish faith in secret). Juhasz, *Jewish Wardrobe*, p. 336.

25 See the entry for the little girl's outfit from Iran in 'Childhood' (p. 34). Reza Shah Pahlavi abolished traditional dress in favour of Western-style clothing, in a move to 'modernize' and unite Iran. See Vogelsang-Eastwood, 'Iranian Urban Dress', pp. 303–04, who refers to the jacket as an *alkaleq*.

26 1967 was the year of the Arab–Israeli war, when many refugees fled to Jordan. Today, there are around 6,400 registered refugees at the Aqabat Jaber camp, 45 per cent of whom are under the age of 14; <http://www.unrwa.org/newsroom/features/aqbat-jaber-refugee-camp?id=106> (accessed 17 January 2017). The YWCA became actively involved in the plight of the Palestinian refugees in around 1949–50.

27 Yusofi, 'Clothing xxvii', who says they were also called *ayāzī* or *ayāsī*. Vogelsang-Eastwood and Vogelsang, *Covering the Moon*, p. 160, include images from miniature paintings and a fourteenth-century account mentioning their use at the court of Tamerlane.

28 The *pīcha* was worn well into the twentieth century. The production of the horsehair mesh was a delicate and difficult process. For a fuller discussion see Vogelsang-Eastwood and Vogelsang, *Covering the Moon*, pp. 158–63. A Jewish Iraqi version from the 1920s is illustrated in Juhasz, *Jewish Wardrobe*, pp. 132–33.

29 Ruete, *Memoirs*, pp. 145–46. Generic terms for face-masks in the region are *burqa'* and *baṭṭūla*. For a discussion of these and other face-masks see Vogelsang-Eastwood and Vogelsang, *Covering the Moon*, esp. pp. 139–40; and Richardson and Dorr, *Craft Heritage*, pp. 434–35, 492.

30 Comparable examples are found in the Arab and Turkish worlds. For a detailed discussion of the history of the *rūband* and other forms of veiling in Islamic cultures see Vogelsang-Eastwood and Vogelsang, *Covering the Moon*, esp. pp. 164–68.

31 The grille is framed with bands of silk embroidery. Both types of embroidery are categorized as 'white-work embroidery'. For the techniques and examples see Wearden and Baker, *Iranian Textiles*, pp. 54, 126–27.

32 For a painted image of a woman from the Qajar period wearing a *chādor* and holding up her *rūband* see **15**, Introduction, p. 21.

33 Yusofi, 'Clothing xxvii'. For a good illustration of the way a *rūband* was worn with the *chādor* see Nabholz-Kartaschoff and Langer, *Pfauen, Blüten & Zypressen*, pp. 74–75.

34 The *bishts* worn by the Druzes in Galilee, northern Palestine, were tighter fitting and finer than those made in Nablus in central Palestine. Weir, *Palestinian Costume*, pp. 49–51. Weir includes an image of a Druze sheikh wearing a complete outfit.

35 The Druze religion dates back to the eleventh century and emphasizes an esoteric interpretation of the Qur'an and devotion to God through heart and mind above ritual practices. Although the mountainous terrain of their homelands shielded the Druzes from direct Ottoman control, as a minority community some members practised religious dissimulation to safeguard themselves from persecution. Firro, 'Druzes (Durūz)'. For a discussion of aspects of Druze dress see Weber and Vogelsang-Eastwood, 'Snapshot'; Klink, 'Beyond the *ṭanṭur*'. According to Zeina Klink-Hoppe, distinctive styles of dress were worn only by initiated Druzes, while uninitiated members did not dress differently from other communities (personal communication, 25 April 2017).

36 Weir, *Palestinian Costume*, pp. 58–61. For the Jewish tradition see Juhasz, *Jewish Wardrobe*, pp. 64–77.

37 Inscribed inside the head-cloth is: 'Worn by all young village men.'

38 The label on the peg-board reads: 'Abyssinian monk's hat,' but a Greek Orthodox bishop's headdress seems more likely. Nothing is written inside the headdress.

39 The inscriptions on the peg-board and inside the hat specify a 'Strict orthodox Pollish [*sic*] Jew.'

40 The inscription inside the hat is: 'Town porter looking smart.'

41 The inscription inside the hat is: 'Fellah bound to follow laws that the order of Sultan Abd il-Kader requires.' This probably refers to the Qadariyya Sufi order named after its founder, the theologian and Sufi saint 'Abd al-Qadir al-Gilani/Jilani (d. 1166).

42 The inscription inside the hat is: 'Religious Moslem (in old days only Moslems might wear green).'

43 The inscriptions on the peg-board and inside the hat are: 'Moslem caretaker of holy places; Moslem guard of holy places and mosques. Writer of charms.'

44 The inscription inside the hat is: 'City Moslem. Koran student. Learned man.'

45 The inscription inside the hat is: 'Bethlehem village and district. Moslem and Christian. A family man.'

46 According to Jenny Balfour-Paul, the *korta* was still worn in the 1980s and embroidered by professionals in town; she mentions that it was sometimes worn inside out as a daily dress to protect the embroidery. She also witnessed the Hakami women working in the Zabid indigo-dyeing workshop, manufacturing the silver-wrapped braid. Balfour-Paul, *Indigo*, p. 133. Sorghum is *durra* in Arabic and millet is *dukhn*; my interpretation of the patterns has yet to be verified.

47 According to Sheila Paine, flashes of red colour on Yemeni garments are amuletic; embroidered decoration itself can form an amulet by its positioning, colour or pattern, and complicated, dense patterns serve to confuse evil spirits. Paine, *Amulets*, pp. 104, 147. For a discussion of Bayt al-Faqih dress and the association with farmers' wives see Ransom and Vogelsang-Eastwood, 'Embroidery from Yemen', pp. 548–51; Gillow, *Islamic Textiles*, pp. 142–43.

48 According to Martha Mundy it was only at her marriage that a woman received the elaborate head-piece. She also mentions that the *maghmūq* was introduced around 1900 and was dyed locally in Sana'a by male dyers. Mundy, 'San'ā' Dress', pp. 534–35. For the dyeing process see the same volume, pp. 265–67. Some women continued to wear the *maghmūq* in the early twenty-first century, but it has been largely replaced by several other forms of veiling adopted from Turkey, Saudi Arabia, Egypt and Syria. For a discussion see Lindholm, 'Yemeni Dress', pp. 233–35; Kennedy, *Flower of Paradise*, pp. 55–57.

49 This *maghmūq* was collected in the field by Martha Mundy between 1973 and 1977. Ransom and Vogelsang-Eastwood, 'Embroidery from Yemen', pp. 539–40; Ransom, *Silver Treasures*, pp. 32–33; Gillow, *Islamic Textiles*, pp. 138–40 (he refers to it as a *mamour* and the head-piece as *rsaja*). Its name may derive from the Arabic word *ghāmiq* ('dark colour').

50 Unusually, the ubiquitous black outer garment ('*abāya*), worn throughout the Gulf region and beyond, is missing. The more common form of face-mask is the indigo-dyed and burnished golden *burqa'* or *baṭṭūla*. (see p. 113, second from top), with very wide eye-openings and a thin frame that skims across the eyebrows, nose, cheeks and mouth, though its use is gradually being confined to the older generations. For a discussion of veiling in this region see Vogelsang-Eastwood and Vogelsang, *Covering the Moon*, esp. pp. 131–38; El Guindi and al-Othman, 'Dress from the Gulf States'; El Mutwalli, *Sultani*, vol. 2, pp. 265–300.

51 Richardson and Dorr, *Craft Heritage*, pp. 424–25, 492–93. For images of an Omani woman making the hand-plaited trim (*tallī*) and the cushions and threads used for the trim see **6** and **7**, Introduction, p. 14.

52 This face-mask was collected by Alexandra Porter directly from Bedouin women at the Al Ain market in 2011. According to Reem El Mutwalli's extensive research on the *burqa'* in the UAE, since the 1990s and with the decline in its popularity fewer people are skilled at hand-making *burqa's*. As a result, skilled craftsmen from the Philippines have also taken on the trade. El Mutwalli, *Sultani*, esp. pp. 288–91.

53 This is according to Vogelsang-Eastwood and Vogelsang, *Covering the Moon*, pp. 177–79. They also mention that other Sunni groups in the region prefer a long, squarish, black *burqa'*, similar to that of Qatar. This red *burqa'* is made of black cotton, lined in white cotton and is designed to cover the eyes, cheeks and nose. It was collected by Sheila Paine at Minab market in 1992, and she noted that some examples were embellished with cross-stitch embroidery and sequins.

54 Richardson and Dorr, *Craft Heritage*, pp. 344–45. For a full discussion see the case study by Dawn Chatty on the Harasiis tribe of central Oman, 'The Burqa', esp. pp. 141–43. This *burqa'* is lined on the back with masking tape, possibly as a stiffener, or to prevent the transfer of indigo onto the skin, though it was customarily considered prestigious to have the blue rub off on the skin.

55 The basting stitches are left intact, which may have been a custom. This style of decorative patchwork coat went out of fashion in Lower Galilee in the mid-1800s in favour of Ottoman-style *entari* coats (called *qumbāz*), but they continued to be worn in Upper Galilee until the 1920s. The coat was worn over narrow-legged, embroidered trousers and a plain long-sleeved dress (*thawb* or *qamīs*). Weir, *Palestinian Costume*, pp. 78–85; Weir, *Palestinian Embroidery*, pp. 15–16; Weir, *Embroidery from Palestine*, pp. 24–27.

56 Weir, *Palestinian Costume*, pp. 32–33, 78–79; Weir, *Embroidery from Palestine*, pp. 32–33. For examples of other *durā'a* from Galilee, including one made of raw silk with purple Syrian brocade, see Munayyer, *Traditional Palestinian Costume*, pp. 81–83.

57 The garments belonged to Fakhria Shasha's grandmother (1861–1951), who died at the age of 90. By the 1930s, urban Christian communities in Iraq had completely abandoned Ottoman dress in favour of European-style clothing. Al-Khamis and Hami, 'Iraqi Dress', p. 264. The trousers (As1973,03.1) are not visible in the photo. The sleeves of the chemise are shown peeping out of the cuffs of the jacket, and the waistcoat's gilt-thread-wrapped buttons are just seen. Images of all the garments are on the museum's website under registration numbers As1973,03.1–7.

58 Micklewright, 'Tracing the Transformations', pp. 38–41.

59 Pio and Vogelsang-Eastwood, 'Embroidery from Iraq', pp. 477–80.

RELIGION AND BELIEF, pp. 120–41

1 See the excellent article by Toorawa, 'Clothing'.
2 The family are also referred to as the *Ahl al-bayt*, 'People of the House'. For a discussion of the account known as the *ḥadīth al-kisā'*, 'Tradition of the cloak', see Sharon, 'People of the House'.
3 The Ka'ba measures 12 metres long by 10 metres wide by 15 metres high. According to Muslim tradition, Abraham and his son Isma'il rebuilt the Ka'ba as a sanctuary of monotheism.
4 The 'Abbasid caliphs (r. 750–1258) in Iraq had the *kiswa* dyed black to reflect their dynastic colour, whereas the Fatimid caliphs (r. 969–1171) in Egypt commissioned white *kiswas* for the same reason. The *kiswa* reverted to black under the Mamluk dynasty (r. 1250–1517) and it has remained so until today. For fuller discussions see Porter, 'Textiles of Mecca and Medina'; Mackie, *Symbols of Power*, pp. 22–26; <http://www.britishmuseum.org/explore/themes/hajj/the_sacred_textiles_of_mecca.aspx>.
5 Smaller panels are made to adorn the corners and other sections of the *kiswa*, and other textiles are made for the inside of the Ka'ba. A cover is also made for the *maqām Ibrāhīm*, a monument marking Abraham's footprints, where he stood when he rebuilt the Ka'ba. According to Louise Mackie, the year-long process requires over one hundred master craftsmen (only men produce the *kiswa*) to manufacture around 760 metres of cloth weighing over 2 tonnes (2,000 kg). Mackie, *Symbols of Power*, p. 26.
6 For examples of a range of media see Suleman, ed., *Word of God*.
7 In contrast, the Sunni model privileges the consensus of the community on matters of authority, rather than an individual's lineal blood ties to the Prophet. Several aspects of Shi'a material culture and ritual are explored in Suleman, ed., *People of the Prophet's House*.
8 Presented by the Khalili Family Trust on the occasion of the exhibition 'Hajj: Journey to the Heart of Islam' in 2012, in honour of Neil MacGregor, OM, director of the British Museum (2002–15). It was made either in Istanbul or in Cairo and probably hung near the prayer niche (*miḥrāb*) of the mosque.
9 The saying (*ḥadīth*) of the Prophet is in the red panel at the top. The Qur'anic verses include Q.49:3 at the top and Q.59:22–24 along the vertical borders. The roundels include the names of Allah, Muhammad and the first four caliphs, alongside Selim's name, which appears twice (under the lamp within the green pendant, with the date of production, and in the cartouches at the bottom). See 'Politics and Conflict', pp. 182–83, for a *sitāra* commissioned by Selim's successor.
10 For examples of other Qajar-period prayer mats see Wearden and Baker, *Iranian Textiles*, pp. 60–61, 136–37.
11 See the discussion of the history and permissibility of this distinctively Shi'a ritual practice in Gleave, 'Prayer and Prostration', esp. pp. 241–43. Some *mohrs* are also made from the soil of the Iranian city of Mashhad, where the eighth Twelver Shi'a imam, Imam Reza, is buried.

12. The largest two groups are the Pashtuns and the Tajiks. Hazaras are thought to be of Turco-Mongolian descent and speak a Persian dialect. Their turbulent history is marred by several wars, displacement, and social, religious, economic and political discrimination. Monsutti, 'Hazāra ii'.
13. The cloth was collected in NWFP, Pakistan, by M. G. Konieczny. Hazara women also embroidered colourful pouches to hold Karbala soil collected by pilgrims. Paine, *Embroidery from Afghanistan*, pp. 14, 76–77, 80–81; Gillow, *Islamic Textiles*, pp. 224–25. According to Alessandro Monsutti, in recent times the Hazaras have increasingly identified with the tragedy at Karbala as a reflection of their own painful history. Monsutti, 'Hazāra iii'. Hazrat 'Abbas was also the imam's half-brother. Calmard, ''Abbās b. 'Alī b. Abū Ṭāleb'.
14. This prayer rug was probably manufactured in China. The souvenir gift pack includes the rug, a set of prayer-beads, a small bottle of perfume and a prayer cap. These and other items were collected by Qaisra Khan for the museum while on ḥajj in 2010; she was project curator for the 2012 exhibition 'Hajj: Journey to the Heart of Islam'.
15. They were also used for seafaring. See Canavas, 'Compass'.
16. The cloak is further ornamented with needle-lace insertions and silk tassels. For comparative examples of white-work embroidery from Iran, dated 1800–70, see Wearden and Baker, *Iranian Textiles*, pp. 120–23. The proverb from ancient Egypt translates as: 'Silence is more profitable than abundance of speech'. The Hebrew text is the *Leviticus Rabbah* from the *Midrash*. A modified version of this adage also appears in Arabic on a ceramic dish from tenth-century Iran as: 'He who speaks, his speech is silver, but silence is a ruby, with good health and prosperity' (British Museum, 1958,1218.1).
17. See Atasoy, 'Dervish Dress', for a discussion of all the garments worn by the Mevlevi dervishes, esp. pp. 258–61 for drawings of headgear.
18. Atasoy, 'Dervish Dress', pp. 266–67.
19. He makes them from double-layered felt that is burnished and singed together, dressed with bone glue and set on wooden forms. Bunn, *Nomadic Felts*, p. 91; Atasoy, 'Dervish Dress', p. 266. These hats were collected in the field by Selçuk Gürışık.
20. Jirousek, 'Historical Survey', pp. 118–19; Bunn, *Nomadic Felts*, p. 91.
21. For the history of indigo in the Arab world and the dyeing process see Balfour-Paul, *Indigo*, esp. p. 133 for references to the Jabal Haraz style of dress and trousers. See also Ransom and Vogelsang-Eastwood, 'Embroidery from Yemen', pp. 543–45; Paine, *Amulets*, p. 139.
22. Unfortunately, the jacket's original owner and the context of its production are unknown. For early and late medieval examples of inscribed objects on a range of media, including textiles, see Blair, *Islamic Inscriptions*, esp. pp. 104–05 for the use of the word 'āfiya on a metal dish.
23. Collected by Sheila Paine; see *Amulets*, pp. 122–25. For more examples of children's *kurtas* and *doghas* see 'Childhood', pp. 30, 38–39. For the use of hair on another Turkmen textile see 'Marriage and Ceremony', p. 70.
24. Translation of an Arabic mourning or wailing song from Artas, adapted from Granqvist, *Muslim Death and Burial*, p. 63. Granqvist published her findings on the birth, marriage and death rituals of Muslims in Artas in several volumes between 1932 and 1965.
25. These samples were hand-stitched by a village woman named Hamdiye Sanad especially for Granqvist's research. Granqvist described Hamdiye as a 'great source of information on ancient customs, and on all the daily happenings in the village'. The loin-cloth, sponge, soap and towel were not usually buried with the corpse but were presented to the person washing the body. However, an unmarried girl was sometimes buried with a piece of soap and a comb. Some women were also buried with square cloths for menstruation and a needle and thread. Granqvist, *Muslim Death and Burial*, pp. 9, 59, 62–63.
26. For the Arabic names of individual garments and a detailed account of the cleansing and preparation rituals see Granqvist, *Muslim Death and Burial*, esp. pp. 55–74.
27. For a discussion of the amuletic use of animal horns and antlers around the world see Paine, *Amulets*, pp. 110–16; this object was collected by Sheila Paine and is published in *ibid.*, p. 113.
28. For a discussion and comparative examples see Marchese and Breu, 'Protecting the Populace', pp. 109–13.
29. For example, he made a breast for a woman who had a lumpectomy. See Bunn, *Nomadic Felts*, p. 91. These and a collection of contemporary felts from across Turkey were collected by the practising felt artist Selçuk Gürışık.

HOUSE AND HOMESTEAD, pp. 142–75

1. Translation from Bunn, 'Nomad's Apprentice', p. 78.
2. Burckhardt, *Arabic Proverbs*, p. 37. There are also Farsi and Arabic versions of this Turkish maxim. I wish to thank Zeina Klink-Hoppe for pointing out the Arabic version to me (personal communication, 27 April 2017).
3. Bilgi and Zanbak, *Skill of the Hand*, p. 17.
4. *Ibid.*, pp. 9–10, 24–25.
5. For a detailed discussion of the Turkmen yurt with images see Andrews, 'Türkmen Tent'. For a discussion of the Bedouin tents of Jordan see Weir, *Bedouin*, pp. 19–20, and bibliography.
6. Two Mamluk-period knitted cotton socks are in the Metropolitan Museum of Art's collections (nos 27.170.95, 27.170.96; for images see the collections online), and another example belongs to the Textile Museum in Washington, DC (no. 73.698).
7. Western socks are knitted from the cuff and worked down the leg to the heel, thus creating a centre back 'seam', which is absent in Eastern socks. For detailed instructions on knitting socks starting from the toe, and excellent photos, see Gibson-Roberts, *Ethnic Socks*, pp. 9–13, 63ff.
8. As part of its acquisition strategy, the British Museum has made it a point not to collect carpets from the Islamic world, to avoid duplicating efforts and resources with the Victoria and Albert Museum. Exceptions include the war rugs from Afghanistan, which are discussed in 'Politics and Conflict', pp. 194–97.
9. Stephanie Bunn covers all of these regions in her *Nomadic Felts*. See also Bunn, 'Kirghiz Felt Carpets'.
10. This piece was collected by Sheila Paine. For the motifs see Harvey, *Traditional Textiles*, p. 114; Paine, *Embroidery from Afghanistan*, p. 14. For similar examples used to decorate the bedding pile (*jük* or *chuk*) see Fitz Gibbon and Hale, *Uzbek Embroidery*, pp. 61, 73, 97, 174. For a detailed explanation of the netting and tassels see *ibid.*, pp. 192–96.
11. Bilgi and Zanbak, *Skill of the Hand*, pp. 15, 19, 23.
12. Bilgi and Zanbak, *Skill of the Hand*, pp. 28–30, 224–40. This napkin previously belonged to the late Winnafreda, Countess of Portarlington (d. 1975), Australian heiress and wife of the sixth Earl of Portarlington.
13. Such murals gradually replaced tiling in interior decoration. Bilgi and Zanbak, *Skill of the Hand*, pp. 46–47, 192–211. An unfinished motif in dark pink on the far right, resembling a minaret, may represent the workshop emblem. This further suggests that the napkin was used for ritual ablutions. For workshop emblems see Bilgi and Zanbak, *Skill of the Hand*, pp. 37, 298–301.
14. Hand towels are usually fringed and are sometimes made of self-patterned damask linen or cotton with stripes or small designs. This one has a diamond-shaped brocade pattern. See Bilgi and Zanbak, *Skill of the Hand*, pp. 27–28, 224–40. A zigzag satin-stitch border in silver-wrapped thread embellishes the lower edges.
15. The term *dastarkhān* and its variants are used across South and Central Asia to refer to table-cloths and floor-spreads laid out for dining. For woven examples see Meller, *Silk and Cotton*, p. 239. Dost Muhammad is thought to have owned this *dastarkhān*, and it may have been produced between 1817 and 1819, when he lived in Kashmir – an area famed for its *aari* (tambour-work) embroidery. It could also have been made by embroiderers in Afghanistan familiar with the technique, or from neighbouring Kashmir. The floor-spread was acquired by Major John Goodday Strutt Gilland (d. 1848), following the siege of Ghazni in 1839 during the First Anglo-Afghan War (1839–42).
16. Published in Weir, *Palestinian Embroidery*, p. 42. For the stitches see Skinner, *Palestinian Embroidery Motifs*, pp. 79, 92, 144–45.

17 Kawar, *Threads of Identity*, pp. 130, 132–33. For examples of modern cushions prepared for bridal trousseaus in the 1960s–1970s, and those produced in the Palestinian refugee camps in Beirut see *ibid*., pp. 413, 425. See also the cushion in 'Politics and Conflict', pp. 202–03.

18 They were collected by Pip Rau in Afghanistan and published, with close-up details, in Paine, *Embroidery from Afghanistan*, pp. 30–31. Similar examples are in Harvey, *Traditional Textiles*, plates 86–87. Tents were usually set up and dismantled by the women.

19 The designs are outlined in chain-stitch and filled in with slanting buttonhole-stitch or angled blanket-stitch. A large number of these were collected by Pip Rau in Afghanistan in the 1960s–1970s and purchased by the British Museum in 2002. Several are published, with close-up details, in Paine, *Embroidery from Afghanistan*, pp. 44–45 (this one).

20 The subject is studied in detail in Fitz Gibbon and Hale, *Uzbek Embroidery*. For illustrations of older and more recent *jüks* in yurts and homes see *ibid*., pp. 59, 66–67, 73, 97.

21 Meller, *Silk and Cotton*, pp. 206–07. Sheila Paine is of the opinion that these motifs are talismanic and powerful representations of shamanism, which protect the family's home and textile wealth (Paine, *Embroidery from Afghanistan*, pp. 14, 44), whereas Kate Fitz Gibbon and Andrew Hale (*Uzbek Embroidery*, p. 127) argue that the power of these images lies in their rigorous forms, dynamic combinations and tribal affiliations, and not in any talismanic function.

22 Posey, 'Lakai Uzbek Embroideries'.

23 This *segusha* was collected by Janet Harvey and illustrated in her book *Traditional Textiles*, plate 170. See also Fitz Gibbon and Hale, *Uzbek Embroidery*, pp. 92–97; Meller, *Silk and Cotton*, pp. 236–37. Zeina Klink-Hoppe pointed out to me that the shape of the *segusha*, when tucked into the bedding pile, resembles a *tumar* (triangular amulet) and, therefore, the entire hanging itself may be used as a protective amulet (personal communication, 27 April 2017).

24 Yurts were fully assembled and dismantled by the women of the household, with very little help from the men. Andrews *et al*., *Turcoman of Iran*, pp. 10, 13, 49.

25 Soumak weaving involves wrapping coloured weft threads over and under the warp threads to create a raised, embroidery-like pattern, while strengthening the weave. Soumak weaving leaves a ragged underside, unlike kilims, which are smooth on both sides but not as strong. For an explanation of tribal *göls* see Harvey, *Traditional Textiles*, pp. 44–45.

26 The census confirmed around one million Yörük (or Yürük) in total, of whom ten thousand are identified as fully nomadic and the remainder categorized as 'semi-nomadic' or 'fully settled'. For these figures and their history see Kellner-Heinkele, 'Yörük'.

27 Brocade construction on flatweaves is sometimes confused with soumak weaving. Marla Mallett describes the most common type of brocade as 'overlay-underlay', where the weft thread goes over three warps, then under three warps, and back over the top again. For illustrated explanations of the various types of tribal weaves across the Islamic world see Mallett, *Woven Structures*, and her website <http://www.marlamallett.com>.

28 Rams' horns are called *kocak*, *koshkar* or *kochkor müyüz* and appear on material culture across Central Asia. Bunn, *Nomadic Felts*, pp. 140–41. Although they may look similar at first glance, one of the main differences between Kyrgyz and Kazakh felts is the liberal use of appliqué on the latter. Kyrgyz *shyrdaks* or mosaic felts are made from pieces of felt that are fitted together like a puzzle and stitched onto a backing felt with further quilted and couched cord decorations.

29 Bunn, *Nomadic Felts*, p. 68. According to Stephanie Bunn, she acquired this felt from a young Kazakh woman, who had made it herself while she was staying in Karakalpakstan. For an embroidered Kyrgyz example glorifying the Soviet Union see 'Politics and Conflict', pp. 210–11.

30 This bag was collected and published by Janet Harvey, *Traditional Textiles*, pp. 89–90, and plate 108.

31 Goldstein and Çağatay, 'Turkmenistan on a Plate'. The pot holders were made with a matching, square bridal pouch, used by the bride to carry ceremonial bread to the wedding. See the British Museum's collections online, As1973,09.179; Andrews *et al*., *Turcoman of Iran*, pp. 73–74; Harvey, *Traditional Textiles*, plates 83–84.

32 *Shyrdaks* are often made as wedding gifts for daughters. Girls interested in felt-making begin to assist their mothers at around the age of 12, thus allowing the skills to pass on from mother to daughter. The pressed felt (*ala ki'iz*) takes only two weeks to produce, but will last for around five years. See Bunn, *Nomadic Felts*, for a full discussion, including the process, pp. 59–64. It is briefly explained in note 28.

33 Jangyl Alibekova (also spelled, Alibyekova/Alibiekova) has sadly died. She received medals for her work during the Soviet period. The Kyrgyz inscription on this felt translates as: 'At-Bashi District 08, Acha-Kaiyndy village, Alibekova Jangyl, 1938' (her date of birth). I wish to thank Mukaddas Muborakshoeva for helping me to decipher and translate this inscription. For a discussion of Alibekova's work and her photos see Bunn, *Nomadic Felts*, pp. 63–64; Bunn, 'A "Making Point of View"', pp. 33–35.

34 Andrews *et al*., *Turcoman of Iran*, p. 55; Parham and Asatryan, 'Carpets and Carpet-Making'.

35 This bag was made as one of a pair, and Peter Andrews suggests that they are associated with the Yomut Gocuq tribe. Andrews *et al*., *Turcoman of Iran*, pp. 53, plate 7b.

36 Published in Paine, *Embroidery from Afghanistan*, pp. 56–57. Fitz Gibbon and Hale, *Uzbek Embroidery*, pp. 85–86.

37 This ritual took place if the deceased was a young man. For a detailed account of Lakai rites of passage and examples of beautiful *daours* see Fitz Gibbon and Hale, *Uzbek Embroidery*, esp. pp. 85–87, 107, 177–78. See also Meller, *Silk and Cotton*, pp. 242–43.

39 *Buzkashī* (literally 'goat-dragging') was once an equestrian folk game, which has now become an institutionalized sport across Central Asia. Essentially, mounted horsemen compete to take control of the carcass of a freshly killed goat or calf and place it in a goal. Whitney Azoy, 'Bozkaši'.

39 The collection includes the full set of trappings. See also Meller, *Silk and Cotton*, pp. 241, 244–49; Harvey, *Traditional Textiles*, plate 48.

POLITICS AND CONFLICT, pp. 176–211

1 This information is adapted from Ghada al-Qaddumi's English translation of the tenth-century Arabic *Kitāb al-Hadāyā wa al-Tuhaf* as *Book of Gifts and Rarities* (1996), pp. 204–05. See also Mackie, *Symbols of Power*, p. 85, for a similar but later quotation from Ibn Khaldun. The Caliph Hisham (r. 724–43), based at his capital city, Damascus, was the son of the Caliph 'Abd al-Malik, the patron of the Dome of the Rock in Jerusalem. His reign is considered as the final period of prosperity and splendour of the Umayyad caliphate.

2 Stillman, Sanders and Rabbat, 'Ṭirāz'. For similar examples and a fuller discussion see Mackie, *Symbols of Power*, esp. pp. 117–20; Martiniani-Reber, Cornu *et al*., *Tissus d'Égypte*, esp. p. 259.

3 The numerous Iranian and Turkic ethnic groups in Afghanistan include the Pashtuns, Tajiks, Turkmen, Hazaras, Baluch, Nuristanis, Uzbeks and Kyrgyz. Karzai himself is a Durrani Pashtun. See the discussion of Karzai's clothing by Vogelsang, 'Political Clothing', esp. pp. 10–12.

4 Presented by the Khalili Family Trust on the occasion of the exhibition 'Hajj: Journey to the Heart of Islam' in 2012, in honour of Neil MacGregor, OM, director of the British Museum (2002–15).

5 It was made either in Istanbul or in Cairo, the two Ottoman centres that annually produced the gold-embroidered and brocaded curtains and covers for the sanctuaries at Mecca and Medina, including the *kiswa* or gold-embroidered Ka'ba cover. This curtain was probably hung prominently near the prayer niche (*miḥrāb*) for all to admire.

6 The First Saudi State, or Emirate of Dir'iyya, formed through an alliance between the families of Saud and Al Wahhab, prohibited Muslims from the Ottoman Empire from entering Mecca and Medina; its followers also desecrated the tombs of the Prophet's family ('Ali, al-Hasan and al-Husayn) in Iraq to prevent pilgrimage to them.

7   The verses are framed with crossed swords in gold on red on the lower register. The verses embroidered in the middle register extol God's virtues as 'the Holy One, the Source of Peace (and Perfection), the Guardian of Faith, [and] the Preserver of Safety' (Q.59:22–24). Within the red and green roundels on the top register, the curtain tellingly includes the names of al-Hasan and al-Husayn alongside those of the first four Muslim caliphs: Abu Bakr, 'Umar, 'Uthman and 'Ali. Al-Hasan and al-Husayn were the grandsons of the Prophet, through 'Ali and Fatima (the Prophet's daughter), and they were also the second and third Shi'a Imams after 'Ali. Although the Ottomans were not Shi'a Muslims, they held a deep reverence for the family of the Prophet (*Ahl al-bayt*).

8   Mahmud II initiated the Tanzimat reforms, which greatly affected social and legal aspects of life in the Ottoman Empire, including the adoption of European dress styles.

9   Between 1845 and 1849, British exports to the Middle East had reached a value of more than £3 million a year, three-quarters of which consisted of articles made of cotton. Owen, *Middle East*, p. 45.

10 'Exporting to the Empire'.

11 This type of image was also perpetuated in Orientalist paintings and sculpture. Although incomplete, the Arabic inscripton on the garment's leg was probably a translation of 'Imported by Arab Trading'. The words 'Great Britain' are sewn into the seam and are partially visible. Well-to-do Palestinian men and women started wearing baggy trousers (with drawstring waists) at the end of the nineteenth century in imitation of Turkish officials and as a form of modest dress because of increased contact at this time with other villagers and with foreigners. Weir, *Palestinian Costume*, pp. 54–55.

12 *Ibid.*, p. 28.

13 *Abū mitayn* (i.e. *mia'tayn*) literally means 'father of two hundred', with reference to the stripes. Weir, *Palestinian Costume*, pp. 27–31, 94. Majdal is now part of Ashkelon, Israel. See Levanoni, ''Asqalān'; Büssow, 'Gaza'.

14 Skinner, *Palestinian Embroidery Motifs*, p. 15; Weir, *Palestinian Costume*, p. 115.

15 Chemical or aniline dyes grew in popularity from the late nineteenth century and were widely adopted by the 1920s, supplanting natural dyes by the 1930s. Weir, *Palestinian Costume*, p. 108; Weir, *Embroidery from Palestine*, p. 16.

16 I have identified as many patterns as possible by referring to Skinner, *Palestinian Embroidery Motifs*, and El Khalidi, *Art of Palestinian Embroidery*. Transliterations are based on modern written Arabic, though pronunciations vary in colloquial contexts. The Arabic names for the patterns are: *nudfat al-thalj* (snowflake), *kaffat al-yad* (palm of the hand), *tumm al-sammaka* (snapdragon), *al-nakhl al-'ālī* (tall palm), *al-ward al-rūmī* (Roman rose), *midhrā* (pitchfork), *'aṣā* (stick), *rīsh* (feathers), *iwazz* (geese/swans), *mukḥula* (kohl-pot), *rabāba* (harp), *hudhud* (hoopoe bird), *shajarat al-'aqārib* (tree of scorpions), *mlawlaw* (turning around) and *zanbaq* (lilies/irises). The tall palm motif was an important symbol of villages in the Ramallah area. It should be noted that names of motifs were fluid, changing through time, and sometimes the same name could be applied to different motifs (personal communication from Shelagh Weir).

17 I am deeply indebted to Louisa Macmillan for sharing her analysis of the inscriptions, portraits and flags on this scarf with me. It was collected by Mark Littlewood (d. 2004) in southern Yemen in the 1960s.

18 The 1958–61 union of Egypt and Syria as the United Arab Republic (UAR) is reflected by Egypt's two-star flag on the scarf. North Yemen later joined the UAR and adopted a similar flag with one star, as shown.

19 For full discussions see Jankowski, 'Pan-Arabism'; and Haklai, 'United Arab Republic'.

20 The names and political titles are translations of the Arabic inscriptions on the scarf. The scarf was probably produced when all the leaders were in power, hence between September 1963 (when Ben Bella was elected president of Algeria) and August 1964 (when Fu'ad Chehab stepped down as president of Lebanon).

21 Most Yörüks are Sunni Muslim, but some are Alevi, as are members of the sedentary Kurdish population in that region. See Kellner-Heinkele, 'Yörük'. The Alevis are a number of heterogeneous, socio-religious communities in Turkey and the Balkans, who practise a form of esoteric Islam centring on the figure of Imam 'Ali. Dressler, 'Alevīs'.

22 Lenin was the mastermind behind the 1917 October (Bolshevik) Revolution in Russia, and the architect and first head of the USSR. I wish to thank Mukaddas Muborakshoeva for deciphering the Russian inscription for me. It is inscribed with the year 1870 and the name 'V. I. Lenin', and includes Turkmen amuletic motifs of horned animals, triangles and flowers.

23 Edgar, 'Portrait of Lenin', pp. 181–83.

24 It is inscribed 'al-Farabi, Qaz Mu', an acronym for Qazakhstan Memleketi Universitet (Kazakh State University). In 1993 it was renamed al-Farabi Kazakh State National University, and in 2001 the name was altered to al-Farabi Kazakh National University (Kaz NU). Further thanks go to Mukaddas Muborakshoeva for her assistance in deciphering the inscription.

25 Kamil Aliyev (1921–2006), a world-famous Azerbaijani carpet weaver and artist, was renowned for his portrait carpets from the 1960s. He was commissioned by the Azerbaijani president Heydar Aliyev (d. 2003) to produce a portrait carpet of Bill and Hillary Clinton for the president's state visit to the USA in 1997. <https://www.azer.com/aiweb/categories/magazine/ai103_folder/103_articles/103_kamil_aliyev.html>.

26 Ghezelayagh has worked with female felt-makers and embroiderers in Iran since 2003.

27 Afnan lived in Haifa, Beirut, Washington, Kuwait, Paris and London, often having to relocate owing to political circumstances. Issa, ed., *Maliheh Afnan*, pp. 141, 150–51.

28 An undecipherable inscription in Farsi, possibly the weaver's signature, appears on one corner in the detail.

29 Single-page painting, mounted on a detached album folio, of Rustam slaying the White Div; ink, opaque watercolour and gold on paper, Qazvin, Iran, 1576–77. H 21.5 cm × W 31.8 cm (painting), 1937,0710,0.327, bequest of Charles Hazelwood Shannon.

30 There are several Farsi inscriptions (some garbled and reversed) around the main scene, including the words 'Afghanistan', 'Kabul', 'soldier', '1379' and 'October 23'.

31 Rahbar has made fifty-two flags in total and *Texas Flowers* is no. 22. Grenier, 'When History Encounters Aesthetics'.

32 The bolero is constructed from seven pattern pieces, based on the design of a round-necked chest panel of a Palestinian village dress, and the tied tassels create flaps that recall the winged sleeves of Palestinian dresses. The star-keys also represent 'death stars' or explosions in the sky. In Nasser-Khoury's own words: 'The omnipresence of death in daily life as a result of the Israeli Occupation has thrown society into a perpetual state of mourning and loss. [My collection] flaunts, in stubborn protest, the last thing that Palestinians ironically still own: their doom.' Rigby, 'Palestinian Fashion Designer's…Debut'.

33 The Arab Revolt in Palestine (1936–39) was aimed at British colonial rule and the exponential increase of Jewish immigrants entering Palestine. Rooijakkers, 'Palestinian Scarves', p. 183.

34 Weir, *Palestinian Costume*, pp. 68–71. The Lebanese–Palestinian artist Mona Hatoum (b. 1952), has produced a black and white keffiyeh by embroidering long strands of dark hair onto plain white cotton (*Keffieh 1993–9*), throwing the dominating masculine associations of the scarf into question. According to Louisa Macmillan, the red keffiyeh or *shimāgh* worn by King Hussein (r. 1952–99) became a marker of Jordanian national identity and a statement in favour of the monarchy (personal communication, 30 January 2017).

35 They were referred to as *kūfīya* (usually with a checked or fishnet pattern) and *ḥatta* (usually plain). The former term seems to originate from the city of Kufa, Iraq. In the 1930s younger generations started to abandon the fez and turban in favour of the head-cloth as a sign of Palestinian solidarity. Weir, *Palestinian Costume*, pp. 68–69.

36 *Kūfīya* is the preferred term in Palestine, Syria and Lebanon. The term *ḥatta* in these regions usually refers to the plain white head-cloth.
37 *Ghuṭra* is used in western Iraq and the Najd region of Saudi Arabia. In the UAE, Kuwait and Bahrain the term *ghuṭra* usually refers to the preferred plain white head-cloth.
38 *Shimāgh* is the term used in Jordan, Saudi Arabia and UAE, where the head-cloth is usually red and white. See Chico, 'Turban and Male Headgear', pp. 481–82.
39 *Mashada* is the term used in Yemen, where the head-cloth is worn in different colours, including printed modern versions. I wish to thank Leila Ingrams for this information.
40 Nineteenth-century head-ropes were thicker than later examples. See Weir, *Palestinian Costume*, p. 67.
41 Warp ikat is the technique of binding and dyeing the patterns onto warp threads several times before they are set on the loom (weft ikat also exists, and double ikat involves pre-dyeing resist patterns on both warp and weft threads). Ikat produces patterns with soft edges, hence is described as 'cloudy' in Persian. For the Central Asian technique and guilds see Hasson, *Ikat*, pp. 67–73. For the various types of ikat (*adras*, *shāhi*, *aṭlas*, *yakruya* and *baghmal*) see Meller, *Silk and Cotton*, pp. 54–65.
42 I have not found standardized names for *abr* patterns. The watermelon design has also been referred to as a sun, poppy, pomegranate or drum motif. See Shamukhitdinova, 'Ornamental Layout', pp. 45ff.
43 Sumner with Feltham, *Beyond the Silk Road*, p. 34; Malik, 'Uzbek Textiles', p. 379.
44 A *munisak* was once a requirement for every bridal trousseau and, after marriage, was worn at family festivities and funerals by the mourners and the deceased alike. After the funerary rite, the coat was removed from the corpse and given to the deceased's daughter or the woman who washed the body. Krody, 'Tradition of the Bridal Trousseau', pp. 432–33. *Munisaks* dropped out of fashion by the early twentieth century, after which they were preserved only by elderly women for their burial ceremonies. Meller, *Silk and Cotton*, p. 55; Sumner, 'Dress from Tajikistan…', p. 373.
45 The silk edging seems to have been attached directly onto the coat while it was being woven (usually by a team of two or three women). For the complex technique, called 'loop manipulation', see Meller, *Silk and Cotton*, pp. 36, 105; Fitz Gibbon and Hale, *Uzbek Embroidery*, pp. 193–94.
46 Meller, *Russian Textiles*, pp. 80–81.
47 For a similar example of a true bridal tent-hanging from Kazakhstan see 'Marriage and Ceremony', p. 71. For a discussion of propaganda textiles from this era see Bogoslovskaya, 'The Soviet "Invasion"'.
48 The absence of Azerbaijan is odd and inexplicable. The emblems for the republics of Tajikistan, Uzbekistan, Kyrgyzstan and Turkmenistan also feature cotton plants, and the last includes a Turkmen rug, which looks more like a Kyrgyz felt mat on this embroidery, reflecting the maker's background.

Bibliography

Al-Banna-Chidiac, Hana. *L'Orient des femmes: vu par Christian Lacroix*. Paris, 2011

Al-Khamis, Ulrike, and Saad Lafta Hami. 'Iraqi Dress', *Berg Encyclopaedia of World Dress and Fashion*, vol. 5: *Central and Southwest Asia*, ed. Gillian Vogelsang-Eastwood. Oxford and New York, 2010, pp. 262–74

Amighi, Janet Kestenberg. 'Kerman xiii. Zoroastrians of 19th-Century Yazd and Kerman', *Encyclopaedia Iranica*, available online at <http://www.iranicaonline.org/articles/kerman-13-zoroastrians> (accessed 28 January 2017)

Andrews, Mügül, and Peter Andrews. *Türkmen Needlework: Dressmaking and Embroidery among the Türkmen of Iran*. London, 1976

Andrews, Peter. 'The Türkmen Tent', *Turkmen: Tribal Carpets and Traditions*, ed. Louise W. Mackie and Jon Thompson. Washington, DC, 1980, pp. 40–59

Andrews, Peter, et al. *The Turcoman of Iran*. London, 1971

Arakelova, Victoria, and Mushegh Asatrian. 'Amulets, Fortune-Telling, and Magic: Iran, the Caucasus, Central Asia, and Afghanistan', *Encyclopedia of Women & Islamic Cultures*, ed. Suad Joseph, Brill Online, 2009, available at <http://dx.doi.org/10.1163/1872-5309_ewic_EWICCOM_0157b> (accessed 18 December 2016)

Arthur, Linda B., ed. *Undressing Religion: Commitment and Conversion from a Cross-Cultural Perspective*. Oxford and New York, 2000

Atasoy, Nurhan. 'Dervish Dress and Ritual: The Mevlevi Tradition', trans. M. E. Quigley-Pinar, *The Dervish Lodge: Architecture, Art, and Sufism in Ottoman Turkey*, ed. Raymond Lifchez. Berkeley, 1992, pp. 253–68

Balfour-Paul, Jenny. *Indigo in the Arab World*. Richmond, 1997

Betteridge, A .H. "Arūsī', *Encyclopaedia Iranica*, vol. 2/6, pp. 666–70, updated version available online at <http://www.iranicaonline.org/articles/arusi-the-secular-wedding-celebration-which-follows-the-wedding-contract-ceremony-aqd-q> (accessed 31 January 2017)

Betteridge, A. H., and H. Javadi. "Aqd', *Encyclopaedia Iranica*, vol. 2/2, pp. 189–91, updated version available online at <http://www.iranicaonline.org/articles/aqd-marriage-contrucl-rnarriagc-contruct-ceremonv> (accessed 29 July 2016)

Bier, Carole, ed. *Woven from the Soul, Spun from the Heart: Textile Arts of Safavid and Qajar Iran, 16th–19th Centuries*. Washington, DC, 1987

Bilgi, Hülya, and İdil Zanbak. *Skill of the Hand… Delight of the Eye: Ottoman Embroideries in the Sadberk Hanım Museum Collection*. Istanbul, 2012

Blair, Sheila S. *Islamic Inscriptions*. Edinburgh and New York, 1998

Bogoslovskaya, Irina. 'The Soviet "Invasion" of Central Asian Applied Arts: How Artisans Incorporated Communist Political Messages and Symbols', *Textile Society of America 13th Biennial Symposium Proceedings*, Washington, DC, 18–22 September 2012, Paper 660, pp. 1–13, available online at <http://digitalcommons.unl.edu/tsaconf/660> (accessed 10 February 2017)

Bulookbashi, Ali A., and Pouyan Shahidi Marnani. 'Circumcision', *Encyclopaedia Islamica*, ed. Wilferd Madelung and Farhad Daftary, Brill Online, 2016, available at <http://referenceworks.brillonline.com/entries/encyclopaedia-islamica/circumcision-COM_05000092> (accessed 1 February 2016)

Bunn, Stephanie. 'Kirghiz Felt Carpets', *HALI*, 93 (July–August 1997), pp. 84–89

Bunn, Stephanie. 'A "Making Point of View": Deep Knowledge from Local Practice, with Special Reference to Felt-Makers in Kyrgyzstan', *Journal of Museum Ethnography*, 24 (2011), pp. 23–40

Bunn, Stephanie. *Nomadic Felts*. London, 2010

Bunn, Stephanie. 'The Nomad's Apprentice: Different Kinds of "Apprenticeship" among Kyrgyz Nomads in Central Asia', *Apprenticeship: Towards a New Paradigm of Learning*, ed. Patrick Ainley and Helen Rainbird. London and New York, 2014, pp. 74–85

Burckhardt, John Lewis. *Arabic Proverbs, or The Manners and Customs of the Modern Egyptians*. London, 1830

Büssow, Johann. 'Gaza', *Encyclopaedia of Islam, THREE*, ed. Kate Fleet, Gudrun Krämer, Denis Matringe, John Nawas and Everett Rowson, available online at <http://dx.doi.org/10.1163/1573-3912_ei3_COM_27380> (accessed 1 July 2016)

Calmard, J. ''Abbās b. 'Alī b. Abū Ṭāleb', *Encyclopaedia Iranica*, vol. 1/1, pp. 77–79, updated version available online at <http://www.iranicaonline.org/articles/abbas-b-ali-b-abu-taleb> (accessed 10 January 2017)

Campbell, Kay Hardy. 'The Gown that Steals your Heart', *Aramco World* (March–April 2016), pp. 22–33

Canavas, Constantin. 'Compass', *Encyclopaedia of Islam, THREE*, ed. Kate Fleet, Gudrun Krämer, Denis Matringe, John Nawas and Everett Rowson, available online at <http://dx.doi.org/10.1163/1573-3912_ei3_COM_25561> (accessed 11 January 2017)

Chatty, Dawn. 'The Burqa Face Cover: An Aspect of Dress in Southeastern Arabia', *Languages of Dress in the Middle East*, ed. Bruce Ingham and Nancy Lindisfarne-Tapper. London and New York, 1997, pp. 127–48

Chico, Beverly. 'The Turban and Male Headgear', *Berg Encyclopaedia of World Dress and Fashion*, vol. 5: *Central and Southwest Asia*, ed. Gillian Vogelsang-Eastwood. Oxford and New York, 2010, pp. 477–84

Crowfoot, Grace, and Phyllis Sutton. 'Ramallah Embroidery', *Embroidery*, 3 (March 1935), pp. 25–37

Diba, Layla S. 'Clothing x. In the Safavid and Qajar Periods', *Encyclopaedia Iranica*, vol. 5/8, pp. 785–808, updated version available online at <http://www.iranicaonline.org/articles/clothing-x> (accessed 3 February 2016)

Dressler, Markus. 'Alevīs', *Encyclopaedia of Islam, THREE*, ed. Kate Fleet, Gudrun Krämer, Denis Matringe, John Nawas and Everett Rowson, available online at <http://dx.doi.org/10.1163/1573-3912_ei3_COM_0167> (accessed 19 July 2016)

Dundes, Alan, ed. *The Evil Eye: A Casebook*. New York, 1981

Ed. 'Māshā' Allāh', *Encyclopaedia of Islam*, 2nd edn, ed. P. Bearman, Th. Bianquis, C. E. Bosworth, E. van Donzel and W. P. Heinrichs, available online at <http://dx.doi.org/10.1163/1573-3912_islam_SIM_5002> (accessed 8 August 2016)

Edgar, Adrienne. 'Portrait of Lenin: Carpets and National Culture in Soviet Turkmenistan', *Picturing Russia: Explorations in Visual Culture*, ed. Valerie Ann Kivelson and Joan Neuberger. New Haven, CT, 2010, pp. 181–84

Ekhtiar, Maryam D., et al. *Masterpieces from the Department of Islamic Art in the Metropolitan Museum of Art*. New Haven and London, 2011

El Guindi, Fadwa, and Wesam al-Othman. 'Dress from the Gulf States: Bahrain, Kuwait, Qatar, United Arab Emirates', *Berg Encyclopaedia of World Dress and Fashion*, vol. 5: *Central and Southwest Asia*, ed. Gillian Vogelsang-Eastwood. Oxford and New York, 2010, pp. 247–49

El Khalidi, Leila. *The Art of Palestinian Embroidery*. London, 1999

El Mutwalli, Reem Tariq. *Sultani, Traditions Renewed: Changes in Women's Traditional Dress in the United Arab Emirates during the Reign of Shaykh Zayid bin Sultan Al Nahyan, 1966–2004*, vols 1–3. Abu Dhabi, 2011

'Exporting to the Empire: Labels of the British Cotton Trade', Bodleian Library, University of Oxford, 2009, available online at <https://johnjohnson.wordpress.com/2009/04/30/exporting-to-the-empire-labels-of-the-cotton-trade/> (accessed 22 June 2016)

Firouz, Iran Ala, and Mehremonir Jahanbani. 'Clothing xviii. Clothing of the Baluch in Persia', *Encyclopaedia Iranica*, vol. 5/8, pp. 826–29, updated version available online at <http://www.iranicaonline.org/articles/clothing-xviii> (accessed 3 February 2016)

Firro, Kais M. 'Druzes (Durūz)', *Encyclopaedia of Islam, THREE*, ed. Kate Fleet, Gudrun Krämer, Denis Matringe, John Nawas and Everett Rowson, available online at <http://dx.doi.org/10.1163/1573-3912_ei3_COM_26097> (accessed 1 August 2016)

Fitz Gibbon, Kate, and Andrew Hale. *Uzbek Embroidery in the Nomadic Tradition: The Jack and Aviva Robinson Collection at the Minneapolis Institute of Arts*. Minneapolis, 2007

Ghezelayagh, Bita. *Namad: A Persian Journey in Felt*. Glasgow, 2009

Gibson-Roberts, Priscilla A. *Ethnic Socks and Stockings: A Compendium of Eastern Designs and Technique*. Sioux Falls, 1995

Gillow, John. *Textiles of the Islamic World*. London, 2010

Gleave, Robert. 'Prayer and Prostration: Imāmī Shi'i Discussions of *al-Sujūd 'alā al-Turba al-Ḥusayniyya*', *The Art and Material Culture of Iranian Shi'ism: Iconography and Religious Devotion in Shi'i Islam*, ed. Pedram Khosronejad. London, 2012, pp. 233–53

Goitein, Shelomo Dov. *A Mediterranean Society: The Jewish Communities of the Arab World as Portrayed in the Documents of the Cairo Geniza*, vol. 4: *Daily Life*. Berkeley, 1983

Goldstein, Darra, and Ergun Çağatay. 'Turkmenistan on a Plate', *Saudi Aramco World* (January–February 2006), pp. 10–19

Gordon, Stewart. 'Khil'a: Clothing to Honor a Person or Situation', *Berg Encyclopaedia of World Dress and Fashion*, vol. 5: *Central and Southwest Asia*, ed. Gillian Vogelsang-Eastwood. Oxford and New York, 2010, pp. 462–67

Görünür, Lale. *Women's Costume of the Late Ottoman Era from the Sadberk Hanım Museum Collection*. Istanbul, 2010

Granqvist, Hilma. *Muslim Death and Burial: Arab Customs and Traditions Studied in a Village in Jordan*. Helsinki, 1965

Grenier, Catherine. 'When History Encounters Aesthetics', *Sara Rahbar: I Have No Faith Left for the Devil to Take*, ed. Elaine W. Ng. New York, 2011, pp. 20–29

Günay, Umay, et al. *Costumes historiques des femmes turques*. Istanbul, 1986

Ḥāfiẓ, Shams al-Dīn Muḥammad. *The Collected Lyrics of Háfiz of Shíráz*, trans. Peter Avery. Cambridge, 2007

Ḥāfiẓ, Shams al-Dīn Muḥammad. *Dīvān-i Ḥāfiẓ*, ed. Muhammad Qazvini and Qasim Ghani. Tehran, 1999

Haklai, Oded. 'United Arab Republic', *International Encyclopedia of the Social Sciences*, 2008, available online at <http://www.encyclopedia.com/doc/1G2-3045302848.html> (accessed 11 July 2016)

Harvey, Janet. *Traditional Textiles of Central Asia*. London, 1996

Hasson, Rachel. *Ikat: Kaleidoscope of Colors. Silk Fabrics from Central Asia*. Jerusalem, 2004

Helms, Laura McLaws, and Venetia Porter. *Thea Porter: Bohemian Chic*. London, 2015

Hillenbrand, Robert, et. al. *The Sarikhani Collection: An Introduction*. London, 2011

Hunte, Pamela. 'Clothing xix. Clothing of the Baluch in Pakistan and Afghanistan', *Encyclopaedia Iranica*, vol. 5/8, pp. 829–33, updated version available online at <http://www.iranicaonline.org/articles/clothing-xix> (accessed 1 August 2016)

Inal, Onur. 'Women's Fashions in Transition: Ottoman Borderlands and the Anglo-Ottoman Exchange of Costumes', *Journal of World History*, 22 (2011), pp. 243–72

Ipek, Selin. 'Ottoman Fabrics during the 18th and 19th Centuries', *Textile Society of America 13th Biennial Symposium Proceedings*, Washington, DC, 18–22 September 2012, Paper 697, pp. 1–8, available online at <http://digitalcommons.unl.edu/tsaconf/697> (accessed 1 April 2016)

Issa, Rose, ed. *Maliheh Afnan: Traces, Faces and Places*. London, 2010

Jankowski, James. 'Pan-Arabism', *New Dictionary of the History of Ideas*, 2005, available online at <http://www.encyclopedia.com/doc/1G2-3424300567.html> (accessed 11 July 2016)

Jirousek, Charlotte. 'Historical Survey of Textiles and Dress in Turkey', *Berg Encyclopaedia of World Dress and Fashion*, vol. 5: *Central and Southwest Asia*, ed. Gillian Vogelsang-Eastwood. Oxford and New York, 2010, pp. 113–20

Jirousek, Charlotte. 'Ottoman Influences in Western Dress', *Ottoman Costumes: From Textile to Identity*, ed. Suraiya Faroqhi and Christoph K. Neumann. Istanbul, 2005, pp. 231–51

Juhasz, Esther, ed. *The Jewish Wardrobe: From the Collection of the Israel Museum, Jerusalem*. Milan and Jerusalem, 2012

Kahooker, Neda. 'Zoroastrian Marriage Apron, World Stories: Young Voices Gallery', Brighton Museum & Art Gallery, 17 April 2014, available online at <http://brightonmuseums.org.uk/discover/2014/04/17/zoroastrian-marriage-apron-world-stories-young-voices-gallery/> (accessed 29 December 2016)

Kawar, Widad Kamel. *Threads of Identity: Preserving Palestinian Costume and Heritage.* Nicosia and London, 2011

Kawar, Widad, Layla Pio and Gillian Vogelsang-Eastwood, 'Embroidery from Syria', *Encyclopedia of Embroidery from the Arab World*, ed. Gillian Vogelsang-Eastwood. London and New York, 2016, pp. 444–75

Kellner-Heinkele, Barbara. 'Yörük', *Encyclopaedia of Islam*, 2nd edn, ed. P. Bearman, Th. Bianquis, C. E. Bosworth, E. van Donzel and W. P. Heinrichs, available online at <http://dx.doi.org/10.1163/1573–3912_islam_SIM_8023> (accessed 19 July 2016)

Kennedy, John G. *The Flower of Paradise: The Institutionalized Use of the Drug Qat in North Yemen.* Dordrecht, 1987

Klink, Zeina El-Khouri. 'Beyond the *ṭanṭūr*: Female Attire Traditions in 19th-Century Mount Lebanon', DPhil diss., University of Oxford, 1999

Krody, Sumru Belger. 'The Tradition of the Bridal Trousseau', *Berg Encyclopaedia of World Dress and Fashion*, vol. 5: *Central and Southwest Asia*, ed. Gillian Vogelsang-Eastwood. Oxford and New York, 2010, pp. 430–34

Krody, Sumru Belger. 'Turkish Embroidery', *Berg Encyclopaedia of World Dress and Fashion*, vol. 5: *Central and Southwest Asia*, ed. Gillian Vogelsang-Eastwood. Oxford and New York, 2010, pp. 121–25

Levanoni, Amalia. ''Asqalān', *Encyclopaedia of Islam, THREE*, ed. Kate Fleet, Gudrun Krämer, Denis Matringe, John Nawas and Everett Rowson, available online at <http://dx.doi.org/10.1163/1573-3912_ei3_COM_23106> (accessed 1 July 2016)

Lewis, Reina, ed. *Modest Fashion: Styling Bodies, Mediating Faith.* London and New York, 2013

Lindholm, Christina. 'Yemeni Dress', *Berg Encyclopaedia of World Dress and Fashion*, vol. 5: *Central and Southwest Asia*, ed. Gillian Vogelsang-Eastwood. Oxford and New York, 2010, pp. 231–37

Mackie, Louise W. *Symbols of Power: Luxury Textiles from Islamic Lands, 7th–21st Century.* New Haven and London, 2015

Mackie, Louise W., and Jon Thompson. *Turkmen: Tribal Carpets and Traditions.* Washington, DC, 1980

Maitdinova, Guzel. 'Clothing xv. Clothing of Tajikistan', *Encyclopaedia Iranica*, vol. 5/8, pp. 818–22, updated version available online at <http://www.iranicaonline.org/articles/clothing-xv> (accessed 1 August 2016)

Malik, Carter. 'Uzbek Textiles', *Berg Encyclopaedia of World Dress and Fashion*, vol. 5: *Central and Southwest Asia*, ed. Gillian Vogelsang-Eastwood. Oxford and New York, 2010, pp. 377–82

Mallett, Marla. *Woven Structures: A Guide to Oriental Rug and Textile Analysis*. Atlanta, 2000

Marchese, Ronald T., and Marlene R. Breu. 'Protecting the Populace: Blue Beads and other Amulets', *The Fabric of Life: Cultural Transformations in Turkish Society*, ed. Ronald T. Marchese. Binghamton, NY, 2005, pp. 99–126

Martiniani-Reber, Marielle, Georgette Cornu et al. *Tissus d'Égypte: témoins du monde Arabe, VIIIe–XVe siècles. Collection Bouvier.* Geneva, 1993

Mazdapour, Katayun. 'Zoroastrian Women: Overview', *Encyclopedia of Women & Islamic Cultures*, ed. Suad Joseph, Brill Online, 2016, available at <http://dx.doi.org/10.1163/1872–5309_ewic_EWICCOM_0155> (accessed 18 December 2016)

Meller, Susan. *Russian Textiles: Printed Cloth for the Bazaars of Central Asia.* New York, 2007

Meller, Susan. *Silk and Cotton: Textiles from the Central Asia that Was.* New York, 2013

Micklewright, Nancy. 'Tracing the Transformations in Women's Dress in Nineteenth-Century Istanbul', *Dress*, 13 (1987), pp. 33–43

Monsutti, Alessandro. 'Hazāra ii. History', *Encyclopaedia Iranica*, vol. 12/1, pp. 81–85, updated version available online at <http://www.iranicaonline.org/articles/hazara-2> (accessed 10 January 17)

Monsutti, Alessandro. 'Hazāra iii. Ethnography and Social Organization', *Encyclopaedia Iranica*, vol. 12/1, pp. 85–90, updated version available online at <http://www.iranicaonline.org/articles/hazara-3> (accessed 10 January 2017)

Mottahedin, Zala, and Eqbal Yagma'i. 'Cosmetics', *Encyclopaedia Iranica*, vol. 6/3, pp. 301–03, updated version available online at <http://www.iranicaonline.org/articles/cosmetics-pers> (accessed 18 December 2016)

Munayyer, Hanan Karaman. *Traditional Palestinian Costume: Origins and Evolution.* Northampton, MA, 2011

Mundy, Martha. 'Ṣan'ā' Dress, 1920–1975', *Ṣan'ā': An Arabian Islamic City*, ed. R. B. Serjeant and Ronald Lewcock. London, 1983, pp. 529–41

Nabholz-Kartaschoff, Marie-Louise, and Axel Langer. *Pfauen, Blüten & Zypressen: Persische Textilien der Qajaren-Zeit (1788–1925)*. Zurich, 2005

Owen, Roger. *The Middle East in the World Economy, 1800–1914.* London and New York, 1981

Paine, Sheila. *The Afghan Amulet: Travels from the Hindu Kush to Razgrad.* London, 1994

Paine, Sheila. *Amulets: A World of Secret Powers, Charms and Magic.* London, 2004.

Paine, Sheila. *Embroidery from Afghanistan.* London, 2006

Pardoe, Julia. *The City of the Sultan, and Domestic Manners of the Turks, in 1836.* London, 1837

Parham, Cyrus, and Mushegh Asatryan. 'Carpets and Carpet-Making', *Encyclopaedia Islamica*, ed. Wilferd Madelung and Farhad Daftary, Brill Online, 2016, available at <http://referenceworks.brillonline.com/entries/encyclopaedia-islamica/carpets-and-carpet-making-COM_05000068> (accessed 7 September 2016)

Pio, Layla, and Gillian Vogelsang-Eastwood. 'Embroidery from Iraq', *Encyclopedia of Embroidery from the Arab World*, ed. Gillian Vogelsang-Eastwood. London and New York, 2016, pp. 476–92

Porter, Venetia. 'Textiles of Mecca and Medina', *Hajj: Journey to the Heart of Islam*, ed. V. Porter. London, 2012, pp. 256–65

Posey, Sarah. 'Lakai Uzbek Embroideries from Uzbekistan', *Embroidery*, 54 (January 2003), p. 34

Ransom, Marjorie. *Silver Treasures from the Land of Sheba: Regional Yemeni Jewellery.* Cairo and New York, 2014

Ransom, Marjorie, and Gillian Vogelsang-Eastwood. 'Embroidery from Yemen', *Encyclopedia of Embroidery from the Arab World*, ed. Gillian Vogelsang-Eastwood. London and New York, 2016, pp. 520–59

Richardson, Neil, and Marcia Dorr. *The Craft Heritage of Oman*, vols 1–2. Dubai, 2003

Rigby, Neville. 'Palestinian Fashion Designer's Uncompromising Debut', *Electronic Intifada*, 24 February 2011, available online at <https://electronicintifada.net/content/palestinian-fashion-designers-uncompromising-debut/9244> (accessed 16 June 2016)

Rooijakkers, Tineke. 'Palestinian Scarves and Flag Dresses', *Berg Encyclopaedia of World Dress and Fashion*, vol. 5: *Central and Southwest Asia*, ed. Gillian Vogelsang-Eastwood. Oxford and New York, 2010, pp. 183–86

Ruete, Emily (Princess Salme). *Memoirs of an Arabian Princess from Zanzibar*. New York, 2009

Scarce, Jennifer M. *Women's Costume of the Near and Middle East*. London, 1987

Schimmel, Annemarie. *A Two-Colored Brocade: The Imagery of Persian Poetry*. Chapel Hill and London, 1992

Shamukhitdinova, Lola. 'Ornamental Layout of Central Asian Ikats', *Modernity of Tradition: Uzbek Textile Culture Today*, ed. Gabriele Mentges and Lola Shamukhitdinova. Münster, 2013, pp. 41–52

Sharon, M. 'People of the House', *Encyclopaedia of the Qurʾān*, ed. Jane Dammen McAuliffe, available online at <http://dx.doi.org/10.1163/1875-3922_q3_EQSIM_00323> (accessed 12 January 2017)

Shirazi, Faegheh. *The Veil Unveiled: The Hijab in Modern Culture*. Gainesville, FL, 2001

Skinner, Margarita. *Palestinian Embroidery Motifs: A Treasury of Stitches, 1850–1950*. London, 2007

Spies, O. 'Mahr', *Encyclopaedia of Islam*, 2nd edn, ed. P. Bearman, Th. Bianquis, C. E. Bosworth, E. van Donzel and W. P. Heinrichs, available online at <http://dx.doi.org/10.1163/1573-3912_islam_SIM_4806> (accessed 31 January 2017)

Spring, Christopher. *African Textiles Today*. London, 2012

Spring, Christopher, and Julie Hudson. *Silk in Africa*. London, 2002

Stehlin-AlZadjali, Julia M. *The Traditional Women's Dress of Oman*. Muscat, 2010

Stillman, Yedida Kalfon. *Palestinian Costume and Jewelry*. Albuquerque, NM, 1979

Stillman, Yedida K., Paula Sanders and Nasser Rabbat. 'Ṭirāz', *Encyclopaedia of Islam*, 2nd edn, ed. P. Bearman, Th. Bianquis, C. E. Bosworth, E. van Donzel and W. P. Heinrichs, available online at <http://dx.doi.org/10.1163/1573-3912_islam_COM_1228> (accessed 24 December 2016)

Stillmann, N. A. "Khilʿa', *Encyclopaedia of Islam*, 2nd edn, ed. P. Bearman, Th. Bianquis, C. E. Bosworth, E. van Donzel and W. P. Heinrichs, available online at <http://dx.doi.org/10.1163/1573-3912_islam_COM_0507> (accessed 10 August 2016)

Suleman, Fahmida, ed. *People of the Prophet's House: Artistic and Ritual Expressions of Shiʿi Islam*. London, 2015

Suleman, Fahmida, ed. *Word of God, Art of Man: The Qurʾan and its Creative Expressions*. Oxford, 2007

Sumner, Christina. 'Dress from Tajikistan and Uzbekistan', *Berg Encyclopaedia of World Dress and Fashion*, vol. 5: *Central and Southwest Asia*, ed. Gillian Vogelsang-Eastwood. Oxford and New York, 2010, pp. 369–76

Sumner, Christina, with Heleanor Feltham. *Beyond the Silk Road: Arts of Central Asia from the Powerhouse Museum Collection*. Sydney, 1999

Tarlo, Emma. *Visibly Muslim: Fashion, Politics, Faith*. Oxford and New York, 2010

Toorawa, Shawkat M. 'Clothing', *Encyclopaedia of the Qurʾān*, ed. Jane Dammen McAuliffe, available online at <http://dx.doi.org/10.1163/1875-3922_q3_EQSIM_00083> (accessed 11 January 2017)

Vogelsang, Willem. 'Political Clothing in Afghanistan', National Museum of Ethnology, Leiden, n.d., pp. 1–16, available online at <http://www.academia.edu/5560474/Political_clothing_in_Afghanistan>

Vogelsang-Eastwood, Gillian. 'Dress from Kazakhstan', *Berg Encyclopaedia of World Dress and Fashion*, vol. 5: *Central and Southwest Asia*, ed. Gillian Vogelsang-Eastwood. Oxford and New York, 2010, pp. 383–88

Vogelsang-Eastwood, Gillian. 'Dress from Kyrgyzstan', *Berg Encyclopaedia of World Dress and Fashion*, vol. 5: *Central and Southwest Asia*, ed. Gillian Vogelsang-Eastwood. Oxford and New York, 2010, pp. 389–99

Vogelsang-Eastwood, Gillian. *Embroidery from the Arab World*. Leiden, 2010

Vogelsang-Eastwood, Gillian. 'Iranian Urban Dress', *Berg Encyclopaedia of World Dress and Fashion*, vol. 5: *Central and Southwest Asia*, ed. Gillian Vogelsang-Eastwood. Oxford and New York, 2010, pp. 298–307

Vogelsang-Eastwood, Gillian. 'Prince for a Day: Turkish Circumcision Outfits' (TRC Gallery, August–October 2010), in Textile Research Centre, Leiden, *Exhibitions, 2009–2010*. Leiden, n.d. [2016], pp. 30–35

Vogelsang-Eastwood, Gillian. 'Saudi Arabian Dress', *Berg Encyclopaedia of World Dress and Fashion*, vol. 5: *Central and Southwest Asia*, ed. Gillian Vogelsang-Eastwood. Oxford and New York, 2010, pp. 223–30

Vogelsang-Eastwood, Gillian. 'Snapshot: Colonel and Mrs. Dickson's Embroidered Garments from Kuwait', *Encyclopedia of Embroidery from the Arab World*, ed. Gillian Vogelsang-Eastwood. London and New York, 2016, pp. 585–89

Vogelsang-Eastwood, Gillian. 'Turkmen Dress and Embroidery', *Berg Encyclopaedia of World Dress and Fashion*, vol. 5: *Central and Southwest Asia*, ed. Gillian Vogelsang-Eastwood. Oxford and New York, 2010, pp. 355–68

Vogelsang-Eastwood, Gillian, and L. A. F. Barjesteh van Waalwijk van Doorn. *An Introduction to Qajar Era Dress*. Rotterdam, 2002

Vogelsang-Eastwood, Gillian, and Willem Vogelsang. *Covering the Moon: An Introduction to Middle Eastern Face Veils*. Leuven, 2008

Wearden, Jennifer. *Decorative Textiles from Arab & Islamic Cultures: Selections from the Al Lulwa Collection*. London, 2015

Wearden, Jennifer, and Patty Baker. *Iranian Textiles*. London, 2010

Weber, Heike, and Gillian Vogelsang-Eastwood. 'Snapshot: Druze Dress', *Encyclopedia of Embroidery from the Arab World*, ed. Gillian Vogelsang-Eastwood. London and New York, 2016, pp. 209–11

Weir, Shelagh. 'Beauty and Meaning: The British Museum Collection of Palestinian Costume', *Middle East in London*, 7 (August–September 2011), pp. 14–15

Weir, Shelagh. *The Bedouin*. London, 1990

Weir, Shelagh. *Embroidery from Palestine*. London, 2006

Weir, Shelagh. *Palestinian Costume*. London, 1989

Weir, Shelagh. *Palestinian Embroidery*. London, 1970

Whitney Azoy, G. 'Bozkaši', *Encyclopaedia Iranica*, vol. 6/4, pp. 425–26, updated version available online at <http://www.iranicaonline.org/articles/bozkasi-lit> (accessed 12 September 2016)

Wiedemann, E., and James W. Allan. 'al-Kuḥl', *Encyclopaedia of Islam*, ed. P. Bearman, Th. Bianquis, C. E. Bosworth, E. van Donzel and W. P. Heinrichs, available online at <http://dx.doi.org/10.1163/1573-3912_islam_SIM_4487> (accessed 9 August 2016)

Yusofi, Golam-Hosayn. 'Clothing xxvii. Historical Lexicon of Persian Clothing', *Encyclopaedia Iranica*, vol. 5/8, pp. 856–65, updated version available online at <http://www.iranicaonline.org/articles/clothing-xxvii> (accessed 14 January 2017)

Zimney, Michelle. 'Islam: Saints and Sacred Geographies: Mashriq', *Encyclopedia of Women & Islamic Cultures*, ed. Suad Joseph, Brill Online, 2016, available at <http://dx.doi.org/10.1163/1872-5309_ewic_EWICCOM_0606b> (accessed 18 December 2016)

Acknowledgments

If I were to liken writing this book to delivering a baby, then it goes without saying that I had several determined but compassionate midwives to ensure its safe delivery. I thank them all for their support and patience: my dear friend and colleague Helen Wolfe, to whom the book is dedicated, Jonathan Tubb, Irving Finkel, Claudia Bloch and, especially, Shelagh Weir. I would also like to thank Michael Row, who is responsible for the beautiful photography, Paul Goodhead for the wonderful map and Ray Watkins for the elegant design. I also wish to acknowledge a number of colleagues from the former British Museum Press who were involved at the start of the project: Coralie Hepburn, Kate Oliver, Emma Poulter and Axelle Russo-Heath. I wish to express my deepest gratitude to Susannah Lawson, Rosemary Roberts and Susanna Ingram from Thames and Hudson for seeing the project to completion with such enthusiasm and attention to detail.

I relied on a number of colleagues and friends for their assistance and advice on specific aspects of the book, or simply for moral support, and I owe them my deepest appreciation: Ladan Akbarnia, Omar Ali-de-Unzaga, Joan Bishop, Dominic Parviz Brookshaw, Kay Hardy Campbell, Rosemary Crill, Alexandra Fletcher, Sara Forster, James Hamill, Zeina Klink-Hoppe, Imogen Laing, Louisa MacMillan, Aisa Martinez, Chris Michaels, Mukaddas Muborakshoeva, Venetia Porter, Jennifer Scarce, St John Simpson, Gillian Vogelsang-Eastwood, Susan Walby and Jennifer Wearden.

Finally, I wish to thank my family in London, Toronto and Chantilly for their continuous support and patience, especially my mother who instilled a love of textiles in me from an early age. Words fail me in thanking Khadija and Aly, who bore the brunt of my stress during the writing of this book.

Picture Credits

All works illustrated in this book are from the collection of the British Museum, unless otherwise stated.

INTRODUCTION

Fig. 16, p. 22, Photo © Paul Quezada-Neiman/Alamy Stock Photo.

Fig. 17, p. 23, Photo © Raymond Tang/Alamy Stock Photo.

CHILDHOOD

Fig. 20, p. 28, Photo © Jonathan Baldock and used by permission.

MARRIAGE AND CEREMONY

Fig. 23, p. 46, Courtesy of Library of Congress Prints and Photographs Division, LC-DIG-ppmsca-09951-00227.

Inset, p. 72, Courtesy of the Peter the Great Museum of Anthropology and Ethnography (Kunstkamera), Russian Academy of Sciences. MAE RAS: № 418-1.

STATUS AND IDENTITY

Fig. 25, p. 80, Photo © Abedin Taherkenareh / REX.

HOUSE AND HOMESTEAD

Fig. 33, p. 145, Courtesy of Library of Congress, Prints & Photographs Division, Prokudin-Gorskii Collection, LC-DIG-ppmsc-04412.

Fig. 34, p. 146, Courtesy of Library of Congress, Prints & Photographs Division, Prokudin-Gorskii Collection, LC-DIG-prokc-20090.

POLITICS AND CONFLICT

Fig. 37, p. 180, Photo © Chris Hondros/Getty Images.

Fig. 39, p. 181, Photo © Peter Macdiarmid/Getty Images.

Inset, p. 203, Photo: Tarek Moukaddem © Trustees of the British Museum. Courtesy of OmarJoseph Nasser-Khoury.

Index

Page numbers in *italic* refer to the illustrations

'abāya/'abā *see under* cloaks
Adile Sultan, princess
    how to wear the *üçetek* ('triple-skirt') *entari* 80
Afghanistan 7, 30, 32
    bedding-pile hanging (*segusha*) *160*, 161
    chapan (Karzai's) *180*, *181*
    child's over-shirt (*kurta*) 30, *30*
    embroidered bodice of Kuchi dress *2*, 4
    fertility charm (*tumar*) 26, *27*
    floor-coverings (*dastarkhān*) 146, *152*, 153, *153*
    head- and plait-covers (*kultapüshak/kallapüshak*) 61, *61*
    horse blanket (*daour/dauri*) 173, *173*
    horse headdress *172*, 173
    kohl holder (*sormadān*) 65, *65*
    marriage canopy and cover (*bugjama/bugzhoma*) 60, *60*
    national dress, attempt by Karzai to create 180
    prayer cloth (*mohr posh*) from Ghazni 124, 130, *130*
    qarākulī (lamb's fleece hat) 180, *181*
    Qur'an bag *125*
    Soviet invasion 180, 195
    tent-hangings (*at torba ilgitsh/at torba ilgich*) 157, *157*, 158, *158*, *159*
    triangular cloth amulet *38*, 39
    war rugs 176–77, *194*, 195, *195*, 196, *196*, *197*
Afnan, Maliheh (artist, 1935–2016) 193, *193*, 222 n. 27
Alaïa, Azzedine (designer, b. 1940) 19
Alfred Ernest Albert, Prince 84
'Ali b. Abi Talib (fourth caliph and first Shi'a imam, d. 661) 31, 122, 124, *190*, 191, 222 n. 7
amber beads *202*, 203
amuletic coats *see under* coats
amuletic over-shirts *see under* over-shirts
amulets 26, 27, 29, 76, 124
    Afghanistan *27*, *38*, 39
    alum *26*, 27
    dogha 27, *38*, 39, *120–21*, 137, *137*
    Iran 104, *174*, *175*
    nazarlık 140, *141*
    Oman 28
    Palestine 26
    talismanic goat's skull 140, *140*
    tumar 26, 27, *38*, 39
    Turkey 140, *141*
    Turkmen *27*, *38*, 39, *120–21*, 137, *137*, 140, *140*
    Turkmenistan *120–21*, 137, *137*, 140, *140*
    Yemen 134, *134*
animal-trappings/hangings *see under* camels; horses
appliqué
    Iran *167*, 167
    Kuwait 94, *95*
    Kyrgyzstan *168*, *169*
    Oman 113
    Palestine 82, 114, *114*, *115*
    Saudi Arabia 182, *182*, *183*
    Uzbekistan 61, *61*, *164*, 165, *165*
    Yemen 10, *50*, 51
'Arafat, Yasser (PLO chairman, 1929–2004) 180, *180*, 204
Armenia 7
    priest's cowl 107, *107*
    theological student's hat 107, *107*
    trousseau 46, 48, *48–49*
Association for the Development of Palestinian Camps *see* INAASH
Atabay *see* Yomut (Atabay) *under* Turkmen people

aṭlas see satin
'Awlaqi tribe, former Western Aden Protectorate, Yemen
    dress 10, *10*
    kohl holders 65, *65*

Ba'th Party 188
badla (metal-strip embroidery) 64, *64*, 100, *101*, 118, *118*, 150, *150*, *151*
bags
    kitchen utensil bag 166, *166*
    Qur'an bag 124, *125*
    saddlebag (*çarkh horcin/khorjīn*) 170, *170*
    spindle bag (*ig serk/ig torba*) 170, *171*
    storage bags and sacks (*çuval/karçin*) 162, *162*, 163, *163*
    tent-pole bags (*okbash*) 144, *156*, 157
    wedding mirror bags (*ā'ina bokche*) 46, *46*, 70, *70*
Bahrain 7
    Over-dress (*thawb al-nashal*) 84, *84*, *85*, 94
Balkan dress 98, *99*, 99
Baluch people
    child's dress (*dishdāsha/pashk*) 32, *32*
    dress 82
    face-coverings (*burqa'*) 113
    kohl holder (*sormadān*) 65, *65*
    textiles 199
    woman's dress (*dishdāsha/pashk*) 94, *94*
bathhouse 150
baṭṭūla see under face-coverings
beads/beadwork 27, 29
    Afghanistan *2–3*, 30, *30*, *38*, 39, *125*, *160*, 161
    Iran *174*, 174
    Kazakhstan *42–43*, 72, *72*, *73*
    Oman 36, *36*
    Palestine 65, *65*, 68, 69, 81, *202*, 203
    Saudi Arabia 37, *37*
    Tajikistan 33, *33*, *123*, *149*
    Turkey 29, 140
    Turkmenistan 39, *39*
    Uzbekistan *160*, 161
    Yemen *50*, 51, 65, *65*, *110*, 111, *111*
    see also under glass
bedding pile (*jük/chuk*) 146, 149, 158, 161
bedding-pile hangings (*segusha/saye qosha*) *160*, 161
Bedouin 13, 19, 94
    burqa' 81, 112, *112*, 113, *113*
    dolls 102, *102*
    handkerchief *45*, 46
    head-cloths (keffiyeh) *107*, 180, 204, *204*
    head-rope ('aqāl/'iqāl) 204, *204*
    image of Bedouin on horseback 184, *184*
    rugs 16
    tents 146
    thawb 74, *75*
bells *2*, 27, 30, 81
belts 86, *86*
bibs (*kirlik*) 39, *39*
bicycle saddlebag *see* saddlebag *under* bags
Binzagr, Safeya (artist, b. 1940) 21
bisht see under coats
black
    and white cord imitating snakes 26, *27*, *120–21*, 122, 137, *137*
    and white kefiyyeh, symbol of Palestinian identity 180, *180*, 204, *204*
    threads imitating hair 61, *61*
    worn by young women 59

blue
    glass beads for protection 26, *27*, 29
    indicator of woman's marital status 74
    indigo *50*, 51, 58, *74*, 76, *76*, 108, 113, *113*, 117, *117*, 124, 134, *134*, 174, *174*, *175*, 184, *185*, 204, *205*
    worn by young women 59
bodice 62, *62*, 118
bonnets 26, 27, 31, *31*
    see also caps; fezzes; hats; headdresses; turbans
braid 33, *36*, 69, 99, 100, *100*, 104, 108, *108*, *109*
brass
    chains *110*, 111, 134, *135*
    kohl container 65, *65*
    sequins 134, *134–5*
bridal dress and textiles *5*, 21, 44–77, *45–77*, 74, *74*, 90, 91, *91*, 96, *96*, 100, *101*, 104, 108, *114*, *115*
    see also dowries; trousseaus
bridal headdresses *see under* headdresses
Britain
    British fashion, influence of 40
    cotton trade 185
    uniforms, influence of 17, 69
brocade 26, 33, *33*, *36*, 52, *52*, *53*, 61, 83, *83*, 116, *116*, *164*, 165, *165*
    see also silk
Bukhara 7
    Bukhara couching *172*, 173
    Bukharan embroidery (*zardūzī*) 15, 61, *61*
    head- and plait-covers (*kultapüshak*) 15, 61, *61*
    man's ceremonial robe (*chapan*) 52, *52*, *53*,
    man's ikat robe (*chapan*) *206*, 207
    woman's ceremonial robe (*chapan*) 54, *55*, *55*
    woman's ikat robe (*munisak*) 207, *207*, *208–09*
burkini 23, *23*
burqa' see under face-coverings
buttons *2*, 34, 39, *39*, 100, *101*, *136*, 166, *166*, *174*, *175*
Byzantine artistic influence 191

camel hair *see under* hair
camels
    camel motif on rug 196, *196*
    camel neck-hanging (*duye bashlyk*) *174*, 174
    camel trappings 137, 145
    ridden in circumcision rites 28, 31
    ridden in wedding celebrations 66, 137, 145, 174
canopies, wedding *see* wedding canopies
canvas 96
caps 77, *77*, *123*
    börk 39, *39*
    chach kep 58, *58*
    lachak 91, *91*
    libda/libbada (porter's cap) 107
    prayer cap 124
    skullcaps 29, *29*, 39, 58, 77, *77*
    ṭāqiyya 36, *36*
    see also bonnets; fezzes; hats; headdresses; turbans
Carmelite missionaries 119
carnelian 27, 30, *30*, 82, *174*, *175*, 217 n. 54
Centre for Omani Dress, Bait Al Zubair Museum (Muscat) 19
chādor see under cloaks
chapan see under robes
charms *see* amulets
chemises 119, *119*
    gömlek 86, *87*, 99, *99*
    pīrāhan 34, *34*, 100

qamīsa 62
    see also dresses; over-shirts; robes; tunics
children's dress 26–41, *26–41*, 77, *77*, 137, *137*, 145
children's toys 112, *112*
Christian dress 64, *64*, 69, *107*, 119, *119*
Church Missionary Society 212
Church's Ministry among Jewish People 31, 34, 212
chyrpy see under cloaks
ciphers, imperial *see tughra*
circumcision 28, 31, 145
cloaks 21, 122
    'abāya/'abā' 19, *19*, 23, *51*, 76, *76*
    chādor 21, *105*
    chyrpy 59, *59*
    hooded cloak 132, *132*
    namad (shepherds' cloak) 17, *18*, 192, *192*
clogs, women's (*qabqab/nalin*) 150, *150*
coatdresses *see under* dresses
coats 40, *40–41*
    amuletic 28, 33, *33*
    bisht 106, *107*
    çabūt 100, *100*
    durā'a 116, *116*, 117, *117*
    overcoats 86
    qumbāz 117, *117*
    see also dresses; jackets
coins 34, *35*, 65, *65*, 68, 69, 81, 83
    coin pendants *2*, 30, *82*
    coin tokens *27*, 28, 31, *31*, 68
copper
    beads *202*, 203
    gilt-copper-wrapped thread (*kılabdan*) 88
coral *42–43*, 72, *73*, 217 n. 54
cosmetics 48, 65
cotton
    European cotton 69, *69*, 184, *184*
    indigo-dyed cotton 58, *58*, 74, *74*, 108, 113, *113*, 114, *114–15*, 117, *117*, 124, 134, *134*, 174, *174*, 184, *185*, 204, *204–05*
    locally produced 116, *116*, 184, *185*,
    mercerized cotton thread 96, *97*, 117, *117*
    Russian cotton 52, *53*, *54*, 55, 174, 207, *207–09*
    sateen (*tubayt*) 96
cowls, pointed (*veghar*)
cowrie shells *2*, 27, 28, 30, *30*, *31*, 39, *39*, *50*, 51, 65, *65*, 124, 140, *141*, 166, *166*
Crowfoot, Grace (textile archaeologist, 1879–1957) 15, 16
curtains (*sitāra*) 126, *126*, *126*, 182, *182*, *183*
    see also wedding curtains
cushion covers 145, *154*, 155, *155*, *203*, 203

damask 150, *151*
Debenhams 23
dervishes 1, 4, 124, *124*, 133, *133*, 140
    see also Sufi (mystics)
diamantes 33, *33*
Dickson, Violet (author, d. 1991) 94
DKNY 23
Dolce & Gabbana 23
dolls 34, *35*, 102, *102–03*, 112, *112*
Dominican missionaries 119
Dost Muhammad Khan (Emir of Afghanistan, r. 1826–39, 1842–63)
    floor-spread (*dastarkhān*) *152*, 153, *153*
dowries 14, 44, 46, 157, 158, 167, 198
    see also trousseaus
dresses 119, *119*

INDEX 229

abū thail ('father of the tail') 51
coatdresses 62, *62*, 92, *92*
dishdāsha (or *pashk*) 32, *94*
jillāyeh 74, *74*, 82, 114, *114*, *115*
kandūra 112, *112*
korta 108, *108*, *109*
kurta chakan 56, *56*
thawb 19, 21, 23, 37, *50*, 51, 74, 75, 184, *185*, 186, *186*, *187*
thawb malak 66, *66*, *67*
thawb al-nashal 20, *21*, 84, *84*, *85*
zanna/zinna 134, *134*
see also chemises; coats; robes; tunics
Druze dress 82, *106*, 107, 116, *116*

East India Company 62
Egypt 7, 188
 bridal trousseau 44
 Cairo 7, 44
 ceremonial robe (*'abāya/'abā'*) 76, *76*
 Coptic textiles 19, 107, *107*
 scarf with political portraits 188, *188*, *189*
 skullcap 77, *77*
 socks 146
 spangled hat 77, *77*
 tasselled cap 77, *77*
 ṭirāz, Fatimid 178, *179*
 textile museum 19
emblems, tribal see tribal emblems
embroidery, importance and learning the skill 14–17, 46–7, 74, 82–83, 91, 119, 145–46, 150, 155–58
embroidery sampler 16
embroidery stencils and pattern templates 77, 150, 158, 169
embroidery stitches and motifs
 animal horn *18*, 39, *39*, 59, *59*, 70, *70*, *156*, 157, 158, *158*, *173*, *173*
 apple (*tuffāh/sīb*) 61, *61*
 bachelor's cushion 15, *16*
 bindalli embroidery 77, *77*
 bird *5*, 31, *31*, 91, *91*, 216 n. 43
 bird of Paradise (*'asfūr al-janna*) 67, 216 n. 43
 boteh *92–3*, 93, 100, *101*, *152*, 153, *153*
 box-stitch 94
 Bukhara couching *172*, 173
 candlestick (*sham'addānāt*) *154*, 155
 cat *90*, 91
 cauliflower (*qarnabīṭ*) *16*
 chain-stitch *39*, *47*, 71, *71*, 113, *113*, 153, *153*, 210, 211, *211*
 chicken feet *16*
 couched embroidery 17, 47, 66, 69, *69*, 77, 77, 98, 99, *99*, 100, *101*, 108, *108*, *109*, 123, 128, *128*, *164*, 165, *172*, 173
 cow's eye (*'ayn al-baqara*) *16*
 cross-stitch 74, 96, *96*, 97, 117, *117*, *125*, 149, *149*, *154*, 155, *155*, 157, *157*, 160, 161, *202*, 203
 cypress tree (*sarū/sarv*) 16, *16*, 91, 150, *151*
 dīval embroidery 77, *77*
 drawn-threadwork 114, 150, *151*
 eggs in a pan 15, *16*
 eye (*'ayn*) 31, *31*
 feathers (*rīsh*) 186
 fish (*samak/māhī*) *5*, 91, *91*
 flowers *78–79*, 86, 87, 91, *91*, 100, *100–01*, 118, *118*, 128, *128–29*, *142–43*, 150, *150–51*, *152–53*, 182, *182–83*, 186, *186–87*
 garden *152*, 153, *153*
 geese (*iwazz*) 186, *187*
 harp (*rabāba*) 186, *187*
 hoopoe bird (*hudhud*) 186, *187*
 insects 157, *157*, 173, *173*
 key of Hebron (*miftāh al-khalīl*) *16*
 key of the heart (*miftāh al-qalb*) 216, n. 43
 kohl-pot (*mukhula*) 186, *187*
 ladder-stitch 59, *59*
 leech in the rose (*'olaiq fi'l-ward*) *16*
 lilies/irises (*zanbaq*) 186, *187*
 moon (*qamr*) 4, *5*, 26
 moon of Bethlehem (*qamr bait lahm*) *16*
 moon of Ramallah (*qamr rām allāh*) *16*
 necklace (*qilāda*) 94, *95*, 184, *185*
 old man's teeth (*asnān al-'ajūz*) 15, *16*
 palm of the hand (*kaffat al-yad*) 186
 pitchfork (*midhrā*) 186
 pomegranate (*ramān/anār*) 100, *101*
 pulled threadwork 105, *105*
 Roman rose (*al-ward al-rūmī*) 186
 satin-stitch 17, 66
 skull *202*, 203
 slices (*shaqahāt*) *154–55*, 155
 snake and the serpent (*al-hayya wa'l-'arbīd*) *16*
 snapdragon (*tumm al-sammaka*) 186, *187*
 snowflake (*nudfat al-thalj*) 186, *187*
 star (*najm*) 26
 star-keys (*mafātīh al-nujūm*) *202*, 203
 stick (*'aṣā*) 186
 sun (*shams*) 4, *5*, 15, 26, *90*, 91, 158, *158–59*
 swans (*iwazz*) 186, *187*
 tall palm (*al-nakhl al-'ālī*) *16*, 186
 tree of scorpions (*shajarat al-'aqārib*) 186
 true tree (*shajar ṣādiq*) *16*
 tulip (*lāla*) 17, *18*, 59, *59*, 100, *101*
 turning around (*mlawlaw*) 186
 vine-scrolls 56, *57*, 118, *118*
 zardūzī (Bukharan embroidery) 15
 zartoshtī dūzī (Zoroastrian needlework) 4, *5*, *90–91*, 91
 see also appliqué; see also under gold; silver
entari see under robes
Ersari tribe see under Turkmen
Ethiopian priest's hat 107, *107*
Europe
 European cotton 69, *69*, 184, *184*
 Europeanization of dress 82, 88, 89, 100, 118, 119, 133
 influence on embroidery 119, 180, 186
'evil eye' ('eye of envy') 26, *26*, 30, 31, 39, 47, 56, 65, 69, 76, 108, 111, 124, 137, 140
ex-votos 140
eye motifs, amuletic 29, 31, *31*

face-coverings 82
 barakoa 104, *104*
 baṭṭūla 113, *113*
 burqa' 81, 112, *112*, 113, *113*
 chashmāvīz 104
 niqāb 112, *112*
 pīcha 104, *104*
 saif malik 104, *104*
face-veils 48, 83, 104
 maghmūq 110, 111, *111*
 ra's maghmūq 110, 111, *111*
 rūband 21, 105, *105*, 215 n. 13, 218 notes 30–33
al-Farabi, Abu Nasr Muhammad (philosopher, d. 950) 191, *191*
Al-Farabi Kazakh State University 191
Fatima (daughter of the Prophet, d. 632) 122, 124
Fatimid dynasty (r. 909–1171)
 ṭirāz with bird and hare motifs 178, *179*
feathers
 on camel neck-hanging 174, *174*, *175*
 on kohl holders 65, *65*
 on wedding mirror bag 70, *70*
 ostrich 65, *65*
felt 140, 146, 157
Iran 1, 4, 17, *18*, 167, *167*, 190, *190*, 192, *192*
Kazakhstan 71
Kyrgyzstan 168, 169, *169*
Palestine 28, 31, *35*, 107
Turkey 124, 133, *133*, 141, *141*, 190, 191
Uzbekistan *156*, 157, *164*, 165, *165*
fertility 26, 27, 30, 56, 58, 59, 70, 91, 137, 207
fezzes (*ṭarbūsh*) 28, 31, *31*, 107, 133, *133*
 see also bonnets; caps; hats; headdresses; turbans
Firdawsi (poet, d. 1020) 196
flags 188, *189*, 198–9, *198–201*, 204, *204*
floor-coverings 146
 dastarkhān *152*, 153, *153*; *shyrdak* 168, *169*, *169*
France
 burkini ban 23, *23*
 cotton thread 117
 embroidery schools set up by missionaries 119
 French fashion, influence of 40
 French weavers in Istanbul 88

funerary dress 124, 173, 207, *207*, *208–09*
 model funerary garments and accessories 138, *138–39*
fur 26, 107

garnet 82
Georgian dress 48
Ghezelayagh, Bita (artist, b. 1966) 17, *18*, 192, *192*
ghutra see under head-cloths
Gibran, Kahlil (poet, 1883–1931) 26
gilt-metal
 braid 99, *99*, 100, *100*
 cords 66, *66*, 68, *78–79*, 86, 98, 99, *99*, 100, *101*
 embroidery 14, 15, *20*, *52*, 53, *54*, 55, 61, *61*, 76, 76, 77, 77, *78–79*, 84, *84*, *85*, 98, *99*, 99, 113, *113*, *118*, *119*, 150
 lace 62
 Selimiye fabric 88, *88*
 spangles 7, 77, *84*, 98, 99, *99*, 104, *104*
 tassels 28, 104, *104*
 threads 204, *205*
 wire 77, 126, *126*, 182, *182*
 see also gold
glass
 beads on amulets 27, *38*, 39, *141*
 beads decorating bags *125*, 166
 beads decorating clothing *2–3*, *26*, 30, *30*, 36, 37, *37*, *50*, 51
 beads decorating hangings 149, *160*, 174
 beads decorating headgear 68, 69, 72, 73, 81, *123*
 beads decorating kohl holders 65, *65*
 blue beads for protection 26, *27*
 Bohemian glass 174
 set into charms 30, *30*
goat hair see under hair
goat's skull 140, *140*
gold
 beads 72, *73*
 braid 33, 99
 brocade 26
 cords 86, 99, *99*, 100, *101*
 gold leaf 138, *138*
 gold-strip embroidery 64, 118, *118*, 150
 lace 62, *63*
 pendants 72, *73*
 spangles *20*, *85*, 99, *99*, 104, *104*, 150, *150*
 tassels 28
 see also gilt-metal
Granqvist, Hilma (anthropologist, 1890–1972) 138
grave-clothes see funerary dress
Greek Orthodox bishop's headdress 107, *107*
Greek priest's hat 107, *107*
green
 amuletic beads 72, *73*
 use in funerary dress 138, *139*
 Zoroastrian festive colour 80, 82, 91
gul-i perons ('dress flowers') *2*

Hafiz (medieval Persian poet, d. 1390) 9
hair
 camel 133, 204
 goat 163, *172*, 173, 204
 horsehair 104, *104*, *156*, 157
 human 39, *39*, 70, *70*, *120–21*, 124, 137, *137*
hairstyles 58
hajj see pilgrimage
hammām see bathhouses
handkerchiefs *45*, 46, 64, *64*
hand motif, amuletic 29
hand towels 145, 150, *150*, *151*
al-Hasan b. 'Ali (Shi'a imam, d. 669–70) 122
hats *1*, 29, 77, *77*, 83, 107, *107*
 kolāh 100, *101*
 kulutiyya 25, *36*
 qarākulī (lamb's fleece hat) 180, *181*
 shtrayml (Hasidic Jew's hat) 107, *107*
 sikke (dervish's hat) *1*, 124, *124*, 133, *133*
 see also bonnets; caps; fezzes; headdresses; turbans
Hazara people 124, 130, *130*, 220 nn. 12–13
head- and plait-covers (*kultapüshak/kallapüshak*) 15, 29, 58, 61, *61*, 72, *72*, 83

head-cloths
 ghutra 112, *112*, 204
 keffiyeh 180, *180*, 204, *204*, *205*
 kūfīya/hatta 107, *107*, 204
 mashada 204
 shimāgh 204
headdresses 29, 45, 58, 145
 bridal 15, 34, *35*, *42–43*, 58, *58*, 68, 69, 72, *72*, *73*
 see also bonnets; caps; hats; turbans
head-ropes ('*aqāl/'iqāl*) 107, *107*, 112, *112*, 204, *205*
headscarves 11, *12*, 21, *50*, 51, 83
 hijāb 23
head-shawls 56, *94*
 kimma 29
 shādar/chādar 94
 sitāra 111
head-veils 34, *35*, 48, 72, *72*
 khirqa 66, *66*
 shayla 112, *112*
henna *12*, 13, 138
hijāb see under headscarves
Hilfiger, Tommy 23
Hisham b. 'Abd el-Malik (Muslim caliph, r. 724–43), introduction of *ṭirāz* 178
hooded cloaks see under cloaks
hoods (*gargūsh/qarqūsh*) 82, 83, *83*
horn, ram's/animal 39, *39*, *28*, 70, *70*, 140, *140*, 164, *164–65*, 170, *206–09*, 207
horses 173
 horse blanket 173, *173*
 horse headdress *172*, 173
 horsehair 104, *104*, *156*, 157
 ridden in circumcision rites 28, 31
 ridden in wedding celebrations 66, *172*
 saddlebags 170
 used in funerary rites 173
al-Husayn b. 'Ali (Shi'a imam, d. 680) 122
Hussein (King of Jordan, r. 1952–99) 188, *188*, 222 n. 34

ikat
 Afghanistan 61, *61*
 India 19
 Kazakhstan 72, *73*
 Palestine 114, *114*, *115*
 Southeast Asia 19
 Syria 117, *117*
 Tajikistan *123*
 Uzbekistan 52, *52*, *53*, 55, 61, *61*, *206*, 207, *207*, *208–09*
INAASH (Beirut) 16, 203, *203*
 see also Lebanon
India
 brocade 19, 83, *83*
 embroidery 64, 84
 ikat 19
 Jewish community in Surat, Bombay and Calcutta 62
 Kashmir floor-covering *152*, 153, *153*
 Kashmir shawls 93
 silk 19, *54*, 55, *55*
 Suri silk (cotton) for export to Oman 37
indigo see under blue; cotton
inscriptions on textiles *1*, 4, *8*, 9, 17, *18*, 31, *31*, 64, 64, 76, 76, 77, 77, 122, *123–24*, 126, *126–27*, 132, *132*, *136*, *168–69*, 169, 178, *179*, 182, *182–83*, 184, *184*, 188, *188–89*, *190–91*, *190–91*, 192–97, *192–97*, *210–11*, 211
insignias see *tughra*
Iran 7
 amulets 104, *174*, *174–75*, 199, *199–201*
 bicycle saddlebag (*çarkh horcin/khorjīn*) 170, *170*
 bridal headdress 58, *58*
 camel neck-hanging (*duye bashlyk*) 174, *174*
 cap (*börk*) 39, *39*
 child's bonnet 31, *31*
 cloak (*chādor*) *21*
 cloak (*namad*) 17, *18*, 19, 192, *192*
 cloak, hooded 132, *132*
 dervish hat *1*, 4
 face-covering (*pīcha*) 104, *104*
 face-mask (*burqa'*) from Minab, Persian Gulf 113, *113*
 face-veil (*rūband*) 105, *105*
 girl's chemise, split-skirt and leggings 34, *34*

230 INDEX

headscarf 12
portrait rug of Ayatollah Khomeini *190*, 191
pot holders (*tutaç*) 167, *167*
prayer mat (*sajjāda*) 128, *128*, *129*
purse *147*
socks 146, *147*
spindle bag (*ig serk*/*ig torba*) 170, *171*
storage bag (*karçín*) 162, *162*
trousseau 46, 48, *48–9*
wedding mirror bag (*ā'ina bokche*) 70, *70*
woman's coat (*çabūt*) 100, *100*
woman's coatdress from Kirman *13* (detail), *92*, *93*, 93
woman's jacket (*arkhāloq*/*nīm-tana*) and cap from Mashhad 100, *101*
woman's trousers (*çulvar*) 100, *100*
woman's trousers (*châqchūr*/*châqsūr*) 105, *105*
Zoroastrian dress from Yazd or Kirman *4*, *5*, 80, 82, *90*, 91, *91*
Iran–Iraq War 180, 192
Iraq 7
adoption of European-style dress 89, 118–19
bride's handkerchief or kerchief (*mandīl*) from Mosul 64, *64*
Christian woman's festive or wedding attire from Mosul 118, 119, *119*
Esther Manassah, Jewish bride from Baghdad 62
flag 188
hooded cloak *132*
Jewish bridal outfit (bodice and coatdress) from Baghdad 62, *62*, *63*, 216 n. 36
üçetek ('triple-skirt') *entari* from Mosul 89, *89*
Islamic dress 11, 13, 21–3, 61, 83, 107
Israel 7, 184, 212, 218 n. 26, 222 n. 13

jackets 48, 119, *134*
arkhāloq/*nīm-tana* 100, *101*
cepken 86, *98*, 99, *99*
taqṣīreh *17*, 69, *69*
see also coats
Jerusalem and Middle East Church Association 107, 212
Jerusalem and the East Mission 184, 212
jewellery 26, 29, 44–45, 48, 69, 83, 94, 95, 124, 145, 184, *185*
Jewish
bride 62
dowries 44
dress 10, 61, *61*, 62, *62*, *63*, 83, 107, *107*, 216 notes 35–37
Hasidic Jews 107, *107*
Sephardic Jews 62
jihāz see trousseaus
Jordan 7, 16
Bani Hamida Women's Weaving Project (Makawir) 16
handkerchief *45*
textile museum 17

Ka'ba (Great Mosque, Mecca) *122*, 122, 123
belt (*ḥizam*) 123
curtain (*sitāra*) 123
kiswa (covering) 122, *122*, 123
kaftan *see under* robes
Karbala 128, 130, 220 n. 13
prayer-stones 128, *128*, 130, *130*
Karzai, Hamid (political ruler, r. 2001–14)
style of dress 180, *181*
Kashmir shawls 93
Kazakh people
bridal headdress (*saukele*) 72, *72*, *73*
tent-hanging (*tus ki'iz*) 71, *71*, *164*, 165, *165*
yurts 71
Kazakhstan 7
bridal headdress (*saukele*) 72, *72*, *73*
portrait rug of al-Farabi 191, *191*
Soviet emblem 211, *211*
tent-hanging (*tus ki'iz*) 71, *71*
keffiyeh *see under* head-cloths
kerchiefs 64
keys 16, 192, *192*, *202–03*, 203
Khomeini, Ayatollah (political ruler, 1900–89) *190*, 191
kitchen utensil bags *see under* bags
knitting *147*, 147

kohl holders 65, *65*
kurta see over-shirts
Kuwait 7
over-dress (*thawb*) 94, *95*
Kyrgyz people 144
bridal headdress (*saukele*) 72
children's dress 29, *29*
hats and headdresses 29
married woman's cap (*chach kep*) 58, *58*
women's dress 29
Kyrgyzstan 7
floor-coverings 146
Jangyl Alibekova (felt-maker, b. 1938) *168*, 169, *169*, 221 n. 33
married woman's cap (*chach kep*) 58, *58*
mosaic floor-felt (*shyrdak*) from At-Bashi *168*, 169, *169*
skullcaps 29
Soviet emblem 211, *211*
tent-hanging *210*, 211, *211*

lace 62, 118, 119
Lacroix, Christian (designer, b. 1951) 19
Lakai tribe *see under* Uzbek people
leather 150, *150*
Lebanon 16
bolero jacket *202*, 203
cushion cover from INAASH, Beirut 203, *203*
Druze community 107
Nazmieh Salem (Palestinian embroiderer) from INAASH *202*, 203
silk-floss threads 117
leggings *34*, 34
see also trousers
Lenin, Vladimir (political ruler, 1870–1924) *190*, 191
linen 66, *66*, 150, *151*, 179, 186, *187*
loofah sponge *138*
lurex thread 33, *108*, 109

Mahmud II, Sultan (Ottoman ruler, r. 1808–39)
curtain commissioned for the Prophet's Mosque, Medina 178, 180, 182, *182–83*
introduction of Europeanized dress code 133
mantles *see* cloaks
Marks & Spencer 23
marriage 14, 29, 44–47, 74, 145
see also bridal dress; marital status *under* status and identity
marriage apron *4*, *5*
marriage canopies *see* wedding canopies
Mawlana (Mevlana) Jalal al-Din Rumi (mystic, d. 1273) 133
Mecca 7, 122, *122*, 123
prayer rug 131, *131*
qibla compass, direction of Mecca 131, *131*
see also Ka'ba
Medina 7, 122, 123
see also Prophet's Mosque
menopause 83, 138
men's dress 83
Afghanistan *181*
Egypt 76, *76*
Iran *1*, *4*, 132, *132*
Iraq 132, *132*
Palestine *106*, 107, *107*, 180, 184, *184*, 204, 205
Syria 76, *76*, *106*, 107
UAE 112, *112*
Tajikistan *123*
Turkey 77, *77*, 133, *133*
Uzbekistan 52, *52*, *53*, *206*, 207
Yemen 51, *51*
see also caps; hats
mercerized cotton thread 96, 117
metallic threads *see* gilt-metal threads
miḥrāb (prayer arch/niche) 128, *128*, 219 n. 8
mirror *31*, 44, 46, *46*, 70, *70*, 155, 166
see also wedding mirrors
missionaries 13, 119, 180, 186
Modanisa Modesty Fashion Show *22*
modest fashion 19–23
mosaic floor-felt *see shyrdak under* floor-coverings
mother-of-pearl 27, 100, *101*, 134, *134*, *135*, 150, *150*, 174, *174*, *175*

Muhammad *see* Prophet Muhammad
Musée du Quai Branly (Paris) 19
Museum of Egyptian Textiles (Cairo) 19
Museum of National Dress (Tashkent) 19

napkins 145, 150, *151*
Nasir al-Din Shah (Qajar ruler, r. 1848–96)
encouraged Europeanized fashions 100
introduced modified tutu skirt 34
Nasser-Khoury, OmarJoseph (designer, b. 1988) 16, *202–03*, 203
9/11 21, 192, 198
niqāb see under face-coverings

Oman 7
amulets *28*
Baluchi child's dress (*dishdāsha*) 32, *32*
Baluchi woman's attire from Muscat 94, *94*
Bedouin face mask from central Oman 113, *113*
braid-cushion from Nizwa 14, *14*
Centre for Omani Dress 19
dress (*abū thail*) from Dhofar 51
face-mask (*burqaʾ*) from Dhofar 113, *113*
face-mask (*saif malik*) from Muscat 104, *104*
girls *28*, 28–29
head-shawl (*kimma*) from Sur 28–9
Suri silk (cotton) imported from India 36, *36*
toddlers' hats from Nizwa, Sur and Muscat 29, 36, *36*
trouser cuffs from Nizwa 14, *14*
orange face-coverings 113
Oscar de la Renta 23
Ottoman Empire 15, 19, 40, 77, 80, *126–27*, *182–83*
coins *81*, 83
dress 80, 82, 86, 89, *98*, 99, *99*
uniforms, influence of 17, 69, 108
see also Turkey
overcoats *see under* coats
over-dresses *see thawb* (*thob*) *under* dresses
over-shirts (*kurta*) 27, 30, *30*, 39, *39*, 137, *137*
Özbek, Rifat (designer, b. 1953) 19

paisley motif *see boteh under* embroidery stitches and motifs
Palestine 7, 13
Bedouin dress (*thawb*) 74, *75*
Bedouin face-cover (*burqaʾ*) *81*
bridal headdress (*shaṭweh*) from Beit Jala or Bethlehem *68*, 69
bridal headdress (*wuqāyat al-darāhim*) from Samu'a, Hebron Hills *68*, 69
child's bonnet *26*, 27
cushion covers (*wisādāt*) *154*, 155, *155*, 203, *203*
dolls 34, *35*, 102, *102–03*
dresses (*thawb*) 184, *185*, 186, *186*, *187*
Druze dress *106*, 107, 116, *116*
embroidery sampler from Ramallah *15*, *16*
fez 28, *31* (circumcision cap), 107, *107*
flag 204, *204*
funerary garments (models) from Artas *138*, 138, *139*
hats 83, 107, *107*
head-cloths (keffiyeh) 180, *180*, 204, *204*, 205
head-veil (*khirqa*) 66, *66*
jacket (*taqṣīreh*) from Beit Jala or Bethlehem *17*, 69, *69*
kohl holders (*mukhula*) 65, *65*
Majdal/Mejdel dress (*thawb*) and textile industry 184, *184*
men's trousers (*sirwāl*/*libās*/*elbās*) 184, *184*
unisex bolero jacket *202*, 203, *203*
wedding dress (*thawb malak*) 46, 66, *66*, *67*
woman's ceremonial/festive dress (*jillāyeh*) 74, *74*, 82, 114, *114*, *115*
Palestine Liberation Organization (PLO) 180
pan-Arabism 188
paper
foiled paper 58, *58*
for inscriptions in amulets *26*, 27
People of the Cloak 122
Persia *see* Iran

pilgrims and pilgrimage 34, 102, 107, 122, *122*, 123, 126, 131
pins, amuletic usage 27
plait-covers *see* head- and plait-covers
plastic
amulets *141*
beads and pendants on a headdress *68*, 69
dolls 112, *112–13*
kitchen utensil bag 166
kohl holder 65, *65*
prayer rug 131
plastrons 118, *118*
PLO *see* Palestine Liberation Organization
pockets 32–3, *32–3*, 94, *94*, 100, *101*
polyester *102–03*, 131
pomegranate flower motif, ikat design 207, *207–09*
pompoms 26, 27, 166, *166*
Porter, Thea (designer, 1927–2000) 19, *19*
porter's cap *see libda*/*libbada under* caps
portrait rugs *see under* rugs and mats
pot holders (*tutaç*) 167, *167*
prayer arch/niche (*miḥrāb*) 128, *128*, 219 n. 8
prayer caps *see under* caps
prayer cloths 130, *130*
prayer rugs and mats *see under* rugs and mats
prayer-stones 128, *128*
printed textiles 11, *11*, 14, *14*, 34, *34*, 46, *46*, 48, *48*, 54–5, 55, 131, *131*, 174, *174*, 184, *184*, 188, *188–9*, 207, *207–09*
Prophet Muhammad (d. 632) 11, 27, 122, 219 nn. 7, 9, 221 n. 6, 222 n. 7
Prophet's Mosque (Medina) 123
curtain (*sitāra*) 126, *126*, *127*, 178, 182, *182*, *183*, 219 notes 8–9
protection *see* amulets
purses 11, *12*, 13, 48, *48–9*, 91, *91*, 146, *147*

Qajar *12*, 21, *13*, *21*, 34, 82, 93, 105, 124, 217 n. 16, 218 n. 32
Quaker missionaries 186
Qur'an 27, 29, 33, 39, 76, 76–7, *122–24*, *122*, *125–27*, 126, 132, *132*, 178, *179*, 180, 182, *182–83*
Qur'an bags *see under* bags

Rahbar, Sara (artist, b. 1976) 180, 198, *198*, 199, *199*, *200–01*
rayon 100
red
bridal or festive colour 56, 72
symbol of fertility 56, 58, 59
Shi'a face-coverings 113
Turkmen preference for colour 100
worn by young women 59
Zoroastrian festive colour 80, 82, 91
Reza Shah Pahlavi (political ruler, r. 1925–41)
abolished non-European dress styles 100
religion and belief *122–41*, 123–41
see also amulets
robes
chapan 52, *52*, *53*, *54*, 55, *55*, 180, *181*, *206*, 207
entari (kaftan) 86, 119
jūkāniyya (a robe for playing polo) 44
khil'a (robes of honour) 44, 51, 178, 215 n. 16
munisak 207, *208–09*
üçetek ('triple-skirt') *entari* 80, 86, *86*, 88, *88*, 89, *89*
see also chemises; dresses; over-shirts; tunics
rugs and mats
garden carpets 195
prayer rugs and mats *see under* rugs and mats 124, 128, *128*, *129*, 131, *131*
portrait rugs 180, *190*, 191, *191*
war rugs 176–77, 180, *194*, 195, *195*, 196, *196*, *197*
Russian textiles 52, 55, 174, 207; *see also under* cotton

Sadberk Hanim Museum (Istanbul) 19
saddlebags *see under* bags
Safavid
silk *8*, 9–10, 213 n. 6
samplers 15, *16*
sashes *98*, 99, *99*, 119
satin 40, *40*, 52, *52*, 65, 74, 77, *77*, *94*, 96, 114, *114*, *115*, 116, *116*

INDEX 231

satin with birds' tongues pattern (lisān al-ʿaṣfūr) 117, *117*
see also silk
Saudi Arabia 7
  Art of Heritage Group 213 n. 15
  curtains (sitāra) 126, *126, 126*, 182, *182, 183*
  festive over-dress (thawb al-nashal) 20, 21, *21*
  girl's dress (thawb) from Bani Malik tribe 29, 37, *37*
  head-rope 204, *205*
  Mansoojat Foundation 213 n. 15
  over-dress (thawb) 94
Saz, Leyla (author, b. 1936) 80
scarf with political portraits 188, *188, 189*
seeds 140, *140*
Selim III, Sultan (Ottoman ruler, r. 1789–1807)
  curtain commissioned for the Prophet's Mosque, Medina 123, *126–27*, 219 notes 8–9
  development of silk industry and *Selimiye* fabric 88
sequins and spangles 20, *20*, 33, *33*, *50*, 51, 61, *61*, 65, *65*, 77, *77*, 84, *84–5*, *98–9*, 102, *102*, 104, *104*, 113, *113*, 134, *135*
Shah ʿAbbas (Safavid ruler, r. 1587–1629) 9, 213 n. 6
Shāhnāma ('Book of Kings') 196, *196*
shepherd's cloak *see namad under* cloaks
Shiʿa
  beliefs 122, 124, 128, 130, 219 n. 11, 220 n. 13
  dress and textiles 31, *31*, 113, *113*, 128, *128*, 130, *130*, *190*, 191
silk
  abū mitayn (silk-striped fabric) 184, *185*, 222 n. 13
  indigo-dyed *50*, 51, 76, *76*,
  named after Sultan Selim III (*Selimiye*) 88, *88*
  jacquard silk 94, *95*
  production 66, *66–7*, 88, *88*, 89, *89*, 100, *100*, 174, *174–5*, 218 n. 23
  taffeta 65, 66, 74, 89, 100, *101*, 114, *114*, 115, *154*, 155, *155*
  tussah silk 92, *92–3*
  see also brocade; satin
silver
  alloy 30
  braid 108, *108*, *109*
  chains 81, *82*
  embroidery 14, *15*, *50*, 51, *51*, 61, *61*, 64, *64*, 76, *76*, 77, *77*, 84, *84*, *85*, *98*, 99, *110*, 111, *111*, *126*, *127*, 128, *128*, 150, *151*
  pendants 28, 58, *58*, *82*, 217 n. 54
  silver-strip embroidery 64, *64*, 100, *101*, 104, *104*, *108*, *109*, *151*
  spangles 61, *61*, 77
  tassels 72, *72*, *73*
  wire 182, *182*
skirts 34, *34*, 100
skullcaps *see under* caps
snake motifs, amuletic 26, 58, *58*, *120–21*, 124 , 137, *137*
socks 146, *147*
soumak weaving 162, *162*
souvenirs 18, *18*, 34, 102, 112
Soviet Union 16, 180, 191, 211
spindle bags *see under* bags
spindles 170, *171*
spoons 166, *166*
status and identity 21, 40, 51, 61, 80–83, 104, 113, 114, 140, 150, 178, 180, 204, 207
  adulthood 26, 28–29, 31
  marital 29, 58, 69, 74, 111, 113
storage bags and sacks *see under* bags
Sufi (mystics)
  dress 1, 4, 107, *107*, 132, *132*
  Mevlevi order 124, *124*, 133, *133*, 140
sūzanī 19, 46, 47, *47*, 56, *56*, 198
Syria 7, 188
  ʿabāya/ʿabāʾ 76
  Aleppo, Homs and Damascus, centres of textile production 96, 117
  dress from Saraqib with embroiderer's signature 96, *96*
  Druze dress 106, *107*
  Fatima al-Qasim, Syrian embroiderer from Saraqib 96, *96*
  flag 188
  wedding coat from Al-Sukhnah 96, *96*
  woman's festive coat (*durāʿa*) 117, *117*

woman's inscribed jacket 136, *136*
taffeta 65, 66, 74, 89, 100, *101*, 114, *114*, 115, *154*, 155, *155*, 218 n. 19
  see also silk
Tajikistan 7, 30
  boy's amuletic coat from Panjakent 28, 33, *33*
  cap *123*
  children's dress 29
  head- and plait-covers (*kultapūshak/kallapūshak*) 61
  Soviet emblem 211, *211*
  sūzanī 46, 47, *47*
  tent-hanging 148, 149, *149*
  wedding canopy (*bolim posh*) 56, 57
  wedding ceremony 46
  wedding dress (*kurta chakan*) from Kulob 56, *56*
  women's dress 29
tallī see gold-strip embroidery *under* gold; silver-strip embroidery *under* silver; trims/edging
tapestry weave 51, 76, *76*, 106, *106*, 170, *171*, *179*
tassels
  beaded *2–3*, 4, 38, 39, *39*, 124, *125*, *148–9*, 149, *160–1*, 161
  bridal context 45, 46, 58, *58*, 60, *60*, 65, *65*, 72, *72–3*, *154*, 155, 166, *166*, 174, *174*
  horsehair *156*, 157
  indigo-dyed 107, *107*
  metal (including silver or gilt-metal) 19, *19*, 28, 31, *31*, 72, *72–3*, 77, *77*, 104, *104*
  on children's clothing *25*, 26, 28, 31, *31*, 36, *36*, 39, *39*, 77, 77
  religious context 124, *125*, 140, *140*
Tekke tribe *see under* Turkmen
tent-hangings 144, 145
  Afghanistan 157, *157*, 158, *158*, *159*
  Kazakhstan 71, *71*
  Kyrgyzstan *210*, 211, *211*
  Tajikistan 148, 149, *149*
  Uzbekistan *164*, 165, *165*
tent-pole bags *see under* bags
tents 163 *see also* yurts
termeh (striped woollen cloth) *12*, 128
thawb (*thob*) *see under* dresses
ṭirāz (inscribed medieval textiles and royal workshops) 178, *179*
Tiraz Centre (Amman) 17, 19
Topkapı Palace Museum (Istanbul) 19
towels, hand *see* hand towels
triangular motif 17, 39, 58, *58*, *120–21*, 74, *75*, 124
tribal emblems (*göl*) 145, 162
trims/edging *10*, 14, *15*, 34, *34*, 48, 52, *52*, 54, 55, 60, *60*, 61, *61*, 76, *76*, 88, *88*, 89, *89*, 99, *99*, 112, *112*, 113, *113*, 116, *116*, 128, *128*, 157, *157*, 170, 207, *207*
  see also tassels
trouser-cuffs 14, 48, 100, *100*, 134, *134*
trousers 48, 119
  chāqchūr/chāqsūr 105, *105*
  çulvar 100, *100*
  libās/elbās 184, *184*
  şalvar 80, 86, 99, *99*
  shalvār 90, 91, 100
  sirwāl (*shalwār*) 32, 184, *184*
  see also leggings
trousseaus 44–47, 65, 66, 69, 74, 91, 144, 145, 150
  model garments 48, *48–9*
  see also dowries
tulle 33, *33*
tunics 82
  qamīṣ 90, 91
  talismanic 192
  see also chemises; over-shirts; robes
turbans 58, 82, 107, *107*, 133, 178, 190, *190–91*, 204
Turkey 7
  bathhouses 150
  child's coat 29, 40, *40–41*
  circumcision ceremony 28
  clogs (*qabqab/nalın*) 150, *150*
  cushions 145
  dervish hats (*sikke*) from Konya and Bursa 133, *133*
  entari from Kütahya 86, *86*
  felt amulet from Balıkesir 140, *141*
  fez 133, *133*
  hand towels 145, 150, *150*, *151*
  houses 145–6

Istanbul 7, 19, 82, 88, 107, *107*
Mehmet Girgiç (felt-maker) 133, *133*
napkins 145, 150, *151*
portrait rug of Imam-Caliph ʿAli from Şanlıurfa *190*, 191
Ramazan Recep (felt-maker) 140, *141*
skullcaps 77
soft furnishings 145
storage sack 163, *163*
textile museums 19
tughra (Ottoman insignia) 150, 182, *182*
üçetek ('triple-skirt') *entari* 80, 86, *86*, 88, *88*
woman's jacket and trousers outfit 98, *98–99*
Turkmen 30, 167
  bib (*kirlik*) 39, *39*
  bridal headdress 58, *58*
  camel-hangings 145, 174, *174*
  cap (*börk*) 39, *39*
  ceremonial cloak (*chyrpy*) 59, *59*
  Ersari 30, *30*, *38*, 39
  fertility charm 26, *27*
  over-shirts (*kurta*) *27*, 30, *30*, *39*, *39*, 137, *137*
  pot holders 167, *167*
  saddlebags 170, *170*
  skullcaps 29, 39
  spindle bags 170, *171*
  storage bag 162, *162*
  talismanic goat's skull 140, *140*
  Tekke 39, *39*, 59, *59*, 137, *137*, 145, *145*, 146
  tent-hangings 144
  triangular cloth amulet *38*, 39
  tribal emblems (*göl*) 145, 162
  wedding mirror bag 46, *70*, *70*
  woman's coat and trousers outfit 100, *100*
  women's embroidered cloaks 17, *18*
  Yomut (Atabay) 39, *39*, 100, *100*, 140, *140*, 162, *162*, 167, *167*, 170, *170*, *171*, 174, *174*
  yurts 145, *146*, 162
Turkmenistan 7
  bib (*kirlik*) 39
  cap (*börk*) 39
  ceremonial cloak (*chyrpy*) 59, *59*
  kitchen utensil bag 166, *166*
  over-shirts (*kurta*) 39, 137, *137*
  portrait rug of Lenin *190*, 191
  talismanic goat's skull 140, *140*
  yurts 145, 146
turquoise beads 73

UAE 7
  face-mask (*burqaʿ*) from Al Ain 113, *113*
  dolls 112, *112*
unfinished hem or embroidery, apotropaic purpose of 30, 47, 71
United Arab Republic 188
USA
  American flag *198–9, 198–199, 200–201*
Uzbek people
  bedding pile 146
  bedding-pile hanging *160–61*, 161
  head- and plait-covers (*kultapūshak*) 61, *61*
  horse blanket 173, *173*
  horse headdress *172*, 173
  kitchen utensil bag 166, *166*
  Lakai 60, *60*, 146, 157, *157*, 158, *158*, *159*, *160–61*, 161, *172*, 173, *173*, 199
  marriage canopy (*bugjama/bugzhoma*) 60, *60*
  Qur'an bag *125*
  tent-hangings 144, 145, 149, *149*, 157, *157*, 158, *158*, *159*
  tent-pole bags *156*, 157
  yurts 146
Uzbekistan 7
  bedding-pile hanging *160*, 161
  chapan (coat or cloak) 52, *52*, *53*, *54*, 55, *55*, *206*, 207
  head- and plait-covers (*kultapūshak*) *15*, 61, *61*
  Soviet emblem *210*, 211
  sūzanī 46, 47, *47*
  Tajik wedding ceremony 46
  tent-pole bags *156*, 157
  textile industry in Bukhara, Samarkand and Marghilan 207
  textile museum 19

wedding canopy (*bolim posh*) 56, *57*
yurts 165
  see also Bukhara

veils, attitudes towards 193
  see also face-veils; head-veils
velvet
  Afghanistan *2*, 26, 61, *61*
  Egypt 77
  Iran 100, *101*
  Palestine 69, 107, *107*
  Russia 52
  Tajikistan 33, *33*
  Turkey 77, *77*, *78–79*, *98*, 99, *99*, 150, *150*
  Uzbekistan 61, *61*, *164*, 165, *165*
  Yemen 65, *65*, *82*, 83

waistcoats 86, 119
wall-hangings *see* tent-hangings
war rugs *see under* rugs and mats
watermelon motif, ikat design *206*, 207
wedding canopies 46, 47, 56, 57, 60, *60*
wedding curtains (*chimilig/chimildik*) 46, *46*
wedding mirrors 46, *46*, 70
wedding mirror bags (*āʾina bokche*) *see under* bags
weddings *see* marriage; trousseaus; dowries
Weir, Shelagh (anthropologist) 13, 66, 107, 212
white
  used in funerary dress 138, *139*
  worn by elderly women 59
  and black cord imitating snakes 26, *27*, *120–21*, 122, 137, *137*
  and black kefiyyeh, symbol of Palestinian identity 180, *180*, 204, *204*
Widad Kawar Home for Arab Dress *see* Tiraz Centre (Amman)
widows 69, 74, 216 n. 47
wool
  busht (hand-woven in Syria and Palestine) 106, *107*,
  broadcloth 17, 69, *69*,
  napped/fulled wool flannel 60, *60*, 72, *72–3*, 157, *157*, 158, *158–9*, *172–3*, 173
  synthetic wool 36, *36*, 113, *113*, 204, *204*
  termeh (striped woollen cloth) *12*, 13, 48, *48*, 128, *128*
  see also felt; pompoms

Xinjiang
  women's and children's dress 29

yellow
  worn by middle-aged women 59
Yemen 7
  Man's ceremonial outer robe (ʿabāya) from Hadramawt 50, *51*
  face-veil with head-piece from Sana'a *110*, 111, *111*
  festive dress (*korta*) from Bayt al-Faqih, Tihama 108, *108*, *109*, 218 n. 46
  festive dress from Yeshbum *10*
  head-cloth (keffiyeh) 204, *205*
  headscarf *11*, 50, *51*
  hood (*gargūsh*) from Sana'a *82*, 83, *83*
  indigo-dyed dress (*zanna/zinna*) from Jabal Haraz 134, *134*, *135*
  indigo-dyed garments 124, 134
  kohl holders from former Western Aden Protectorate 65, *65*
  scarf with political portraits 188, *188*, *189*
  wedding or ceremonial dress (*thawb*) from Hadramawt 50, *51*
  trouser-cuffs from Jabal Haraz 134, *134*
Yomut tribe *see under* Turkmen
Yörük people
  felt amulet 140, *141*
  portrait rug of Imam-Caliph ʿAli *190*, 191
  storage sack 163, *163*
yurts 26, 71, 140, 144, *145*, 146, 157, 162, 165
Yusuf (Joseph, biblical prophet–king) 9, 122
YWCA School 102

Zanzibar 7
  face-mask (*barakoa*) 104, *104*
  Princess Salme of Zanzibar (d. 1924) 104
Zoroastrian dress and needlework *5*, *80*, *82*, *90*, 91, *91*